Towards Cre Learning Sp

In Higher and Further Education there has been considerable recent interest in shifting from formal to informal models of learning. Much current design has tended to rely on the belief that we should be moving away from formal lecture halls and classrooms, towards technology-rich and social learning spaces. This book challenges the underlying assumptions in this approach, arguing that we need a rethinking of the relationships between learning and space.

There remains a surprising lack of underlying analysis about what is changing in learning and teaching practices and about what role architecture has in this process. Architectural provision for the post-compulsory educational sector needs to develop learning spaces based on greater clarity and creativity.

- What kinds of space are we talking about – conceptual, physical, virtual, social, personal?
- What are the relationships between architectural design and learning, teaching and research activities?
- What are the different spaces in which learning takes place and how can we judge their relative effectiveness?

This book first engages with recent educational and architectural theories in a critical way. It then considers alternative ways of mapping relationships between spaces and their occupation so as to better understand the social and spatial practices of learning at a variety of scales. Finally, it explores examples of innovative ways for articulating learning and considers the implications for the development, design and occupation of different learning spaces.

Relevant both to architectural practice and to the education of the next generation of design students, this book integrates issues of education, design and cost. It is a wide-ranging and thought-provoking text which supports a better understanding of how to make enhanced and sustainable spaces.

Jos Boys has a background in architectural practice, research and journalism and is currently Senior Research Fellow of Learning Spaces at the Centre for Excellence in Teaching and Learning through Design (CETLD). She has taught at various institutions, including the Architectural Association, London Metropolitan University and the University of Brighton; and has also been an academic developer for the art and design disciplines. Jos' practice is predominantly community-based and she is particularly interested in exploring the relationships between space and its occupation, not just theoretically but also publicly and practically.

Towards Creative Learning Spaces

Re-thinking the architecture of post-compulsory education

Jos Boys

Routledge
Taylor & Francis Group

LONDON AND NEW YORK

First published 2011
by Routledge
2 Park Square, Milton Park, Abingdon, Oxon OX14 4RN

Simultaneously published in the USA and Canada
by Routledge
711 Third Avenue, New York, NY 10017

Routledge is an imprint of the Taylor & Francis Group, an informa business

Cover photo: Jos Boys. Interior by Ben Kelly Design, The Public, West Bromwich

Typeset in Univers by Pindar NZ, Auckland, New Zealand

British Library Cataloguing in Publication Data
A catalogue record for this book is available from the British Library

Library of Congress Cataloging-in-Publication Data
Boys, Jos.
Towards creative learning spaces: re-thinking the architecture of post-compulsory
education / Jos Boys.
        p. cm.
    Includes bibliographical references and index.
    1. College buildings. 2. Architecture--Human factors. 3. Architecture and
society. I. Title.
    NA6600.B69 2011
    727—dc22   2010023695

ISBN13: 978-0-415-57062-6 (hbk)
ISBN13: 978-0-415-57064-0 (pbk)
ISBN13: 978-0-203-83589-0 (ebk)

Contents

Illustrations

Tables

Acknowledgements

This book was written with the support of a senior research fellowship from the Centre for Excellence in Teaching and Learning through Design (CETLD). This was a five-year partnership between the University of Brighton, the Royal College of Art, the Victoria and Albert Museum and the Royal Institute of British Architects (RIBA), funded by the Higher Education Funding Council for England (HEFCE) from 2005 to 2010. I would like to thank all my colleagues at these institutions, who formed an important backbone of support to the research here, through their associated projects and activities. Particular appreciation is due to Anne Boddington, Anne Asha, Debbie Hickmott, Clare Melhuish, Hilary Smith, Philippa Lyon, Jane Devine-Meja, Patrick Letschka, Alma Boyes, Cynthia Cousens, Catherine Moriarty, Ike Rust, Chris Mitchell, Beth Cook, Catherine Speight, Rebecca Reynolds, Irena Murray, Paul Snell, Sol Sneltvedt, Clare Chandler, Sina Krause and Roland Mathews at CETLD; and to Tom Hamilton and Diane Brewster at the 'next-door' CETL in Creativity (CETL-C), a collaboration between the University of Sussex and the University of Brighton. I would also like to thank Fiona Duggan, Lars Wieneke, Shirley May and Lyn Nesbitt-Smith. And finally, I must mention my colleagues and students at the British Higher School of Art and Design, Moscow, who have helped me think about learning spaces in a different country and context.

Introduction

Why re-think learning spaces?

There has been increasing interest in learning spaces over recent years. Experts across the fields of architecture, education and estates management are producing a considerable number of publications, and many new and innovative examples have now been built (Joint Information Systems Committee (JISC) 2006, Tertiary Education Facilities Management Association (TEFMA) 2006, Oblinger 2006, Scottish Funding Council 2006, Neary *et al*. 2010). Yet key basic questions about what we mean by 'space' and what matters about it in relation to learning, remain unanswered. What kinds of space are we talking about – conceptual, physical, virtual, social and/or personal? What are the relationships between the nature of these various spaces and how they actually impact on learning activities? What are the different spaces in which learning takes place (both in and beyond the formal teaching environment) and how can we interrogate the effectiveness of different kinds of learning spaces? What needs to change both in the 'conceptual' spaces we have about learning, and in our physical and virtual spaces, in order to enhance learning experiences?

This book will critically explore these issues, particularly in relation to post-compulsory education, so as to better inform many of the contemporary debates on learning spaces across policy, theory and practice; and between designers, clients, managers and users. A key aim is to challenge some of the conventional wisdom about how teaching and learning is – or should be – changing, with its assumptions that the 'answer' lies mainly in providing more informal, flexible and social learning spaces in universities and colleges (JISC 2006; Jamieson 2008). Many recent educational projects for example, have offered learning cafés, informal seating areas, corridor alcoves or social 'hubs'. They have also exploited playful settings, bright colours, natural lighting and softer furnishings. While many of these examples are of a high quality, this book aims to look beyond this 'beanbag' approach to learning space design. It will argue instead for better theoretical frameworks for, and analytical methods of, examining the relationships between space and the activities that go on within it. This will help us better understand both what is *distinctive* about post-compulsory learning, and what *matters* in the design of spaces for learning. To do this *Towards Creative Learning Spaces* is organised around three key themes:

Part 1. *Reviewing our frames*:

This section centres on how we think about and articulate the relationships between learning and built space. It does this by critically exploring how these notions are currently conceptualised by the main subject disciplines involved – architects, educationalists and estates planners – so as to unravel our various assumptions about, attitudes to and discourses around, what is important for the design of learning spaces.

Part 2. *Mapping the terrain*:

This section offers some alternative ways of mapping and analysing relationships between spaces and their occupation, so as to better understand what is distinctive about the social and spatial aspects of teaching, learning and research – across a variety of scales – and to consider the implications for architectural design.

Part 3. *Shifting the boundaries*:

This section explores some possibilities, proposals and case study examples that offer innovative and creative ways of articulating the intersections between post-compulsory teaching, learning, research and the development, design and occupation of the associated spaces.

Towards Creative Learning Spaces is not intended as either a design guidance manual or an illustrated set of good practice case studies. It does not tell architects (or their clients or users) what to do. Rather it aims to discover what are the right sorts of questions to ask, and the important issues to address, in order to create enhanced conditions for learning in our universities, colleges and other educational settings.

The problem with the formal/informal learning divide

In post-compulsory education there has been considerable recent interest in shifting from formal to informal models of learning. As Harrison and Cairns put it:

> Approaches to learning in educational settings are changing. Traditional teacher-centred models, where good teaching is conceptualised as the passing on of sound academic, practical or vocational knowledge, are being replaced with student-centred approaches which emphasise the construction of knowledge through shared situations.
>
> (Harrison and Cairns 2009: 1)

For many educationalists, this requires a move away from formal lecture halls and classrooms towards technology-rich and informal, social learning spaces – a strong driver in many recent building designs and adaptations. These debates are influenced by many disparate sources – from theory (the 'communities of practice' literature of Lave and Wenger 1991; Wenger 1998); and policy (government initiatives on the creative economy, and on lifelong and workplace learning); to new technologies following the success of Web 2.0 applications such as Facebook and YouTube; and pragmatics around space utilisation and costs. But the underlying assumptions and terminology remain seriously under-researched. For example, use of the terms 'formal' and 'informal' learning often 'jump' from describing differences between educational sectors inside and beyond the university to describing types of spaces within a university, to, by implication, describing better and worse kinds of education. This problem can be exacerbated when 'formal' and 'informal' modes of learning are simplistically translated into spatial/representational design metaphors, rather than related through specific, situated learning and teaching practices. In fact, there are several intersecting myths embedded in much current work that urgently need carefully unravelling. These myths are:

- Formal and informal learning are binary opposites.
- Informal learning is good because it is social, personalised and integrates physical and virtual environments.
- Formal learning is bad because it is a one-way transmission of factual knowledge from teacher to learner.
- Teaching and learning in post-compulsory education needs improving.
- It can be improved through the development of both physical and virtual innovative and flexible learning spaces.
- The new generation of students will be 'digital natives' who will demand a different kind of education.
- 'Good' education enables the ability to think critically and solve complex problems, preparing learners for the 'knowledge economy'.

I call these myths, not because they are 'wrong' but because they have become the 'common sense' we think *with* rather than *about*, and thus can all too easily become a substitute for critical analysis. Most importantly, this argument starts from two simplistic generalisations – that most university and college teachers still use and prefer a traditional 'chalk and talk' method, and are resistant to any sort of change; and that university spaces still mainly consist of 'passive' lecture theatres. Such assumptions are hardly ever supported by actual data and tend to ignore more situated and nuanced analysis (Fig. 0.1). They also do not reflect the general experience of teachers or students in higher education (in the UK at least), where ideas about, and support for, active learning have been around for over 30 years. Nor do such assumptions consider the realities of contemporary post-compulsory education in many countries, where the problem of increasing student numbers within a reducing resource framework, continues to make mass lecturing necessary.

First, then, we need to engage with such myths critically, rather than just accepting them as 'common sense'. Second, just as importantly, we need to address the important issues that such myths tend to obscure. *Should* the idea of the university be predominantly about 'preparing students for a knowledge economy' as many policy-makers argue, for example; and, if so, what are the implications both for teaching and learning practices and for the range of associated spaces this might require? What kinds of spaces do new technologies offer? Are these different to

Fig. 0.1
Drawing Studio,
Moscow
Architectural
Institute
(MARKHI),
August 2009.
Photo: Jos Boys.

physical spaces, and what does that mean for learning? And – most crucially for this book – what is it that matters about the design of material (and virtual) space for learning?

To understand this better we need to not just examine the myths, but also to challenge the *underlying structure* of such common-sense ideas about space and learning. Many theorists have revealed the inherent flaws in how we 'normally' order the world through binary oppositions such as formal/informal (Baudrillard 1981; Bourdieu 1987; Bhabha 1994). Linking particular spatial qualities with assumed learning activities via a pattern of associative analogies, and then setting these 'against' an oppositional list may appear to make everyday obvious sense, but is, in fact, a tautological relationship (Fig. 0.2) where each term seems to 'prove' the existence of its (supposed) Other.

Yet such a framework obscures more than it reveals. It makes it easy to be persuaded by such 'obvious' arguments, without demanding evidence in support. In addition, the reliance on this common-sense understanding has allowed the subject of learning spaces to remain worryingly under-theorised, and to frame what is and isn't said, what is and isn't thought about learning and space. In the current context it is urgent that the underlying difficulties with such assumptions are addressed rigorously and critically, so as to prevent simplistic oppositions or associations being made between different types of learning and spaces. We are already discovering that the UK Building Schools for the Future (BSF) capital building programme in the primary and secondary sectors is struggling to produce designs of quality (CABE 2006). The post-compulsory educational sector therefore needs to develop plans for their learning spaces based on greater clarity of, and creativity in, thinking.

Fig. 0.2
Formal and
informal learning
spaces shown
as a pattern of
'either/or' binary
oppositions and
associations.

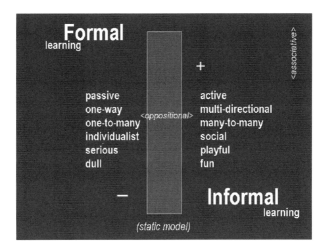

Fig. 0.2
Formal and
informal learning
spaces shown
as a pattern of
'either/or' binary
oppositions and
associations.

Beyond the beanbag?

Here, then, I am arguing that while many of the new learning environments being developed can offer exciting additions to existing spaces, they do not enable a better conceptual framework, appropriate research methods or strategic critique to be developed. This means that current learning space design is based on simplified – and even idealistic or metaphorical – notions of learning space. It may perpetuate our failure to engage with the wide panoply of learning spaces from academic workplaces to research settings, and ignore the continuing need for better-designed formal (and other hybrid) learning spaces. It concentrates on only aspects of learning space design and issues. Yet as well as the formal/informal learning debate, there are many other concerns, including widening participation, communities of practice, inclusive pedagogies, business and community engagement, entrepreneurship, research and consultancy, new technologies, health and wellbeing, resource-effectiveness and sustainability. Finally, it tends to ignore both contemporary shifts in educational theories and practices, and recent ideas in architectural and cultural theory.

This book, then, aims to open up the un-thought-through assumptions about post-compulsory education across its many locations in universities, colleges, libraries, museums, homes and workplaces. This will include facing up to some of the tensions and complexities in relationships between learning and space. These occur at a conceptual level such as, for example, the impossibility of designing a perfect 'fit' between a learning activity and its spaces. And they also occur at strategic and operational levels as in, for example, the contradictions between a recent emphasis on personalised learning and increasing student numbers, and the real difficulties of combining teaching and learning innovations with cost-effectiveness and sustainability agendas.

Re-thinking relationships between space and learning

The key arguments in this book are that we need to:

- better understand the distinctive characteristics of post-compulsory learning by exploring contemporary educational theories and practices and critically engaging with what these can tell us about learning spaces;
- examine how contemporary architectural theory and practice can better inform our understanding of relationships between learning and the spaces in which it occurs;
- better map the relationships between learning and space in post-compulsory education, engaging with many of the methods that already exist (particularly from ethnography and ethnomethodology) which can help us do this;
- consider the intersections between space as a scarce resource and its occupation.

The arguments here will be informed both by the 'communities of practice' and related literature from education (Lave and Wenger 1991; Wenger 1998; Meyer and Land 2003; Barton and Tusting 2005) and what has been called 'the cultural turn' (Jameson 1992; Thrift 2008) which has influenced much contemporary architectural theory (Koolhaas 1997; Tschumi 1994, 1996). In educational theory, teaching and learning are increasingly being framed as a collective practice towards shared social meanings. Crucially such a practice is *situated*, and involves thinking, doing and affective encounters (Austerlitz 2008; Sagan 2009; Savin-Baden 2008). It is also increasingly seen as a transitional process; that is, a liminal space or journey – one of negotiating 'thresholds' or 'sticking places' (Land *et al.* 2005; Meyer and Land 2006; Land, Meyer and Smith 2008).

In architecture, through a critique of older modernist assumptions, there has been a re-conceptualisation of the relationships between space and its activities in three important ways. First, rather than seeing architecture as essentially representational (where meaning-making occurs through what we *see* in a space), it is increasingly understood as non-representational or events-based; that is, meaning-making occurs through the activation of space by our bodies. As part of this framing, space and its occupation are not separate or in a behaviourist stimuli–response relationship, but endlessly informing and influencing each other. Second, this is a non-congruent, partial and situated form of relationship. Rather than articulating space and its occupation as a reflection of each other, particular sets of social and spatial practices must be analysed in context, to unravel the specific and dynamic patterning, which will also always include excesses, overlaps and gaps between the space and the activities taking place. This is often referred to as not the 'either/or' of thinking through binary oppositions but the 'and/and' of uneven and complex intersections. Third, encounters with and in space are neither cerebral nor corporeal but *affective*, where affect is not just articulated as 'emotion' but, as Thrift puts it, 'affect is understood as a form of thinking, often indirect and non-reflective, true, but thinking all the same' (Thrift 2008: 175). Space is therefore one of our means of thinking about the world and of embodying thought into action (Fig. 0.3).

Fig. 0.3
Learning space
shown as a
pattern of 'and/
and' encounters
and practices.

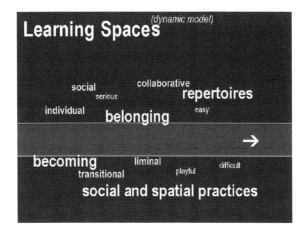

This articulation of a more complex and partial relationship between space and the activities which take place in it means that we can no longer rely on the simplistic and reflective analogies that are used, for example, in the formal/informal divide. Rather than framing learning spaces through the simple binary oppositions of formal or informal, I want to look instead at what Henri Lefebvre famously called a 'spatial triad'. In his book *The Production of Space* (1991) Lefebvre proposed that a better method for analysing the messy complexity of space was to consider it through three aspects, rather than use a simple two-part binary method. Based on his work, I will propose that we can understand space and its occupation better by examining the intersections between:

- the ordinary social and spatial practices of existing communities of practice in education;
- designed learning environments;
- participant perceptions of space, and their engagements with, and adaptations of, both learning spaces and practices.

Importantly, each of these aspects is always situated in relationship to both particular places and people; and no aspect is obvious, congruent or complete, either on its own terms, or with others. These never align (or do so only momentarily) so that the resulting map is what Geertz (1973) terms a 'thick description'. That is, it is a rich and layered account that does not result in a 'solution' or conclusion, but can *illuminate* (Parlett and Hamilton 1972) our decision-making.

The key aim of this book, then, is to explore just what such a shift in conceptual framework and research method *means*. This is, first, about how it will affect our understanding of the relationship between learning and space on a variety of different scales, ranging from the immediate encounters between and across learners and teachers, through to the institutional level, and on to the wider context. And second, it concerns the implications for architecture, both as a 'product' (that is, a particular built landscape) and as a design practice.

7

'Talking back' from an art, design and media perspective

The research behind this book was funded by the Centre for Excellence in Teaching and Learning through Design (CETLD), which is a partnership led by the Faculty of Arts at the University of Brighton in collaboration with the Victoria and Albert Museum (V&A), the Royal Institute of British Architects (RIBA) and the Royal College of Art (RCA). The Centre's learning spaces research has a much wider focus than just the architecture, art, design and media subjects; it starts from the belief that these disciplines can usefully 'talk back' to more mainstream educational and professional theories about learning and space. In many ways, at least on the surface, art and design education does not seem to 'fit' with much that is written about post-compulsory teaching and learning. Teachers within the creative disciplines are often critical of pedagogic theory and even of the use or value of the concept 'learning space' itself (Box 0.1). In fact, the formal/informal learning space divide does not make much sense when dealing with the complexities of the creative subjects' wide range of spaces, from 'conventional' lecture theatres and seminar rooms to studios, workshops and labs. Yet art, design and media education is already often cited as the paradigm for new types of learning, because of its emphasis on open-ended, multi-disciplinary and problem-based learning; on open-plan and studio-based learning, built around collaborative critique and self-reflective iteration.

Learning space is a term bandied about which people think has a shared understanding. I would think of learning space as a physical space where you learn stuff, but it could just be reading a book. It could be somewhere you go to do something or it could be in your head, what you have chosen to do. Mainly, though it is having a particular physical space connected to a task, so going to work is not being at home or going to a jewellery class.

Learning space is not a term I use, I think of it as 'education speak' – quite alien.

Learning is the process whereby a sentient individual or group acquires a new and valuable insight into the properties, constraints and affordances of their (physical, social or cognitive) environments.

Learning space is what is inside you really – and the relationship between that and the physical space, curriculum and timetables.

A good learning space for me is a frame of mind, rather than an actual space. It is internal rather than external.

Learning is engaged awareness (for a purpose?)

The 'learning space' doesn't make any difference *unless* the teacher isn't engaging and then the space *could* become important.

What students want from the space is a different kind of liberation.

Learning happens all the time and everywhere. You can teach something in the studio, but it's waking up in the morning, that's when it 'clicks'.

Box 0.1
Perceptions of the idea of 'learning space': selected quotations from tutors in art and design education (unpublished interview notes, Jos Boys 2008–09).

These subject areas also offer a 'take' on learning that is slightly different from, and can throw light on, other disciplines and on pedagogic theory more generally. Art, design and media education emphasises creativity, which is increasingly considered of value for learning more generally. It focuses on learning by doing – through making and interpretation that necessarily combines verbal and non-verbal communication – offering the potential for richer description and analysis of learning spaces. Finally, it has many existing intersections with vocational, academic, community-oriented, practice-based and professional spaces, which make it relatively easy to think about relationships inside and beyond the campus. In this book, all of these characteristics will be useful in opening up relationships between learning and space more widely, and will also help to highlight creative learning as *already* existing across a range of subjects in post-compulsory education.

Chapter outline

Initially, then, this book will explore how ideas around learning spaces have been framed within contemporary debates and from the viewpoints of different subject disciplines. So, for architects, space is the physical setting in which learning takes place. For educational theorists it may either be absent entirely or is predominantly a conceptual space, leading to the use of abstract terminology for describing aspects of learning. To an estates planner, learning spaces are a limited and costly resource that must be effectively distributed. For teachers and students, learning spaces are a set of given physical, virtual, organisational and durational frameworks into which a variety of activities must be fitted. Rather than assuming a common language, we need to explore, explicitly debate – and even enjoy – the problematic intersections between these different perspectives. At the same time, we need to be examining what is not being said, most crucially in the gaps between 'common-sense' thinking and contemporary theories, both within and across perspectives. Part 1: *Reviewing our frames*, then, critically examines the architectural, educational and estates-based perspectives in turn.

Chapter 1: *Learning spaces from an architectural perspective* shows that there is now a considerable literature written, and built examples designed, by architectural professionals in support of the development of new types of informal, flexible and technology-rich spaces for learning in higher education. This chapter critically explores how these architects link ideas about space (comfort, appearance, appropriateness, etc.) to behaviours, and how they explain processes of design development and realisation. These approaches will then be intersected with contemporary shifts in architectural theory and practices.

Chapter 2: *Learning spaces from an educationalist perspective* begins with an exploration of some of the most important recent educational theories, particularly the idea of 'communities of practice'. Rather than assuming that learning is a kind of circular iterative process, whereby individual intellectual understanding is practised through its application in different contexts and then developed through 'reflection' (Laurillard 2001), these newer approaches treat learning as essentially collaborative and being about social meaning-making. Rather than individual learning conversations between tutor and student, authors and practitioners are exploring the wider processes through which a community of 'knowers' come to inculcate not just knowledge, but also the attitudes and culture of their community to new generations. This leads to a definition of learning as 'increasing access of learners to participating roles in expert performances' (Lave and Wenger 1991: 17). Both this approach and the 'threshold concepts' research (Meyer and Land 2006) (which articulates learning space as centrally a process of transition and liminality) have been very influential. To support students through learning articulated in these ways requires a 'holding environment for the toleration of confusion' (Cousin 2006a). As I have written elsewhere, such a space needs to be 'safe', but not merely a 'comfort zone' (Boys 2008); a place where students feel able to take risks and deal with uncertainty. I suggest that educational concepts such as these help us break out of the simplistic formal/informal divide, precisely because they do not merely generate an obvious pattern of binary oppositions or associative design metaphors. The chapter concludes by exploring how we can map the everyday social and spatial practices of learning so as to understand them better as transitional, liminal and situated processes.

Chapter 3: *Learning spaces from an estates planning perspective* aims to go beyond the traditional oppositional divide between academics and estates managers, by suggesting that the underlying (shared) problem is the lack of a conceptual framework or analytical methods for understanding the inter-relationships between space and its occupation. This is not about reaching a single consensus view or approach, but about working creatively *from* difference. The chapter suggests that rather than taking the route of increased 'flexibility' using space utilisation models, institutions should be developing improved methods for mapping existing and preferred social and spatial processes and practices of learning in post-compulsory education. It is also argued that viewing physical space and its occupation as always partially related, contested and changing can itself actually open up space planning and management to more creative and constructive engagements with teaching, learning and research.

Part 2: *Mapping the terrain* offers a more explicit conceptual framework for thinking about learning spaces, with the aim of also developing richer and more appropriate methodologies for examining how different participants interpret and interact with conceptual, physical and virtual spaces. Too many architectural case studies tend to explain the intention of the space, and show how the design is planned to have these effects, but actually involve little proper research evaluation of spaces in use. And while there are now a number of studies beginning to investigate the student experiences of learning spaces, recent reviews (JISC 2009; Melhuish 2010b) suggest that we are still a long way from having effective ways of understanding how different participants experience the various spaces in which learning takes place, on and off the campus. This is both about complex, layered and informative ways of finding out what already happens and about recognising not just the explicit relationships of learning (course content, curriculum, physical and virtual space, etc.) but also its unspoken interactions (Austerlitz 2008).

Chapter 4: *Getting beneath the surface: re-thinking relationships between learning and space* develops an alternative conceptual framework, based on a critique of the 'communities of practice' literature, intersected with some contemporary aspects of architectural and cultural theory. It explores how key concepts underpinning the 'community of practice' model such as its boundedness, the nature of its transitional journey towards becoming and belonging, and the role of a repertoire in making concrete its social and spatial practices, can offer valuable ways of articulating the spaces of learning in post-compulsory education. It suggests that an adaptation of Lefebvre (1991) offers a potentially creative and constructive means of analysing experiences of space, which goes beyond a simplistic pattern of binary oppositions and instead 'layers' three inter-related aspects: the everyday social and spatial practices of learning; the spaces designed for that learning; and individual 'positionings' in relation to both practices and spaces.

Chapter 5: *On the ground: searching for the student learning experience?* begins by illustrating the problems with existing evaluations of learning spaces, which generally remain poorly theorised and under-researched, despite the availability of many useful methodologies which link space and its occupation across subjects such as ethnography, phenomenology and ethnomethodology (Cousin 2009). It then reviews a recent research project by Clare Melhuish (2010a, 2010b), which uses such an approach to explore whether concepts from the 'communities of practice' model, such as boundary conditions/crossings, iterative encounters and repertoires, can help us elucidate our understanding of experiences and perceptions of learning spaces.

Chapter 6: *Shaping learning: (re)designing the institution* explores how social and spatial practices at the level of the educational institution 'shape' the spaces of universities and colleges. The chapter challenges two conventional assumptions: first, that to develop new and innovative designs we need improved participation and collaboration; and second, that design at the level of the educational institution can be explained as a representation of some aspect of the learning community. Instead the chapter explores how to re-think the architecture of universities and colleges around what *matters* about the design of space for the social and spatial *practices* it orchestrates. This involves returning to the concept of 'communities of practice' and exploring the complexities, conflicts, gaps and unintended consequences where such communities intersect – in organisational cultures, roles and relationships, and specific patternings of activities in one way rather than another. While these issues are neither new to, nor unconsidered by, architects, this chapter examines how understanding non-congruence and a partial translation between and across intentions, representation in form, and lived experiences, impacts on how designers work.

Finally, Part 3: *Shifting the boundaries* offers some examples which help us think about the implications of the arguments made here for learning space design at a variety of levels.

Chapter 8: *Designing learning as a transitional space* opens up different ways of developing new kinds of learning spaces, looking particularly at the immediate level of learning encounters. It brings together ideas and research that articulate learning as a transitional space, and explores what this might mean for design.

Chapter 9: *Hybrid spaces and the impact of new technologies* looks at how new information and communication technologies are affecting the development of both virtual and material spaces. The chapter first critically engages with the concept of affordances; that is, what a medium is 'capable' of. It then explores how articulating ICT (information and communication technology) as a part of the repertoire of educational communities of practice can help us locate it differently in contemporary design debates. The chapter thus offers a critique of some of the simplistic assumptions around the role of technology in learning, and explores some examples that illustrate a richer understanding of the intersections between learning, technology and space.

Finally, Chapter 10: *Creative learning spaces: towards the porous campus?* returns to the level of the educational institution, to explore how engaging creatively and constructively with the conceptual frameworks and methods offered in this book can help us re-think the architectural design of post-compulsory education. It considers some examples of learning spaces both within and beyond the campus, not as preferred 'solutions' but as a way of illuminating the kinds of questions designers, university managers and academics should be asking.

Locating constructive interventions

Towards Creative Learning Spaces aims to be part of the beginning of richer debate and more informed theory and practice around the design of learning spaces in post-compulsory education. Such a re-thinking is essential for many reasons. A better and more creative understanding of the relationships between built space and its occupation is of importance to both educational and architectural theories, where intersections across these disciplines remain poorly conceptualised. Developing frameworks and methods for understanding the everyday social and spatial practices of learning are of value to those who may have previously thought little about the relationships between space and activities, to those who find themselves involved in actual building projects, and to those for whom the practice of architecture and design is central. In integrating issues of education, design and cost, this work also supports the development of a better understanding of how to make enhanced learning spaces that are also resource-effective and sustainable.

But perhaps most crucially, such re-thinking re-introduces to learning space debates and practices the many complex challenges and realities of post-compulsory education in the current period. For it is not just formal or informal learning but the whole shape of higher, further and adult education that is at stake. This means recognising and engaging with the multitude of contested arguments over basic issues such as the status of knowledge, the value of learning, who has access to learning and where and how it occurs. Architecture is not the only – or even the central – mechanism through which such processes as these happen through time and in different places and contexts. But architectural design does have a recognisable and meaningful place. With a better understanding of where that place lies, designers (and clients and users) can take an even more creative and constructive part in the future enhancement of spaces for learning in post-compulsory education.

Part 1

Reviewing our frames

Chapter 1

Learning spaces from an architectural perspective

There are now a considerable number of building designs aimed at creating innovative types of informal, non-hierarchical, flexible and technology-rich spaces for learning in post-compulsory education, both in the UK and globally. Rather than merely list good examples, which can be easily found elsewhere (JISC 2006; Scottish Funding Council 2006; Tertiary Education Facilities Management Association (TEFMA) 2006; Australian Teaching and Learning Council (ATLC) 2007; Oblinger 2006), this chapter aims instead to critically explore some of the underlying conceptual frameworks and assumptions behind these recent architectural projects. In fact, I suggest that a set of new design 'types' is already coming into such common usage as to potentially be the new norm. This raises several questions that are not yet being asked. How do such innovative learning spaces connect ideas about physical space to intended effects on learning? What new typologies are being offered as more appropriate environments for post-compulsory education? Are these new kinds of environments enhancing learning as predicted? Does this recent addition of new types of learning space provide for the full range of learning in post-compulsory education, or are there important gaps and alternatives which are not being considered? And how do these new building designs relate to shifts in contemporary architecture more generally, especially to its most recent theories about, and approaches to, the design of space and its occupation? Ultimately I will argue that in order to answer these questions we need to unravel what matters about space when it comes to learning; that is, to develop a better understanding of how space 'works'.

The impact of the informal learning model on design

In September 2007, a design workshop was organised by architects Wood Bagot in Melbourne, Australia, to 'create a new generation of learning environments on campus which support the shift towards more student-centred, collaborative and problem-based learning approaches' (Jamieson 2008: 2). This workshop started from the 'common-sense' belief, already outlined, that current learning spaces in universities and colleges are no longer adequate for the emerging pedagogies of higher education. Delegates agreed that we are – or should be – moving from a teacher-centric transfer of knowledge (via the archetypical lecture theatre) towards more student-centred, collaborative and problem-based learning approaches. By focusing on the design of the classroom setting 'where the bulk of an under-graduate student's formal educational experience takes place' (Jamieson 2008: 4), the workshop therefore aimed to stimulate thinking about new learning environments, to find more creative ways of engaging participants in the design process, and to find ways of prioritising design in the educational project management process. Participants were invited to imagine new class spaces, based on more informal, flexible and personalised forms of learning. The 'problem' was framed as follows:

> In formal classrooms, in particular, the physical environment is funda-mental to the experience of the student. The physical setting shapes expectations, class size, enables certain possibilities for acting whilst impeding or excluding others, and impacts on matters such as student control and ownership of the setting. More subjectively, the setting is intrinsically linked to student comfort and motivation as it involves fun-damental characteristics such as acoustic quality, thermal and lighting levels as well as decorative aspects such as colour and material finishes that are integral to the occupant's well-being and capability.
>
> (Jamieson 2008: 20)

Thus, the argument goes, a space set up for presentational delivery from the front by one person to large numbers of individuals does not prevent, but may work against, collaborative and small-group activities, especially where furniture and other facilities are fixed. In addition, the occupants of a space are seen to be affected by its environmental qualities, functional and relational capabilities, and by the 'cues' it offers as to what is likely to be going on there. By analysing these conditions and altering them, behaviours can also be altered.

The report's author, Peter Jamieson, proposes that two key disciplines facilitate this type of analysis, each with a discourse that has previously developed independently. These are teaching and learning research (e.g. Entwistle 1984; Ramsden 1992; Prosser and Trigwell 1999) and environmental behaviour and psy-chology (e.g. Canter and Lee 1974; Lawson 2001; Scott-Webber 2004). The former has opened up debates about how to make higher education more student-centred, the latter enables better understanding of how humans relate to the built environ-ment and what this means for the performance of teachers and students in the classroom. Jamieson argues that bringing these disciplines together enables us to understand, for example, 'the need for natural light, the preference for certain colours [and] the issue of 'personal' space (Jamieson 2008: 24). Following Scott-Webber (2004: 6), he proposes that the design task is:

> to create environments capable of supporting intended behaviours. It follows, then, that the role of educators in contributing to the design of improved learning environments should be to articulate the intended

behaviours of the teachers and students in those settings in order to
inform the spatial solutions provided by the design team.

(Jamieson 2008: 25)

As Jamieson emphasises, this is not a simplistic deterministic relationship between
spatial 'cause' and learning 'effect':

Lawson (2001) talks about the designer influencing, but not determining,
behaviour by making a 'move in space that frames or invites behaviour'
and knowing 'when to leave the space more ambiguous' (p. 225). It may
be as much a matter of what we design 'out', as opposed to what we
design 'in', that leads to an effective learning environment. Can we antici-
pate all the needs and intentions of the users (teacher and students)?
Should we even try? Which needs or functions are most important to
accommodate and how do we prioritise these?

(Jamieson 2008: 14)

In addition to this problem of explicitly articulating the complex and partial relationships between behaviours and environment, there is also the difficulty of being
able to analyse precisely what it is that teachers, students and researchers actually
do, and how and why this is changing. Thus, Woods Bagot suggest, an expertise
in educational planning is also required, which can 'translate' between design and
pedagogic languages, both in defining appropriate intended behaviours and in offering relevant design solutions.

All of this can appear so obvious and straightforward, that it hardly
seems worth discussing. Of course we are affected by poor-quality environments
(too hot, too cold, without a view, drab, etc.), and improvements in comfort and
quality are likely to enhance our experiences of a space. Behavioural and environmental psychologists have been attempting to precisely pin down these different
stimuli–response mechanisms, with varying degrees of success, for many years
(Edgerton, Romice and Spencer 2007). Yet, while such approaches have their value
in highlighting the basic functional and physiological dimensions of material space,
they are less useful for unravelling the multiplicity of everyday social and spatial
intersections that occur when particular participant groupings come together and
engage in specific cultural – here learning – practices, embedded in situated contexts. These activities are inherently complex, dynamic, contested and open to many
interpretations simultaneously. What the Melbourne workshop actually illustrates is
both the important but relatively banal qualities that behaviourist approaches can best
address, centring on comfort, 'attractiveness' and flexibility, and the impossibility of
pinning down a standard formula or solution that makes a better, informal learning
classroom.

In fact, here, as in many other arguments in favour of informal learning
spaces, the overall 'solutions' are already given by the initial premise. Because there
is an intended shift away from formal to more informal and student-centred learning
methods, there is a perceived need for new types of non-hierarchical and flexible

classrooms which can both accommodate a greater range of activities and 'promote movement within the space and enable student control over facilities such as tables, chairs, benches, IT devices and learning materials' (Jamieson 2008: 11).

But at the same time, this 'obvious' idea of making more flexible spaces turns out to be itself full of complexities and difficulties. The aim, after all, is to re-think the classroom space such that it 'is likely that a radically different conception of the "classroom" as a learning environment will emerge with inspiration drawn from other successful social, recreational, and workplace environments' (Jamieson 2008: 20). Yet the notion of what flexibility actually means in this context, and how it might lead to such a radical shift, turns out to be deeply problematic:

> What is meant by flexibility? Does it refer to the capacity to move and re-arrange furniture at the discretion of the user, allowing the use to change according to need? Does it refer to the range of activity that can be sup-ported in a single space simultaneously? Alternatively, does it mean that a space is adaptable and able to support pedagogical alternatives – in other words, different modes of teaching and learning?
>
> (Jamieson 2008: 58)

But if flexibility is actually about enabling different modes of teaching and learning, then surely this is an issue of changing educational methods rather than spaces? In fact, what is required is a better understanding of the range of existing and poten-tial teaching and learning modes in any particular situation, as well as the particular spatial and architectural conditions which can support them. Ultimately this is less a matter of generic 'flexibility' than of developing techniques for the creative and constructive mapping of teaching and learning practices and spaces. This will be explored in greater detail in Chapter 5. What is interesting about the Melbourne workshop, as a good example of current debates, is that it mainly exposes how under-theorised the relationship between learning and space remains, and it also often reveals the ambiguities and problems in what is offered up as a common-sense and obvious solution – informal and flexible design.

The architectural practice behind the workshop, Woods Bagot, is an inter-national firm with considerable professional expertise in the area of education. Like many mainstream architect practices, it has built up a body of specialist knowledge by moving easily and eclectically across various approaches and methods, including, but also beyond, behaviourist methods. These architects are strongly aware that architecture is not just about comfort and 'attractiveness', but also, for example, about more strategic concerns, which frame the learning encounter/classroom arrangement such as cost, structural and constructional robustness, management, identity and other institutional agendas. John Holm, also from Woods Bagot, spoke at the Melbourne workshop about how architects must:

> traditionally (do) 'things right', which means ensuring the building is tech-nically correct in terms of variables such as occupancy levels, activities, comfort (temperature, light, ventilation, occupational health and safety,

personal safety) and condition (maintenance, wear and tear, anticipated life expectancy).

But they must also achieve 'organisational outcomes' – much harder to measure – 'such as flexibility (capacity for growth, modification and adaptation), performance (effectiveness of facility in achieving teaching and learning outcomes), and branding (image, design and appropriateness)' (Jamieson 2008: 48).

Here, though, I want to suggest that the common-sense behaviourism of much mainstream architectural practice hides more than it reveals, and to explore how we can think differently about the relationships between learning and space. As I have already noted, whilst it remains important to engage with functional and physiological needs, these should not be assumed as obvious and generic, but as having complex and situated intersections with the *spatial and social practices* through which we 'do learning'. To examine this further I want first to look at the effects such common-sense and behaviourist understandings currently circulating are having on the development of particular building types for post-compulsory education over recent years; and then to consider alternative understandings in contemporary architecture about how space 'works' in relation to its occupation – which, I suggest, can better inform our understandings of, and approaches to, learning spaces.

Towards a new educational building type for post-compulsory education?

An outline review of many of the current examples of new learning spaces in post-compulsory education (Table 1.1) suggests that a particular grouping of design responses is already forming across the sector. When we drew up a taxonomy (Smith and Boys forthcoming) of the building examples that were used again and again to illustrate best practice, certain elements repeatedly occurred. Most of the examples circulating within the UK concentrate on informal learning, often connected to libraries, resource centres and/or student support units. In the US and Australia, there are also many examples related to generating new hybrid research spaces, where different disciplines can intersect and collaborate.

These new kinds of learning spaces offer both design metaphors and physical arrangements, centred on a certain set of associated ideas (Fig. 1.1). Spaces are envisaged as enabling collaboration and interaction (both educational and social), articulated, for example, as 'atrium', 'street', 'hub', 'drop-in centre' and 'learning café'; particular spatial layouts for enabling a range of group and individual study combinations in space, such as learning 'nooks', 'pods' and 'clusters'; a tendency to informal, 'softer' furniture such as beanbags, asymmetric furniture layouts, bright colours and 'landmark' elements such as special features or artist commissions; and finally, what are usually called technology-rich environments.

A good example is Telford College in Edinburgh where, as their website notes:

Table 1.1 Examples of new 'informal' learning space design in the UK.

Learning space	Environment	Design attributes
Saltire Centre, Glasgow Caledonian University (see http://www.gcu.ac.uk/thesaltirecentre/) (2006, BDP architects) Library, atrium, internet café, informal learning, flexible study spaces, technology-rich environment, landmark building, art commission		'Using the idea that learning begins with a conversation, we created a wide range of environments to stimulate thought or discussion. These included group areas, cafés, incidental places on circulation routes, silent 'monk cells' and terraced south-facing garden areas.' (http://www.bdp.com/Projects/By-Name/P-Z/Saltire-Centre/)
Telford College, Edinburgh (see http://www.ed-coll.ac.uk/) (2006, HOK Architects) Social hub, atrium, internet café, learning streets, open-access computer labs, flexible study spaces, technology-rich environment.		'The college includes a wide variety of learning environments equipped with 'touchdown' desks for students to freely use the internet and to work on assignments. Providing natural light and ventilation to the classrooms on either side, the Learning Streets avoids the 'corridor' effect typical of large education establishments.' (http://www.hok.com/)
Learning Grid, University of Warwick (see http://www2.warwick.ac.uk/) (2004, MJP Architects) Library, atrium, student resource centre, informal learning, technology-rich environment, flexible study spaces, artwork commission.		'MJP used a range of screens and furniture to create a loose arrangement of working areas that the students can reconfigure to suit their changing needs. Curves, colours and textured materials are used to create a lively environment – and as a reaction against other facilities which provide dreary rows of computer desks.' (http://www.mjparchitects.co.uk/Learning_Grid.php)

Learning space	Environment	Design attributes
Centre for Inquiry-based Learning in the Arts and Social Sciences (CILASS), and Information Commons, University of Sheffield (see http://www.shef.ac.uk/cilass/) (2007, RMJM architects) Information Commons, open-access computer labs, informal learning, flexible study spaces, technology-rich environment.		'Provides a 24/7 integrated learning environment for undergraduate and postgraduate students. It provides 1,350 new study spaces where students can study individually or in groups, using print and electronic materials. It has been designed to accommodate current and future learning methods and technologies.' (http://www.rmjm.com/projects/information-commons-university-of-sheffield-england)
Techno-café, Department of Computer Science, University of Durham (see http://www.dur.ac.uk/alic/technocafe/) (2006, P H Partnership) Internet café, informal learning, flexible study space, technology-rich environment.		'The client required an innovative computer lab which offered interactive space for people to socialise during group work sessions. Work Pods encapsulating state of the art AV technology and interactive tablet PCs were developed within a modern interior and functional space to offer a hint of techno chic. Pods clad in translucent polycarbonate material, were backlit to provide a soft-lit environment.' (http://www.phparchitects.co.uk/?section=technocafe.php)
InQbate Creativity Zone, University of Sussex (see http://www.inqbate.co.uk/) (2006, University of Sussex) Immersive environment, new technologies, flexible teaching and learning space, teaching creativity.		'Fully technology-enabled, but not technology-driven, the Sussex creativity zone provides teaching staff with personal, pedagogic and technical support, along with resources that can be used in a variety of configurations. It is hoped that this will support more innovative and effective teaching and learning in both the InQbate creativity zone itself as well as other teaching spaces on campus.' (http://www.inqbate.co.uk/content/view/33/97/)

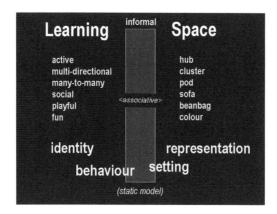

Fig. 1.1
Examples of
associative
design metaphors
for informal
learning spaces.

Learning and study facilities have been extended without the traditional classroom and library environments to give students more freedom to study where it suits them. Two Learning Streets run along the length of the first floor and provide access to computers and group study areas for 4–6 students. The streets are staffed by Learning Resource Centre (LRC) Assistants, so specialist support is always available.

(http://www.ed-coll.ac.uk/content.asp?ArticleCode=185
&par=1)

At Telford, the student social area is part of the main entrance and reception. It is a double-height top-lit and arched space known as the 'hub' (Fig. 1.2), surrounded by a range of services in single-height wings to either side, including Student Services, a hairdressing salon, a beauty therapy salon as well as different food stalls and the college's own restaurant. These facilities are also open to the public, with the explicit intention of 'making the whole campus accessible and welcoming to the wider community'. The learning streets, described above, run either side of this central space and service flexible classrooms (Fig. 1.3).

Similarly we can see a mix of each of these aspects at the Saltire Centre, Glasgow Caledonian University: another frequently referenced example, which is

designed to provide users with a variety of different spaces, from noisy social interaction areas for group work, to places for silent study. The flexibility of the building will also give staff the opportunity to experiment further with student-centred, active learning approaches.

(http://www.gcu.ac.uk/thesaltirecentre/building/index.html)

Like Telford, Saltire also has a central glass atrium and exhibition space, here five storeys high, which 'in addition to providing maximum natural lighting [. . .] will aid natural ventilation and environmental control within the building', which is also linked to a 'street' – a student services mall – this time offering 'a one-stop-shop for our

students, enabling them to access all of the services that they might need in a single location'. There is a 'learning café' for 'relaxed group study space', outdoor terraces, and a variety of seating arrangements and types. The building is a technology-rich wireless environment throughout, so students can use portable IT devices such as laptops, PDAs and tablet PCs anywhere. Finally, Saltire uses the device of a copper-sheathed tower as 'a stunning landmark on the campus', also visible from the motorway and from various sites in the city, 'reaffirming the university's position in the heart of Glasgow', and has commissioned two works by artists (http://www. gcu.ac.uk/thesaltirecentre/building/index.html).

These recent design responses have also been informed by, and are informing changes in other building types, particularly workplaces (Duffy and Powell 1997; Worthington 2006; Myerson and Ross 2006). Here the arguments have been very similar to those in education: that traditional office work used to be mainly about repetitive assembly-line-type tasks, but is now much more centred on what Myerson and Ross call 'knowledge work' based on creativity and interactive information exchange. Rather than gridded cubicles in open-plan offices, then, workplace design is also moving towards informality, shared social spaces, clusters and more informal, playful design (Fig. 1.3). Companies such as Google have been at the forefront of these kinds of approaches (http://www.google.com/corporate/culture.html). In their turn, new workplace specialists have begun to focus on academic workplace provision, although here interestingly, a central concern has been resource efficiency; that is, in reducing the amount of 'inappropriate' individual cellular offices for academics (Harrison and Cairns 2009).

Leaving aside the realities of many workers (in places such as international call centres) who may not have the opportunities to enjoy such creative working environments, these examples – however good – beg some really basic and essential questions. First, is the problem of how ideas about a particular set of activities (learning, working) are translated into physical form; here I will suggest

Fig. 1.4
Creative office design for IQ Marketing, Moscow (Anastasia Panibratova, 2007).
Photograph: Jos Boys.

mainly through the mechanism of metaphor. Second, the implicit use of metaphors as a means of designing, while often potent and relevant, enables us to avoid the issue of what is distinctive (if anything) about the characteristics of post-compulsory learning which might make it different to, for example, the workplace. Third, we need to know more about what matters about space (both physical and virtual) for the specific social and spatial practices of learning. And, finally, we need to have mechanisms for evaluating the effectiveness of the impact of different environments on the quality of learning that takes place in them. How do we know if one 'learning hub' works better than another?

The value and problems of using metaphors for learning

Metaphor is a central, though often not explicit, aspect of architectural design. As Peter Jamieson writes for the workshop with which this chapter began:

> The use of 'metaphor' can provide a basis for individuals and teams (especially when they have little formal design expertise) to engage in the design process and establish a common language. I have used the metaphor of the 'classroom as nightclub or cabaret' as the basis for a recent and extremely effective refurbishment of a traditional classroom into a multi-level collaborative learning environment. Other metaphors I have used include 'classroom as empty space' – a room with little furniture and which conjures up various thoughts of what a student would do and how they would do it; 'classroom as a sandpit' – a space for play and discovery (words that are seldom used when describing learning in higher education); 'classroom as café' – a casual lounge setting with no obvious 'front' of class location.
>
> (Jamieson 2008: 32)

So, the atrium, street or hub both literally represent the idea of inter-mixing, sharing and unexpected encounters, and aim to facilitate it. Ditto, the 'drop-in centre' and 'learning café' and particular spatial layouts for enabling a range of group and individual study combinations in space, such as corridor 'learning nooks' or 'pods' offering a metaphorical image of 'small-groupness' as well as intending to offer locations in which peer-to-peer and informal teacher–student can easily occur. The tendency to informal, 'softer' furniture such as beanbags, asymmetric furniture layouts, bright colours and 'landmark' elements such as special features or artist commissions also speaks of these assumed 'new' types of relationship; as does the associative resonance between new technologies (with their focus on social networking, anytime access and interactivity) and new attitudes to learning.

This leads, in turn, to more questions. First, to what extent are such metaphors shared? While beanbags may well express informal, comfortable, playful and relaxed ways of working to some students, others see them as childish and inappropriate. Second, are there other metaphors that might usefully add to our repertoire for post-compulsory education, as indicated by Jamieson? Softroom, the architects of the Sackler Centre for Arts Education at the Victoria and Albert Museum in London, for example, reference artists' studios as a key metaphor in support of their design (http://www.vimeo.com/5858785). How far might such metaphors go before they cease to have a resonance with a particular design area? How does the underlying associational process work? And perhaps most importantly, what is the relationship between the expressive, representational aspects of such metaphors and their lived experience?

In relation to this last question there remains surprisingly little research. Where work exists it tends to stem from anthropology and ethnography rather than education or architecture. It is deeply critical of the mismatches, particularly in modernist design, between metaphorical intentions and the experiences of everyday life (Boudon 1979; Holston 1989). This underlying tendency for particular problems, where the metaphorical intention is taken as evidence of what actually happens, can actually be illustrated again and again. For example, the idea of the 'street' (which has been a staple of post-war secondary school design in the UK (Saint 1987)) has had many criticisms over the years, but has been re-articulated many times over in new post-compulsory educational buildings. This is not to say that some street-type spaces do not work in educational environments, only that they are often based on the simplistic notion that mere adjacency will, of itself, enable constructive interaction. For, as Nigel Thrift writes, 'these buildings are clearly meant to manipulate time and space in order to produce intensified social interaction so that all manner of crossovers of ideas can be achieved' (Thrift 2008: 44). He lists several buildings in the UK and the USA designed on this basis and goes on to outline their common features:

> First, they will often include an explicit attempt to represent 'life', whether that be swooping architecture, some form of public display of science, or similar devices. Second, they are meant to be highly interdisciplinary. [. . .] Very often, they will place apparently unlike activities (such as computer laboratories and wet laboratories) side by side, or have unorthodox office allocation schedules, all intended to stimulate interdisciplinarity. Third, they are porous. Personnel [. . .] and information constantly flow through them. [. . .] Fourth, in keeping with an architectural rhetoric about changing ways of working which arose in the mid-1980s and is now an established convention, they are meant to encourage creative sociability, arising out of and fuelling further unpredictable interactions. From cafes to temporary dens, to informal meeting rooms, to walkways that force their denizens to interact (Duffy and Powell 1997), the idea is clearly to encourage a 'buzz' of continuous conversation oriented to 'transactional knowledge' and, it is assumed, innovation. Fifth, they are meant to be transparent: there are numerous vantage points from which to spot and track activity, both to add to the general ambience and to point to the values/value of the scientific activity that is going on.

> (Thrift 2008: 45)

But Thrift also goes on to note that 'although these buildings place a clear premium on interdisciplinary discovery, it is often not clear how that process of discovery is being maximised'. He suggests that in addition to the representational/functional/facilitative elements of the architecture itself, the managers of these buildings have also had to implement new *processes* – the designation of explicit 'brokers' and 'pathfinders' to enable cross-disciplinary collaboration, mechanisms to keep people 'on the move so as to avoid group decay and organisational inertia' (p. 46).

Metaphor then is a useful but dangerous tool for designers, their clients and users. It can represent a social-spatial idea and give it the appearance of 'obvious' and 'commonly agreed' reality, especially where it becomes a well-recognised convention through time. But this does not mean that the resulting space is interpreted by all its occupiers in the same way, or that other ways of expressing spatial and social relationships are not possible which are not generated from metaphor; and – most crucially – that the representational image necessarily or transparently translates into an equivalent everyday lived experience. In many ways this is a counter-intuitive idea; we are so used to taking design metaphors as powerful expressions of social reality, linking high-rise housing, for example, to poverty and social deprivation, and suburban estates to middle-class conformity, that we are surprised (and consider it newsworthy) when reality fails to match – for example, where a violent crime happens in a suburban area. But at the same time, we often experience the inconsistencies and tensions between the representational qualities of a space and its lived engagement. In the above example of 'street' designs for new research institutes, many of us would remain unconvinced that merely bringing a variety of people together in close proximity is likely to 'automatically' enhance their relationships, unless there is already a commitment to this end by the individuals involved.

Even more problematically, the use of metaphor can constrain other, more rigorous and theoretical, engagements with space and learning. The 'common-sense' analysis of space, where designs that 'look' informal are somehow assumed to generate informal learning, is tautological (with each 'proving' the other in a closed loop). It seems so obvious that a more 'informal' setting will generate informal learning that we fail to ask deeper questions. For example, if our aim is to help students to learn *how to learn* in this way (that learning is about being collaborative, creative, interactive and lateral) then we may in fact need to develop a highly structured series of development activities. Whether these are considered formal or informal is actually of little consequence. What matters is whether the teaching and learning is of value, and has an effective impact.

This problem with the use of metaphor as a design method is not new to architecture. Along with cultural and critical theorists more generally, designers and critics have long been arguing against exactly this emphasis on representation (where space is articulated as a setting) and towards practices (where space is a process). The key point here is that current concepts about designing for learning – such as flexibility and/or metaphors of informality and playfulness – are deeply flawed conceptually. They are based on underlying common-sense assumptions, usually linked to an un-thought-through reference to behaviourism, which assumes a transparent, direct and obvious relationship both between design intention and lived reality; and between the representational qualities of a space and the practices which occupy it.

Yet, much contemporary architectural practice and theory has been challenging these assumptions, a process that have already been going on since the 1980s. This means that new ideas about learning are still being translated into built form with little or no reference to the most recent developments in architectural theory – and in cultural theory more generally. These have been part of a much wider paradigm shift away from the 'grand narratives' of enlightenment and modernist thinking based on the simple expression of function, coherence and order and towards ideas of hybridity, partiality and dynamism (Harvey 1989; Jameson 1992). This work has been informed by theorists across many disciplines, especially those concerned to deconstruct the assumed coherences between language and meaning (Baudrillard 1981; Derrida 2001) and philosophers such as Deleuze and Guattari (2000) whose writings have a particularly 'spatial' turn. Next, then, I want to explore some of these shifts in architectural theory and practice since the 1980s, and to consider the implications for thinking about the relationships between space and learning differently.

From representations to practices: new architectural approaches

Much contemporary architecture theory has engaged with the problems in modernist and behaviourist thinking about space, exploring ways to articulate relationships between space and occupation less as a stimuli–response mechanism and much more as the dynamic interaction of social and spatial practices. With the shift away from modernist to post-modernist and post-structuralist understandings, space has been increasingly understood as inherently performative and events-based; it is not just a neutral container or 'setting' into which behaviours are 'poured'. This is something much more complex, partial and fluid than any simple cause and effect relationship, however partial. These ideas developed within architecture through the work of architects such as Bernard Tschumi (1994, 1996) and Rem Koolhaas (1997; Koolhaas and Mau 1997). Interestingly, both of these architects have undertaken designs for post-compulsory educational institutions, which – perhaps because they do not fall within the formal/informal design divisions circulating within UK, USA and Australian debates – are not included in the 'standard' reviews of new learning spaces. Can we, then, both inform and shift the learning spaces debate in post-compulsory education, through an engagement with these theorists/designers?

When Bernard Tschumi writes about his practice's scheme for the Le Fresnoy National Studio for Contemporary Arts, Tourcoing, France (1991–97) he calls it 'a strategy of the in-between'. The project was for the conversion of a ten-thousand-square-metre building, to include a school, a film studio, a médiathèque, exhibition halls, two cinemas, laboratories for research and production (sound, electronic image, film and video), administrative offices, housing and a bar/restaurant. Because the existing property was made up of a series of buildings in a variety of relatively poor conditions, Tschumi proposed a big roof over the top, which combined the protection of everything underneath from the weather with an overarching technology-rich infrastructure. As he goes on to describe it:

Conceptually, we see the project as a succession of boxes inside a box.

The outer box is the rectangular, ultra-technological solid of modernity, whose north side is closed. The other sides remain open and provide a view of the old and new buildings. [. . .] Under the large electronic roof are the boxes of the existing building, most hereafter sheltered from the bad weather. [. . .] At the same time, we conceived the new facilities located in the existing volumes as technically autonomous boxes while maintaining the fluidity of the Fresnoy spaces. [. . .]

If the new roof acts as the project's common denominator (a large screen-umbrella), we also sought to accelerate the probability of chance-events by combining diverse elements (umbrella and sewing machine meet on the dissecting table), juxtaposing great roof, school/research laboratory and the old Fresnoy, place of spectacle. [. . .] we can speak of an 'architecture-event' rather than an 'architecture-object'. The interstitial space between the new and old roofs becomes a place of fantasies and experiments (filming and other exploratory works on space and time).

(http://www.archined.nl/oem/reportages/fresnoy/fresnoy3.html)

Here Tschumi is, of course, using the metaphorical qualities of the 'big roof', as well as its functional and organisational characteristics. But his approach also centres on *relationships* rather than behaviours. And in articulating particular relationships between categories of activities, he also offers us gaps – non-defined zones – between these categories, in which non-formalised activities can take place. Thus, rather than designing space for both formal and informal learning as an imposed pattern of intended behaviours and responses, he leaves spaces in-between.

Rem Koolhaas and his practice, the Office of Metropolitan Architecture (OMA), have also undertaken a number of international education-related projects, of various scales, such as Seattle Central Library, Seoul National University Museum in South Korea and Qatar Education City. Here the invited competition entry for a Multi-Media and Information Technology building for the City University of Hong Kong in Kowloon (2004) is of interest, both because it offers an example of Koolhaas's approach and because it deals explicitly with the impact of new technologies at a strategic and expressive level, rather than as something merely added on to existing space. As he writes:

Planning a media building is an instance where the most permanent and spatially defined of disciplines – architecture – meets the most ephemeral and placeless discipline – media. [. . .] How can frequent technological and programmatic change be accommodated in architectural construction? How can a building exemplify and enhance the curriculum for a new media school without limiting its development and misinterpreting its future? How can architecture embody media? How can a building bridge the gap between the local reality of architecture and the global presence of media? Should it?

(http://www.oma.nl/)

In their competition entry OMA argue for a division of building design into 'Hardware' (all the physical elements of the building, architectural and technological), 'Software' (all the programmatic or digital elements providing particular services and all aspects of use, both digital and spatial) and 'Content' (all elements that contribute to the project's identity). As they go on:

> In its founding era, the development of new media was a question of faith; during the internet bubble it became an object of greed, and with the burst of the bubble it turned into a domain of skepticism. While technical abilities are unprecedented, good ideas, sustainable discourse and viable business models are rare. We created a continent of new possibilities and now do not know how to settle it.
>
> Yet, the absence of ready-made solutions puts the school in a unique position. It can draw from its background spanning East and West, art and technology, the public and academic, rather than from the monoculture of NASDAQ, Moore's law and free speech. It can have a focus on communication rather than technology, exchange rather than indoctrination. It can be a trading house rather than a trademark, an engine rather than an icon.
>
> (http://www.oma.nl/)

This meant moving away from designing learning spaces divided up into subject disciplines per se, towards the underlying types of 'study, production and display', which then have both areas of specialisation and areas of interaction. As with Tschumi's Le Fresnoy scheme, concepts within the category 'Hardware' reflect similar contemporary concerns with informal and chance encounters, hybrid relationships and collaboration, and the metaphorical and performative expression of these intended relationships. As Koolhaas goes on, the 'Parts' here are 'a machine for spectacles, a tower for display, a laboratory for production, a hive for study [. . .] and a hypercore connecting and cross-fertilising the different parts – incorporating all programme types' – so not unlike the hubs, clusters and landmarks previously mentioned. But, if the elements are similar, what Koolhaas adds is a simultaneous engagement with the intended processes and practices:

> Instead of defining a building through a room program, we could define it by the services it needs to provide. Many services would not require to be fixed to a room but could be temporarily 'downloaded'. The building then would not be understood by 'use' but by 'uselets'. A classroom for example would be defined as a set of services 'downloaded' and activated by a user (a teacher or student) rather than as a space. Such services might be for example the registration of location and time of a lesson in the school schedule and the building of a way-finding system, access control, a label at the entrance (teacher and course number) and basic teaching infrastructure. A lesson could take place in a theatre, in a museum space, in a laboratory or off-site.

Equally, any physical room could become part of a display sequence, any space a production space and so on. Use so defined is not restricted to the building, but could be invoked while in transit, at a desk during an internship or at a store. Applications can be created by the school, but also by external providers, former students or staff.

(http://www.oma.nl/)

Thus, OMA are proposing a building that can be constantly reconfigured. 'The school could react to trends, strategies and opportunities. It would be a network participating in larger networks of collaboration. It could redefine itself constantly – foregrounding different abilities in different contexts.' This is not flexibility as the potential to move furniture or even as the adaptability to different teaching and learning practices; it is the ability of the whole institution to adapt quickly to changing internal and external conditions.

Beyond settings for learning

These projects – while attempting to reject the representational and metaphorical – both have a strong metaphorical 'centre', showing perhaps that architecture cannot avoid expressing ideas in physical form, however hard it tries. But what these projects also do is to take an approach which goes beyond the notion of formal/informal as a binary opposition or as the 'setting' for learning encounters. Instead they start from the conceptual and strategic, and are also willing to engage in formal and compositional as well as metaphoric understandings of space. In addition, relationships between space and its occupation are articulated via an underlying and explicit conceptual framework, informed by contemporary cultural theory and which both architects have described in various ways in their writings. This is built on three interconnected ideas which attempt to undermine the assumption that design intention and lived reality are interchangeable, that a building can transparently represent its occupation (without any redundancy) or that we have a simplistic stimuli–response relationship to architectural space. Instead, design is articulated as an event-based practice; occupation is envisaged less as a set of functional activities and more as a series of overlapping affective encounters; and physical space is conceptualised as non-congruent with the activities that take place in it. That is, it is seen as having only a partial and uneven effect on occupation, such that there will inevitably be many inconsistencies, and uncontrollable gaps.

Thus, because space is understood as a relationship rather than a setting or entity it can never exist meaningfully separate from the participants that inhabit it, and the situated context in which they (and the space) are operating. This approach will be briefly expanded below, and its potential for informing the design of learning spaces initially considered.

Design as an event-based practice

What is odd in learning spaces debates is that whilst contemporary ideas about teaching and learning have been profoundly influenced by wider shifts in cultural theory, attitudes to how space *works* have remained resolutely stuck in a commonsense, modernist and functional mode. Space is still seen as the setting for behaviours. This is despite the fact that what is often termed the cultural turn, informed by post-modernism and post-structuralism, is also transforming how contemporary architecture is 'thought' across both its theories and practices. So learning space design urgently needs to engage critically, creatively and constructively with these newer theories and methods. What does this mean? Well, first, that the relationship between learning and the spaces in which it takes place is articulated as a series of events, which are inevitably uncontrollable and which do not need to be directly 'matched' with or congruently ordered 'onto' space:

> Thus we arrive at a notion of site as an active and always incomplete incarnation of events, an actualization of times and spaces that uses the fluctuating conditions to assemble itself (Kwon 2004). Site is not so much the result of punctual, external causes, therefore, as it is an insertion in to one or more flows.
>
> (Thrift 2008: 12)

This has had two (uneven) impacts on some ideas about design approaches and methods. First, many architects and designers have been introducing more lateral, even random, concepts to generate form; here summarised succinctly by Helene Frichot:

> The first phase of the diagram describes a practice in which architects have almost always been adept. Taking the given brief for a proposed architectural project, the architect sets to work. First, the functions that the project will accommodate are specified. Second, these functions are arranged according to type. Third, the above arrangements according to type and function take into consideration a given site. [. . .] Finally, the architect discovers he has his container. [. . .]
>
> The second phase of the diagram is where [. . .] the traditional process described above is insufficient. [. . .] The second diagram answers to a force that is preferably derived from outside the field of architecture so as to invest new possibilities into the architectural process. Take your pick – diagrams of solution waves, DNA structures, liquid crystals, geometric processes such as sine waves, fractals, morphing – it is up to you. These diagrams from the outside are then superimposed across the traditional diagram. The idea is to destroy one clarity with another clarity in order to create a blurriness, or what we might call a zone of obscurity [. . .]
>
> (Frichot 2005: 74–5)

In other cases, architects are re-articulating their relationships to clients and users. Atelier D'Architecture Autogeree (AAA), for example, calls their approach *urban tactics* – probably the closest that architecture can get to non-representational practice. AAA do not make architecture, they make space-events and participatory processes:

> A 'self-managed architecture' provokes assemblages and networks of individuals, desires and different manners of making. It is a relational practice, which is not always consensual but at times conflictual, and it is the role of the architect to locate confrontations and accompany subjective productions. Such architecture does not correspond to a liberal practice but asks for new forms of association and collaboration, based on exchange and reciprocity.
>
> (http://www.urbantactics.org)

Thus the architectural process ceases to be based on an assumed consensus between designer, client and user, or a simple 'mapping' of either existing or preferred functions and behaviours. Instead, it is about much more messy, partial (but also creative) relationships and practices.

Occupation as affective encounters

In re-conceptualising the relationship between space and its occupation, theorists and designers are also interested less in function and behaviour and more in meaning and identity. As Hooper-Greenhill writes:

> Behaviourism proposes that learning takes place through a response following a stimulus. According to this simple model of learning, effects are specific reactions to specific stimuli, so that one can both expect and predict a close correspondence between what is learnt and what is taught.
>
> (Hooper-Greenhill 2000: 133)

But, as Hooper-Greenhill goes on to say, our relationships to both space and learning are also active processes, where we bring what we already know (through previous experience) to each new engagement with a situation, activity or space, so as to both make sense of it and to *learn* from it. Here, she suggests the implications for such learning enablement in a museum context where:

> the focus is on how meaning is constructed through social life by active individual agents, within social networks. Meanings are understood to be negotiated through cognitive frameworks, interpretative strategies and interpretative communities, and are plural, contingent and open to challenge. [. . . C]ommunicators act as enablers and facilitators. The task [. . .] is to provide experiences that invite visitors to make meaning through deploying and extending their existing interpretative strategies and repertoires, using their prior knowledge and their preferred learning styles, and testing their hypotheses against those of others, including experts. The task is to produce opportunities for visitors to use what they know already to build new knowledge and new confidence in themselves as learners and social agents.
>
> (Hooper-Greenhill 2000: 139–40)

Design, then, is not just about signs and significations (settings), but the full reg-isters of thought, including affect and sensation. This is particularly relevant to learning at post-compulsory level, which tends to prioritise intellectual thought and self-reflection.

Yet conscious thought – at least when at its most intellectual – has the effect of 'downgrading' the body's own sensory and emotional experiences, so that the endless sensations of touch and smell do not 'interfere' with thinking but are automatic and 'obvious', while everything except the most demanding emotions are likely to also be blocked. As I will show later, research and evaluations of learning spaces often show that neither academics nor students appear to consider physical building design much in relationship to their studies (Temple 2008). For we often live space, as Walter Benjamin famously wrote, 'in a state of distraction' (1999). But as Thrift notes, this does not adequately capture what is actually experienced:

> Nearly all action is joint action, linked to being-as-a-pair, linked to the digestion of the intricacies of talk and body language, even linked to an ambient sense of the situation to hand. This unremitting work of active reaction imposes enormous evaluative demands, equally enormous demands on intermediate memory, and similarly large demands on the general management of attention.
>
> (Thrift 2008: 7)

Thus affective emotions may be implicit, vague and often un-acknowledged but are in fact high-level cognitive abilities, which monitor, interpret and guide us through our encounters with ideas, objects and spaces as well as others. As researchers such as Noam Austerlitz (2008) are showing, 'unspoken interactions' have a central effect on learning, and how effectively it takes place.

In addition, affective engagements are vital to learning because they are a form of thinking through doing; part of our ongoing creative processes of intersecting what is known with what is not, so as to investigate what might be. This is an attitude rather than a concept or process. And while this is happening the experience is less that of a fully 'conscious' mind, than an 'ongoing process of off-balancing, loosening, bending, twisting, reconfiguring and transforming the permeating, eruptive/disruptive energy and mood below, behind and to the side of focused attention' (Schechner 1993: 43, quoted by Thrift 2008: 119).

As I will show later, many educational theorists still tend to separate out thinking/reflecting and doing/practising, even where they acknowledge that this is an artificial division, and they may even treat them as an oppositional pairing (Kolb and Kolb 2005). But these newer understandings, which are, according to Thrift, increasingly underpinned by neurological research, refuse such a division, looking instead to learning concepts such as 'flow', where a student or researcher becomes completely absorbed, physically and mentally, in the activity they are undertaking (Csíkszentmihályi 1996, 1998). These ideas are bringing a renewed interest in the immediacy of embodiment and experience as a fully integrated and situated corpo-real and cerebral engagement with the world. They are expressed not through (or not only through) conscious thought and language but also through non-representational means – through embodiment.

Non-congruence between intention and experience

As I have already said, in the 1980s and 1990s avant-garde and radical architecture was influenced by theories and approaches, particularly from linguistic theory. For writers such as Jean Baurillard and Jacques Derrida there was no direct connection between what the author intended and how a book's narrative was interpreted by its many readers. The idea of 'supplementaries' (Caputo 1996: 278–95) captured something of this non-congruence. This is the concept that rather than there being a match between idea and result which can be analysed and revealed as coherent and complete, there are both 'gaps' and extras in the space in between the 'thing' and its realisation/interpretation/experience. Analysis becomes, in this case, not so much the construction of a recognisable self-contained and stable totality as the 'deconstruction' of several irreconcilable, contradictory and unstable meanings, which are inherent to any act of production and consumption.

How does this inform our understanding of architecture and learning? The aim of building design is still almost invariably seen as attempting to make a best 'match' or fit with the activities that it contains. This appears such obvious common sense that it is hardly ever questioned. As we look at, and participate in, built space, we often note how it does 'not work'; that is, where it fails to perform appropriately in support of the things that we are doing or want to do. But as soon as we begin to unpick the many, partial, complex and often contested processes through which buildings and spaces are achieved, adapted, removed or replaced, we begin to see that designed space is much more ambiguous. It is not a 'fit' between activities and material, spatial and/or aesthetic arrangements; nor is it a direct, transparently obvious correlation between function and form. It is much more about problematic compromises, collisions and unexpected outcomes. The ideas of both event-based design and non-congruence between design intention and its interpretation/experience, try to capture some of this ambiguity and to admit to the impossibility of architectural design even attempting a perfect fit with activities through time.

Towards a better understanding of social and spatial practices

The key underlying argument in this chapter has been that it is precisely the ideas that are affecting attitudes to learning – emphasising the personal, situated, hybrid, informal, interactive – which are also affecting how architecture is being *thought*. Yet, most of the current debate around innovative forms of learning spaces is still being articulated through older modernist ideas and assumptions about how architecture works. These believe that design can provide a direct fit between space and its occupation, and can be designed as a functional and metaphorical response to human behaviour. These ideas are not 'wrong', but they do tend to frame possibilities in particular ways rather than others.

This 'other' way of looking at architecture suggested here is important for two main reasons. First, it enables us to bring to bear a different kind of examination on the intersections of architectural approaches and designs with educational theories and practices, so as to begin to build a richer and more conceptually rigorous conceptual framework around what matters about space for learning, particularly in the post-compulsory sector. Crucially, this is not about creating a design 'guide' or arguing for particular 'solutions'. It is about accepting partiality, conflict and contradictions, working out what are the relevant questions to ask, and exploring what sorts of problem-seeking (rather than problem-solving) methods and techniques can support architectural decision-making.

Second, it locates architectural space as having a complex and uneven relationship with the activities that go on within it, an attitude that opens up the potential for alternative ways of thinking about the architecture of post-compulsory education beyond the formal/informal learning divide. As I will go on to show, this is both about how we might re-articulate learning as a bundling of distinctive social and spatial practices which are nevertheless open to adaptations and transformation; and about how we can incorporate issues about physical (and virtual) spaces that intersect with, but are separate to, the activities of learning itself, such as sustainability and resource effectiveness.

In the rest of this section then, I will first explore what current educational theories can offer to inform architectural approaches to learning space, and then begin to look at the complicated inter-relationships of not just designing and occupying educational space, but also planning and affording it.

Chapter 2

Learning spaces from an educationalist perspective

Just as recent building designs for post-compulsory education have been surprisingly little informed by contemporary architectural theories, so much of the assumed importance of moving from formal to informal learning spaces has little direct connection with current educational theories. It can often seem that education is over-theorised, across a variety of approaches and paradigms (Schunk 2007; Atherton 2009; Learning Theories Knowledgebase 2010) (Table 2.1). Most debates around learning spaces make reference, at least in passing, to constructivist approaches, sometimes also called 'conversational theory'. In her seminal text, *Re-thinking University Teaching* (2001), Diana Laurillard simultaneously attempted to outline a detailed description of post-compulsory learning based on theories of social constructivism, and to understand how new information and communication technologies (ICT) could be best used to support and enhance this type of learning. Her work continues to have considerable impact on debates around the design of both physical and virtual learning spaces.

However, while Laurillard has underlined the importance of both abstract thinking and practical application in learning 'conversations', these aspects could be seen to be artificially separated in her diagrams, and in her examples they are supported by different kinds of tasks (Fig. 2.1). In addition, by focusing on specific learning encounters she does not engage with the wider contexts or processes of learning. In more recent – and equally influential – research, Jean Lave and Etienne Wenger (1991) deliberately aimed to criticise what they saw as the implicit assumptions in this notion of university teaching and learning practices, with its focus on the teacher/learner dyad, and on the division between thinking/reflection and doing/practice. They started instead from the premise that all learning is situated; that is, it cannot be separated from either its participants or the conditions in which it takes place. They were also critical of a formal/informal divide – in this case understood as between formal education 'inside' the academy, and 'informal' learning that takes place outside of it. Their work was therefore also a challenge to assumptions about where learning takes place. For Lave and Wenger, learning is crucially a social practice that does not just happen exclusively in educational establishments, and is

Table 2.1 Different learning theories, adapted from Atherton, J. S., (2009,) 'Learning and teaching: angles on learning, particularly after the schooling years''. Available online at: http://www.learningandteaching.info/learning/site_map.htm (accessed 06/10/10).

Behaviourism	Behaviour modification
	Anticipatory-avoidance learning
	Learned helplessness
Cognitive theories	Aspects of Cognitive theory
	Piaget's developmental psychology
	Assimilation and Accommodation
	Constructivism
	Conversational theory: Pask and Laurillard
	Convergent and Divergent thinking
	Intelligence
	Multiple intelligences
	Personal construct psychology
	Gestalt
Humanistic approaches	Andragogy
	Reflective practice
	Critical reflection
Other angles	Authority and learning
	Deep and surface learning
	Cognitive dissonance
	Experiential learning
	Imitation
	Learning how to learn
	Learning curve
	Situated learning
	Tacit and implicit learning
	Memory
	SOLO taxonomy
	Resistance to learning

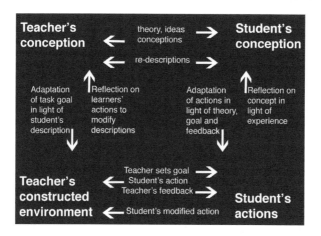

Fig. 2.1 Outline of the social constructivist or conversational framework, adapted from Laurillard (2002).

framed not by learning outcomes but through the negotiation of shared meanings. How, then, might these more recent ideas help us grapple with better understanding the relationships between learning and space?

The situatedness of learning

By exploring learning through work-based activities – based on investigating different kinds of apprenticeships – the authors move beyond a simplistic division between training as the mere process of acquiring specifics through observation and imitation, which have been conventionally set against (and often seen as inferior to) formal instructional learning in the classroom (involving verbal abstraction and reflection). They posit instead a form of learning through doing which is not just observing a task, but participating, initially at the edges, in the whole process – both absorbing and being absorbed by – the culture and operations of a group and/or specialism, that is, joining a community of practice. In this process, understanding and practice are developed through simultaneous interaction. They call this increasing involvement, usually from edge to centre but also in different patterns, legitimate peripheral participation (LPP):

> In any given community of practice the process of community reproduction – a historically-constructed, ongoing, conflicting, synergistic structuring of activities and relations among practitioners – must be deciphered in order to understand specific forms of LPP through time. This requires a broader conception of individual and collective biographies than the single segment encompassed in studies of 'learners'. Thus we have begun to analyse the changing forms of participation and identity of persons who engage in sustained participation in a community of practice: from entrance to newcomer, through becoming an old-timer with respect to newcomers, to a point where these newcomers themselves become old-timers. Rather than a teacher/learner dyad, this points to a richly diverse field of essential actors and, with it, other forms of relationships of participation.
>
> (Lave and Wenger 1991: 55–6)

Their research grew out of sociolinguistics, discourse analysis and cognitive studies as part of a growing body of work which has been exploring the situated character of human understanding and communication and aims to locate learning squarely within processes of co-participation and social meaning-making, not in the heads of individuals. 'Rather than asking what kinds of cognitive processes and conceptual structures are involved, they ask what kinds of social engagements provide the proper context for learning to take place' (Lave and Wenger 1991: 14).

Rather than assuming that learning is an intellectual process which is applied to different contexts, practised and then reflected on by individuals, learning is here seen as already and inherently collaborative. Rather than operating through particular conversations between tutor and student, learning is seen to take place through a community of 'knowers', and this inculcates not just knowledge but also a set of attitudes and a culture. This leads to a definition of learning as 'increasing access of learners to participating roles in expert performances' (Lave and Wenger 1991: 17).

Learning, then, is a centripetal and transitional movement where:

> peripherality suggests that there are multiple, varied, more-or-less engaged and inclusive ways of being located in the fields of participation defined by a community. [. . .] *Changing* locations and perspectives are part of actors' learning trajectories, development of identities, and forms of membership.
>
> (Lave and Wenger 1991: 35–6; original emphasis)

This is both potentially empowering and disempowering. Moves towards more intensive participation are enabled (as are positive choices to exploit a peripheral position), but at the same time the periphery is a place where one is kept from participating more fully. It is also an inside/outside boundary between different communities of practice, which may afford or prevent various forms of overlap and interchange. The concept of LPP, then, tries to capture learning as this developing process of ongoing and embodied engagement with knowledgeable experts (old timers) through increasing degrees of responsibility, understanding and control. Such learning is situated precisely because it has an 'emphasis on comprehensive understanding involving the whole person [. . .], on activity in and with the world; and on the view that agent, activity and the world mutually constitute each other' (Lave and Wenger 1991: 33).

Ultimately they argue that this is not just one form of learning; rather it is a general theoretical perspective 'about the relational character of knowledge and learning, about the negotiated character of meaning, and about the concerned (engaged, dilemma-driven) nature of learning activity for the people involved' (Lave and Wenger 1991: 33).

Despite its difficulties (which will be examined in greater depth in Chapter 4), the concept of communities of practice seems to offer some real purchase on our experiences of teaching and learning. And although Lave and Wenger attempt to make learning in the formal and informal sectors seem very different, many of the aspects they highlight also centrally inform education in universities and colleges. Within post-compulsory education a key aspect for academics is the transfer and development of their subject knowledge from one generation to the next. In addition there is a central concern with the whole person. Few academics would disagree with Lave and Wenger's belief that:

> participation is always based on situated negotiation and renegotiation of meaning in the world. This implies that understanding and experience are in constant interaction – indeed, are mutually constitutive. The notion of participation thus dissolves dichotomies between cerebral and embodied activity, between contemplation and involvement, between abstraction and experience; persons, actions, and the world are implicated in all thought, speech, knowing and learning.
>
> (Lave and Wenger 1991: 51–2)

Situated learning and threshold concepts; on the issue of 'getting it'

At the same time as the 'communities of practice' literature has been developing, there has been another key development in our understanding of learning spaces, which tries to unravel why students often have difficulties 'getting' key concepts. The work of Meyer and Land is here summarised by Glynis Cousin:

> The idea of threshold concepts emerged from a UK national research project into the possible characteristics of strong teaching and learning environments in the disciplines for undergraduate education (Enhancing Teaching-Learning Environments in Undergraduate Courses: http://www. tlrp.org). In pursuing this research in the field of economics, it became clear to Erik Meyer and Ray Land (2003, 2005, 2006), that certain concepts were held by economists to be central to the mastery of their subject. These concepts, Meyer and Land argued, could be described as 'threshold' ones because they have certain features in common.
>
> (Cousin 2006a)

The idea of threshold concepts has the potential to create a bridge between (as well as challenge) the communities of practice model and conversational/constructivist theories. This is because it deals with moments of encounter, within the framing of an academic discipline as a whole. Different subjects have their own threshold concepts, which could be thought of as centrally defining what constitutes any 'locally negotiated regime of competence', that is the knowledge and skills of any specific community of practice.

Meyer and Land suggest five key characteristics for a threshold concept. First, understanding such a concept is transformative, because it requires a real shift in thinking. As Cousin writes: 'this kind of "turn" in understanding a subject marks an important initiation into any subject culture' (Cousin 2006a). Second, a threshold concept is usually irreversible; once understood the learner is unlikely to forget it: although once understood, they may go on to adapt or challenge the concept. Third, such concepts enable a deep knowledge of connections, generally obscured by common-sense understandings. Fourth, a threshold concept is likely to be bounded, in that 'any conceptual space will have terminal frontiers, bordering with thresholds into new conceptual areas' (Meyer and Land 2006: 6). Thus, specific threshold concepts become one of the mechanisms through which a discipline recognises itself and inculcates its disciplinary knowledge and boundaries into the next generation. Finally, a threshold concept is likely to involve forms of 'troublesome knowledge'; David Perkins defines this as 'that which appears counter-intuitive, alien (emanating from another culture or discourse), or seemingly incoherent' (in Meyer and Land 2003: 7). As Cousin puts it:

> [F]rom this view, mastery of a threshold concept can be inhibited by the prevalence of a 'common sense' or intuitive understanding of it. Getting students to reverse their intuitive understandings is also

troublesome because the reversal can involve an uncomfortable, emotional repositioning.

(Cousin: 2006a)

An example of a threshold concept from my own subject area would be drawing technique. Common-sense and intuitive understandings of drawing, which new students often bring to university or college, suggest its use for accurate and figurative reproduction of the 'real'; i.e. that a bad drawing is one where there is not an immediate and recognisable correspondence between what you see 'out there' and what you see in the drawn representation. Enabling students to see and use drawing as a different kind of investigative tool takes time, because many of them find that this is counter to what they think they 'know'. This can be particularly hard for students who draw well 'figuratively' as their representations seem (to them) to get worse before they get better.

Threshold concepts and liminal spaces

Meyer and Land (2006: 22) suggest that this kind of learning – central to the intellectual, personal and professional development at post-compulsory level – involves a transition through a liminal (that is, an ambiguous, seemingly undefined and potentially disorienting) space:

> This space is likened to that which adolescents inhabit, in which they are not yet adults, and not quite children. It is an unstable space in which the learner may oscillate between old and emergent understandings, just as adolescents often move between adult-like and child-like responses to their transitional status. But once a learner enters this liminal space, she is engaged with the project of mastery, unlike the learner who remains in a state of pre-liminality in which understandings are at best vague.
>
> The idea that learners enter into a liminal state in their attempts to grasp certain concepts in their subjects presents a powerful way of remembering that learning is both affective and cognitive and that it involves identity shifts which can entail troublesome, unsafe journeys. Often students construct their own conditions of safety through the practice of mimicry. In our research, we came across teachers who lamented this tendency among students to substitute mimicry for mastery.

(Cousin 2006a)

These authors use the term mimicry as a way of describing how some students may stay at a surface level in their understanding of a concept or approach; that is, as a technique for avoiding 'troublesome knowledge', which challenges their own preconceptions and 'common sense'. They may try instead to just do 'what the tutor 'wants', or to use concepts in a superficial way. Shanahan and Meyer (2006), for example, show how some economics students they studied never really 'got' the idea of 'opportunity cost' – a threshold concept central to understanding aspects of economics – but were nevertheless able to get through a degree programme by undertaking 'learning (as) the product of ritualised performances rather than integrated understandings' (Cousin 2006a).

What, then, are the implications of this research for learning spaces? Meyer and Land (2008: 198) suggest that threshold concepts are like 'jewels' in the curriculum. Teaching and learning at the post-compulsory level should involve tutors understanding what the key threshold concepts are for their subject and developing methods of enabling students to understand and use these at a deep level. Of course, because tutors have often become so used to these key ideas as full members of a community of practice, they may themselves have difficulty articulating them effectively to newcomers, and may not remember what the kinds of anxieties and difficulties such counter-intuitive concepts produced when they were new themselves. To support students through their learning thus requires a 'holding environment for the toleration of confusion' (Cousin 2006a). As I have written elsewhere, such a space needs to be 'safe', but not merely a 'comfort zone' (Boys 2008). It is where students can feel able to take risks and deal with uncertainty, as an essential pre-condition of learning. They need to know that their fellow students are also experiencing difficulties, that mastery of threshold concepts can require a 'letting go' of what they already 'know', and that learning involves much 'looping back' and repetition; that it takes time.

Savin-Baden argues (as do Meyer and Land) that the common structure of many contemporary university and college courses, with their emphasis on discrete learning 'chunks', tied to specific assessment criteria and carefully delineated learning outcomes – a system which was partly influenced by constructivist approaches – in fact does not adequately capture the nature of this type of post-compulsory learning:

> Many students who believe, on joining a course, that they understand what constitutes learning may not realise the challenges and conflicts that may ensue. For most, prior experiences will be of traditional, didactic methods of teaching that offered little opportunity to value their own knowledge and perspectives. However, students who then engage with active forms of learning, such as problem-based learning, are often challenged to explore and to develop their own tacit understandings and to understand the incoherence of these. Making sense of incoherence can be a precarious affair. Experience is not something that can be tied into neat packages, and thus to speak of it is to risk being seen as stupid and incoherent, when it is in fact the reflections upon those experiences which are incoherent. Meanings, particularly about prior experience and learning, seem to need eventually to become coherent in order that they can be interpreted and subsequently valued.
>
> (Savin-Baden 2008: 99)

If, following constructivist models, learning encounters are best framed as a dialogic process between tutor and student (as well as between students themselves), where learners are enabled to 'talkback' their developing understanding of a subject, then Meyer and Land add three important considerations. First, the educational content central to such conversations is not transparent but problematic and (initially at least) may be obscure to the student. Educators therefore need to consider their role as 'translators' of troublesome knowledge. This also underlines the differential relationship between teacher and learner, and concerns what each brings to the subject in hand. Second, learning simultaneously involves intellectual, abstract and verbal interactions as well as emotional, immediate and unspoken ones. Finally, learning happens unevenly. It takes time, and is not necessarily directly correlated with a particular teaching experience. As Thackara notes:

> More than 70% of learning experiences in the modern workplace are informal or accidental, not structured or sponsored by an employer or a school. This kind of learning is pervasive, continuous, and profoundly social. It happens wherever people do their work: on the shop floor, around a conference table, on site with customers, or in a laboratory.
>
> (Thackara 2006: 158)

Unpacking learning as a situated, transitional process

The contemporary research of Meyer and Land, of Wenger and of their colleagues, therefore begins to suggest something about the distinctive conceptual characteristics of learning spaces in post-compulsory education, both at the level of the learning encounter and at the level of the institution. First, learning brings together competencies in knowledge and skills with personal attributes; with, as already noted, an 'emphasis on a comprehensive understanding involving the whole person [. . .], on activity in and with the world; and on the view that agent, activity and the world mutually constitute each other' (Lave and Wenger 1991: 33). It is about becoming and being a geologist or social scientist or designer, not just understanding geology, social science or design. Rather than being seen as obvious, comprehensive or consistent, such a process of inculcation is conceptualised as being uneven, contested and incorporating potential tensions for all its participants. This is both in terms of the bodies of knowledge of a subject, which are not fixed but constantly in flux as alternative approaches are negotiated (a process where education has a major and explicit role in mediating through its processes of teaching and research); and also in terms of educational processes which contain implicit and explicit rules that must themselves be 'learnt' by tutors and students alike, but which can also be challenged, refused or misunderstood.

Teachers, students and student support staff are thus all members of (at least) two intersecting communities of practice: the educational institution and their own specialist subject or subjects. What, then, are the procedures for moving towards full membership of these communities? In ethnomethodology (Garfinkel 1967; Turner 1970; Sacks 1984, 1992) there is a strong thread of work that focuses on how societal membership works:

> Members as social actors assume that the social work is a factual reality which is there for 'anyone' to see, and they regard it as a commonplace, generally taken for granted environment, which no competent member has problems recognizing and acting upon.
>
> (Payne 1976: 33)

Particular social and spatial practices – the rules and conventions of everyday life – become embedded, congealed and 'reified' in our 'normal' actions, in the spaces we occupy and the objects we use in different situations. To become full members, new entrants have to undertake boundary crossing(s) – that is, they must both be allowed in and choose to positively engage with the community being entered. They then begin a process of learning to interpret the 'cues' of that community of practice, its rules, beliefs, habits of thought, preferences, modes of talking and acting, etc. which they must gradually and fully adopt into their own personas. This demands a commitment towards both becoming and belonging as active and ongoing engagements. It sometimes involves challenging, adapting or transforming the existing rules and conventions, which may then become new, shared forms to be passed on, in turn, to newcomers. And as with our normal inattentiveness to the spaces of everyday life as we get used to particular situations, so too, we tend to take on completely the intellectual, social and emotional practices we have learnt and stop noticing them.

It should be noted that this journey from beginner to expert member may not be available to everyone. In university and college education that is explicit; certain criteria (exam scores for example) have to be achieved before access is allowed. But it may also be that certain types of people are *already* kept outside a community of practice as part of its boundary definitions; women, for example, were historically 'obviously' not competent to study at a higher education level. In Harvey Sacks' paper 'On doing being ordinary', he opens up the kind of work ordinariness involves:

> So one part of the job [doing being ordinary] is that you have to know what anybody/everybody is doing: doing ordinarily. Further, you have to have that available to do. There are people who do not have that available to do, and who specifically cannot be ordinary.
>
> (Sacks 1984: 415)

In the work of academics on widening participation for disadvantaged students (such as Olivia Sagan 2008) and my own work on disability (Boys 2009), the ways in which assumptions about 'what is normal' continue to locate some people who 'cannot be ordinary' as learners, are explored. And what seems, on the surface, to be just 'doing learning' is in fact one of the all-encompassing social and spatial practices which ethnomethodologists call 'problematic accomplishments' (Ryave and Schenkein 1974). This is because our everyday social and spatial practices involve a considerable amount of detailed – usually seen but un-noticed and un-commented upon – work. This is the work required in order to maintain the commonplace world where people know what 'anyone' knows and does; often only fully recognised when transgressed either accidentally or deliberately.

Beyond formal versus informal learning spaces (1)

Here, what is important about the work of both Lave and Wenger, and Meyer and Land, to the current debate about learning spaces is that it offers a conceptual model of learning as a dynamic social process. This can therefore supplement the teacher/student dyad, so central to constructivist approaches. In line with much other contemporary cultural theory, this model is complex, non-binary and situated. These theorists show that we need to interrogate each specific learning environment as an intersecting relationship between the concepts we are trying to teach and the underlying social and spatial conventions through which we attempt to get those concepts across. We need to explore how different learning spaces can make participants (tutors as well as learners) feel safe or uncomfortable, and the impact this can have on their learning. If a space is very 'recognisable', for example a lecture theatre, then is it likely that students will fall into standard assumptions about their 'place' as a passive rather than an active learner, and may in fact prefer such a location, since it represents what they already know. On the other hand, the strangeness of having 'standard' routines shifted, without clear alternative rules being offered, may undermine confidence. This suggests that we need to know much more about our conventional routines for producing and recognising the accomplishment of 'doing' learning – and to understand how these can be positively and appropriately adapted and translated across both different physical and virtual spaces.

There is no simple one-size-fits-all answer here. Envisaging specific learning spaces that enable both a sense of belonging, and also 'push' participants beyond their particular comfort zones, seems to hold in tension contradictory trends. In fact, Lave and Wenger's concept of legitimate peripheral participation is one example of just such a learning space. Can such concepts-in-tension, then, inform the design of physical space and if so, how? This will be the theme of the second section of this book.

Beyond formal versus informal learning spaces (2)

The second key point about contemporary educational theories for learning spaces is that they offer the potential to explore not just the enhancement of a series of individual learning encounters, but also wider contexts and agendas. This also switches the angle of view from what I earlier called the 'deficit model of teaching' (that the problem is with what teachers 'normally' do) towards the whole process of post-compulsory educational provision. This includes, for example, ongoing changes in student numbers and attitudes, assessment procedures, similarities and differences across subject disciplines and between universities, and arguments over relationships between research and teaching. As Ronald Barnett has written:

> Not only do universities exhibit diversity between themselves with
> their contrasting missions and internal characteristics, but they are

supremely dynamic organisations. They move, they shape changes as – for instance – their disciplinary base shifts, or their interventions with the wider society take on new forms, or their priorities alter, and in the process, the balance of their activities may even be changed.

A related matter is that of space. If the key activities of the university – research, teaching, management – may be considered as so many shapes forming patterns, different possibilities present themselves as far as space is concerned. It may be said that the history of the university has been the successive introduction of new spaces. [. . .] if we conceive of research and teaching as occupying the spaces of the university then we can ask questions of the following kinds: What are the spaces that these activities occupy? How are they shaped? How do these spaces stand in relation to each other? What is their configuration? Are there spaces for other activities? Are the spaces genuinely open or are they actually closed in some way (by virtue of the ideologies they represent or the resources they demand for their occupation)? Do the actors in these spaces feel that the spaces are theirs to a certain extent? Can new spaces open up within the activities themselves?

(Barnett 2005: 2–3)

Barnett also asks what is 'occluded or distorted, submerged, indistinct or contentious, blurred' within the university, between university and outside world; questions that I suggest a critical engagement with the 'communities of practice' literature can help us respond to constructively and creatively.

Crucially, then, thinking about learning spaces on this institutional and supra-institutional scale means engaging with urgent questions about the status of knowledge and of different forms of learning provision across both various educational services and society as a whole. This is both about how universities, colleges and other forms of post-compulsory education should be 'related' to work, leisure and community engagement (such as via museums and galleries), and also concerns the particular framing of education within universities and colleges, both generally and in relation to specific institutions (for example the 'old' and 'new' universities, or further and higher education). In the UK, this means opening up to debate issues around, for example, widening access to education; vocational and academic forms of study, curriculum design and timetabling; learning outcomes and assessment; and relationships between teaching, learning, research and wider communities and contexts. For example, the notion of 'threshold concepts' also offers a serious critique of the 'bite-sized' and linear 'learning outcomes model'. 'We would argue', write Land *et al.*,

for the notion of learning as excursive, as a journey or excursion which will have intended direction and outcome but will also acknowledge (and indeed desire) that there will be deviation and unexpected outcomes within the excursion; there will be digression and revisiting (recursion) and possible further points of departure and revised direction. The eventual destination may be reached, or it may be revised. It may be a surprise. It will certainly be the point of embarkation for further excursion.

(Land *et al.* 2008: 202)

Savin-Baden offers a related logic for higher education institutions to re-think the qualities of spaces for learning: '[I]f the university is to maintain some leverage in the world of intellectual thought, then it needs to regain learning spaces as places in which in-depth deliberation and intellectual positioning can occur' (Savin-Baden 2008: 141).

As with John Thackara (2006), quoted earlier, the call here is for more iterative, time-rich learning and research environments. Many such arguments have been challenging existing teaching and learning provision in UK universities and colleges recently. These set a valuable context for the current interest in informal and social learning spaces, rather than formal ones. In fact, pitching the debate at this level offers the potential to broaden and deepen not only discussion of the educational issues but also the range of alternative social and spatial practices which might be part of a design response. Some examples of what these arguments suggest for re-thinking the architecture of post-compulsory education will be addressed in the last section of this book.

Beyond formal versus informal learning spaces (3)

Finally, following this discussion of contemporary educational theories, we need to return to issues about how architecture 'works' to support learning. What is most interesting here is that the kinds of 'spatial' terms being used by educationalists – concepts such as liminal or transitional spaces, boundary crossings and thresholds, centripetal movements, and the call for spaces that are 'safe', enabling belonging but not reinforcing comfort zones – do not easily offer the kind of simplistic associative social-spatial metaphors of 'informal' learning. Most importantly, the very underlying structure of ideas, which makes formal and informal oppositional, precisely through an assumed sequence of associated and analogous spatial/aesthetic differences (e.g. uncomfortable/comfortable, one-directional/multi-directional, teacher-led/student-led, serious/playful), just does not work for more complex conceptual spaces such as liminality or transition. These ideas may link to, but cannot be so easily represented through those seemingly obvious design tropes such as 'niche' or 'cluster', 'street' or 'hub', as described in the previous chapter.

This is crucial in developing a deeper understanding of relationships between learning and space. If these concepts are, in some way, distinctive to the experiences of teaching and learning in post-compulsory education, then we cannot, and should not, blur them directly into architectural form. Rather we should explore whether and how such concepts can have an impact on the actual material 'shape' of learning environments (both physical and virtual) as a means of informing the kinds of questions architects – and their clients and users – should be asking, and the possible approaches they can take. The implications of this will be explored throughout the following chapters.

But, first, we also need to consider those aspects of architectural design which are relevant to the design of learning spaces, but are not *only about* learning. As designers and clients well know, space is a scarce and often costly resource. It has particular properties which both 'suggest' what is possible and limit what can be done. The approaches to, and methods for, its procurement and management have developed from a different perspective to either architectural or educational theories and practices; and are often seen as oppositional and problematic to both design and learning processes. But any serious re-thinking of the architecture of post-compulsory education needs to engage with the planning and resource-effectiveness of learning spaces, not just as an 'additional' issue, but as something central to how space works. This is what I will turn to next.

Chapter 3

Learning spaces from an estates planning perspective

This chapter begins by exploring the 'conventional' conflicts between an estates planning perspective and the educationalist and architectural viewpoints previously outlined. This is particularly in relation to arguments over how the costs and value of learning spaces are worked out. Rather than merely repeating the differences, I want to examine how issues of cost-efficiency and resource effectiveness might be more creatively intersected with pedagogic and design concerns. This is not about finding an artificial consensus where the complexities of space and resource management somehow 'fit' neatly together with the particular characteristics of learning, teaching and research, but to accept the different interpretations of what kind of resource space *is* as a basis for asking new kinds of questions about its 'value', both to learning and to the educational institution more widely.

Space conflicts

The most immediate tension between academics' everyday experiences and those of estates planners – at least in the UK – is that to most tutors there never seems to be enough space for teaching and learning in our universities and colleges. However, simultaneously, space occupancy levels in these post-compulsory educational institutions are again and again evidence of chronic under-usage. As Sian Kilner notes in her summary of the research undertaken for the Space Management Group (SMG): 'at the Estates Managers Statistics (EMS) reported utilisation rate of 27 per cent in 2003–04, 3.7 square metres were being provided for every one square metre being used' (SMG 2006a: 11) in the post-compulsory education system. This under-use means that resources, which could be allocated to other aspects of teaching, learning and research, have become tied up in the physical fabric of universities and colleges:

> As currently the average cost of space in UK Higher Education – taking into account capital, depreciation, maintenance and operating costs – is nearly £200 a square metre, achieving the most effective use of this

valuable resource is a key management task.

(Temple 2008: 230)

Of course, while academics and other learning support and administration staff often recognise this push for space efficiencies by increased utilisation, there is also a tendency to view estates managers as a threat, or as people who only see space in the most simplistic cost terms, and whose aim is to make efficiencies by *taking away* existing space. Temple summarises this understanding of the role: 'The technical/administrative specialism of university space planning is concerned with determining the appropriate amount of space to be provided for defined purposes, and maximising its use once provided, by means of various space management techniques' (Temple 2008: 229–30).

For estates teams, stereotypes of academics, learning support and other administrative staff can be equally strong. They are seen as 'claiming' spaces just in case they might need them, but not being capable of articulating what they need them for, or being able to describe what kinds of alternative spaces they require. Estates teams perceive the academics as being unwilling or unable to negotiate, unable to appreciate the strategic issue of costs, and generally being resistant to change of any sort. As Kilner notes, from an estates management point of view, the different experiences of space as simultaneously under-used or over-used are only in part due to the nature of any particular estate's appropriateness or flexibility. This is mainly because of marked differences in predicted and surveyed rates of utilisation, 'which can lead simultaneously to strong perceptions of shortages of space while, at the same time, rooms are empty' (SMG 2006a: 11). That is, spaces are booked for classes and then not used. To which many teachers will retort that if they do not book the best or appropriate spaces, these will not be available when they need them.

While it seems obvious that space planning and utilisation should be matched to the associated teaching and learning practices, there is 'little evidence that such decisions are usually informed by an understanding of the relationships between space and the teaching and learning that go on in it' (Barnett and Temple 2006: 11). In fact, while the importance of understanding this relationship is recognised, anecdotal evidence from my own institution suggests that no-one is certain just *where* such knowledge might be located or developed. Comments from members of the University of Brighton's estates team show a deep interest in the need to connect space management more creatively with the activities that go on in it:

> We need better briefing (from academics), but also a better understanding of relationships between space and activities.
>
> We should know more about what already happens, (and then) what the priorities are and what might change.
>
> There are major opportunities for enhancing learning, (we) could be adventurous.

(Boys 2003–09, unpublished interview notes)

But if estates managers and space planners are keen to know more about the spatial implications of teaching and learning, academics and managers still seem to often assume that their estates departments will provide all the necessary expertise, as if cost-planning was somehow separate from teaching and learning activities:

> Understandably the focus of these professionals is on the reduction of risk and the timely completion of projects within budget. They have never been required to serve as the educational visionaries for the institution – which is precisely what is required when looking to create a 'new generation learning environment'.
>
> (Jamieson 2008: 25)

Space planning and management in universities and colleges, then, sits in an uncomfortable location. It has, and continues to develop, valuable knowledge and tools; yet this expertise is often seen as 'wanting' within the post-educational sector more generally. At the same time, as Barnett and Temple (2006) have noted, there is increasing focus on the quality of the physical assets of universities and colleges, not just in terms of increasing space efficiencies but also because of the importance of marketing and identity, for example, in commissioning 'landmark' buildings (Fig. 3.1), which make considerations of space more central to senior managers. '[T]he challenges of managing an enlarged higher education system should mean that, in future, space issues form a more central component of such studies and of management concerns related to teaching and learning' (Temple and Barnett 2007: 11).

Fig. 3.1
Graduate
Centre, London
Metropolitan
University
(Studio Daniel
Libeskind, 2004).
Photograph:
Jos Boys.

How, then, can we move beyond this endless oppositional swing between stereotypes of money-minded estates managers who do not understand what teaching and learning involves, and academics who are entirely self-centred and self-interested? Here I will suggest we focus instead on the deeper underlying issues. These are, first, that we do not know enough about the particularly distinctive and dynamic patterns of post-compulsory teaching and learning practices and therefore fail to develop sufficiently sophisticated models for their planning and management; second, that concentrating only on efficiency measures such as space utilisation does not enable us to capture either the wider range of potential institutional aims for space, nor does it enable us to articulate how the *effectiveness* of different kinds of space might be judged; and third, that space has properties and qualities over and above the fact of its occupancy – as a scarce material resource – which also have an impact on the design of learning spaces, and need to be taken into consideration.

Currently organisations such as the SMG and the Association of University Directors of Estates (AUDE) in the UK, the Australasian Tertiary Education Facilities Management Association (TEFMA), the Association of Higher Education Facilities Officers (APPA) and the Society for College and University Planning (SCUP) in the USA, are all exploring these concerns. Here my aim is to start from a critical examination of some of this work, so as to further inform the re-thinking of learning spaces in post-compulsory education.

Space as a scarce resource

Contemporary space planning in universities is still informed by the concept of space norms; that is, guidance on room sizes, which was developed over 40 years ago:

> In the UK, from the 1960s, a set of figures calculated from time to time on behalf of the University Grants Committee from survey data – the so-called 'UGC norms' – dominated space planning decisions in universities. These figures effectively determined the site and, to an extent, the design of the new buildings in the period of expansion of higher education in the post-Robbins period and beyond. Even when UGC norms ceased to have official recognition once central funding of capital projects largely ended (and their formal status was only ever that of guidance), they continued to provide university planners with a defensible basis on which to make judgements on space needs.
>
> (Temple 2008: 230)

More recently the SMG in the UK commissioned a series of reports as part of their UK Higher Education Space Management Project (2006b) in order both to move beyond the simplistic assumptions of the space norms model and to examine how newer demands around the sustainability of university and college estates might be incorporated.

This work 'aimed to develop additional guidelines and tools to help to deliver effective space management' (SMG 2006a: 3) and was organised in two phases. Phase One focused on three areas – a review of current space management practice; an examination of the financial requirements for maintaining university estates; and a study of the key drivers for a post-compulsory educational estate, already referred to above. Phase Two of the project explored what the effects might be on space of future changes in higher education, and suggested ways of promoting space efficiency in building design. This work also proposed possible guidelines for a strategic approach to space utilisation. In her research for the SMG project, Kilner found that:

> the absence of sector-wide and up-to-date space standards or norms was repeatedly highlighted as a problem by some survey respondents. Some Higher Education Institutions (HEIs) have developed their own standards or norms, while 45 percent of respondents continue to use norms from the now-defunct University Grants Committee (UGC) and Polytechnics and Colleges Funding Councils (PCFC), or space weightings, in some cases modified by the particular institution. None of these norms has been updated since 1990, and the space standards underpinning them are even older.
>
> (SMG 2006a: 5)

Interestingly, despite their relative inefficiencies in space occupancy, universities and colleges in the UK are already operating at below the original UGC and PCFC space norms:

> The study, assess(ed) the scale of change which has taken place across the sector when measured in terms of performance against the norms: the research compares a reference year (1991–92) with 2003–04. The analysis found that the sector is operating at an average 80 per cent of UGC norms and just under 80 per cent of PCFC norms.
>
> (SMG 2006a: 12)

Kilner also examined the way in which the UGC and PCFC norms were originally derived. As she says, they were a function of a series of coefficients, including:

- total hours of on-campus contact or learning hours per week per student;
- breakdown of those hours into different types of activity, for instance, lecture theatre hours, seminar hours and laboratory hours;
- total hours that space is available per week to be used, for instance 40 hours;
- predicted frequency and occupancy rates for space use; that is, planned utilisation;
- space standards per place in teaching, learning, research and support spaces;
- definition of discrete subject groups or disciplines;
- staff: student ratios by discipline or subject group;
- professorial: other academic staff ratios by subject group;
- academic: support staff ratios by subject group.

> (SMG 2006a: 12)

The basis of these coefficients has, of course, changed considerably since the 1960s. Staff: student ratios have increased so that, for example in my own experience as a student and then an educator in architectural education, norms of 1:8 in the design studio in the 1970s are now more like 1:25. In addition, contact hours have (mainly) decreased and the older patterns of dedicated studio space with a desk per student have been replaced with centralised booking systems and hot-desking. When Kilner looked again at the UGC and PCFC coefficients, she argued that HEIs were now too diverse to make a sector-wide method or single set of norms useful or practical, and proposed instead first that:

> the concepts underlying the development of norms should be retained, because the principles of basing an assessment of capacity or space needs on what activities are to be delivered and how that might be done are still relevant. Without an assessment of this type, it is difficult to know whether an HEI, or any organisation, has broadly the right amount and type of space.
>
> (SMG 2006a: 12)

Kilner notes that the Learning Skills Council (LSC), which runs further education colleges, uses guided learning hours rather than contact hours as a tool. Her international review of space management in Australasia, North America, Hong Kong and Germany found that a range of methods are employed, mostly similar to UK approaches. So, she has developed a new approach to calculate indicative space needs based on the old UGC and PSFC coefficients, but using these as the parameters for an open 'matrix', thereby allowing each university or college to set its own priorities and activity patterns:

> The method [. . .] takes the form of a framework which HEIs can use to generate indicative space predictions for types of space and the student full-time equivalents for all or part of an HEI, based on staff and student numbers and a series of default coefficients to assist calculations. HEIs can override the default settings where they consider that alternatives would better reflect their own circumstances and requirements. The more generously the coefficients are set, the greater the estimated indicative space calculation, and vice versa.
>
> (SMG 2006a: 13)

Kilner's approach therefore, is to enable educational managers and teachers to plot the amount of space and time required for each activity relevant to their own subject area, so as to plan what is needed for teaching and learning in different situations. Thus, there has been an important shift in the underlying UK space assessment models from per-student norms to *activities*.

Interestingly, when Kilner presented this outline framework to a mixed group of art and design academics and estates managers at the *Making Space* conference (University of the Arts, London, July 2009) the debate moved quickly beyond whether such a method offered the kind of transparency, flexibility and adapt-ability Kilner was aiming for, and towards questions about what the distinctiveness of space in post-compulsory education *is*, particularly in art and design education. This was, first, about space defined less by its functional contents and more by the *practices* it enables:

> [F]or some people this is about what the room *has* and for others about what it *does*. I think I'm leaning towards the latter, but this is rather more problematic than the former. A clay room is a room for clay. It has [a] special kit. An art studio is a studio for making art – but it shouldn't have to demonstrate this beyond its designation as a 'making' space. And by 'making' I mean thinking, chatting, reading, drawing, playing, eating, sleeping – whatever it takes! And this is really tricky to explain to someone who is trying to timetable that room in the same way they might timetable a standard classroom.
>
> (http://evocativethings.blogspot.com/search?q=making+space)

Second, it was about space not as a cost to the institution, but as a benefit to the student with its availability a central component to their studies:

> Art spaces must be accessible 24/7 – these spaces provide a *service* – they have to be offered even if not always used. It's not about allocation *of* space, it's about access *to* space [. . .] and I think this should be an entitlement for all art students.
>
> (http://evocativethings.blogspot.com/search?q=making+space)

And, third, it was about how to capture the dynamic patterning of education (as opposed, for example, to employment) with its weekly and yearly cycles related to modules and assessment arrangements:

> We ended up having a discussion about problems of averages and peak-loads. For me, educational courses are more like the bus system than a standard office – there are inherently peaks and troughs through the semester cycle, particularly in the art and design subjects.
>
> (http://spacesforlearning.blogspot.com/2009/07/creative-tension.html)

I came away from the conference thinking that if art and design (and other) academ-ics want to argue their case better, we have to look at methods for space planning which are more complex (that is, can better model the dynamic space/time patterns through the academic cycle), but of course not so complex that they are ineffective predictors. We also have to be able to describe more precisely the space/time pat-terns of teaching and learning. Most importantly, what the debates that day revealed is that rather than representing simple oppositional perspectives between estates managers and the 'rest' as being about wanting more or less space, what is at stake is different modes of articulating what learning space *is*. As one institution puts it:

> [A] university isn't like a supermarket, where you pick your degree off a shelf because you've paid for it; it's more like a gym or a health club, where the university provides the training and the facilities but it's your responsibility to make the best use of them. If you skip all the preparatory reading for class, or try to get by with only the minimum amount of reading, or question-spot for exams rather than developing a proper understanding of the subject, or refuse to engage in discussion and debate, there's a serious risk that you'll still be intellectually flabby and unfit by the end of the course.
>
> The positive side of having fewer scheduled classes is that you have far more freedom to develop your own approach to the subject, pursuing the aspects that particularly interest you, rather than having to stick rigidly to a prescribed reading list and a set curriculum. You can also arrange your work in a pattern that suits you, if you find that you work best first thing in the morning or late at night. One of the most important skills you need to develop at an early stage in university is how to organise your own learning, how to make effective use of the time and resources that are available. It is perfectly possible to keep certain times free for sport, or to reduce your commitments to a minimum for a week so that you can appear in a play, or make time for any other activity, provided that you make up the time somewhere else, and still meet your deadlines.
>
> (University of Bristol Faculty of Arts Undergraduate Handbook, quoted at http://www.bristol.ac.uk/arts/prospective/undergrad/contact.html)

The changing shape of post-compulsory education

Thus, while the research funded by the SMG and similar organisations is a valuable addition to the literature, I suggest that it throws up as many complexities, gaps and contradictions as it solves. According to Kilner, the collection of appropriate and comparable strategic data within universities and colleges remains uneven, with specific and measurable targets rarely found. Her evidence also suggested that the link between space management and academic and financial planning is patchy and inconsistent, and that relevant data tend to be spread piecemeal across the institution, making it difficult to get an overview. What is more, space analysis and planning still tend to relate to general-purpose teaching space (which makes up only 15 per cent of the total net internal non-residential area of the HE estate), rather than relating to more specialist teaching spaces, or research, office and support spaces like libraries and student support facilities.

This inability to achieve useful or comprehensive data reveals, I suggest, not so much individual institutional failings, as the deeper underlying problem of knowing just *what* is to be mapped and *how* this might be done. This is because, as already stated, current changes in beliefs about where learning should take place – with the strong focus moving towards the informal spaces of libraries, resource centres, student support centres and even cafés and corridors – sets up a challenge to the conventional calculations of space utilisation. The impact of thinking about learning space and human interactions is shifting from formal to informal and from specific needs or categories (libraries, lecture theatres) to more flexible spaces. There is a blurring of conventional boundaries, not just learning in teaching spaces, but in the corridor, the café, through the computer and beyond the campus itself. These spaces are also becoming not just about learner–teacher roles and relationships but about health and well-being, community engagement and work-related environments; not just about space usage and cost implications but also about quality of experience, identity and sustainability. Is a student learning when they are drinking a cup of coffee? Or chatting to their friends? How does one cost the value of providing space for community activities? And how exactly is one to map the agglomerations of multiple individual movements from space to space each day? All of these difficulties are exacerbated by the potential of new technologies for shifting aspects of learning into virtual space, which has its own difficult-to-evaluate resource and cost implications.

Rather than an 'automatic' opposition between costs and educational requirements, then, we need to take more notice of how costs are articulated, and explore how these might be better intersected with patterns of learning and teaching. This is a problem *shared* by academics and estates planners because we all still lack relevant frameworks or techniques for mapping the dynamic social and spatial practices of learning. It is also particularly important in the present moment because of the pressure on resources. Space is a sizeable proportion of current budgets, and many universities and colleges are having to make cost cuts. In addition, sustainability of the estate is becoming increasingly central, whilst new technologies offer the potential for more complex and responsive forms of modelling and usage.

However, while this is a shared problem, there is no one 'solution', only partial, contested and difficult choices. This is not only because of differences in perspective but also because of the realities of space as a medium, and of occupation as always in a process of flux through time. Orchestrating effective space utilisation takes place in the context of a particular layout of physical fabric and – through its additions, adaptations and re-arrangements – always within the movement from new, appropriate, valued spaces, to inappropriate and deteriorating ones.

How, then, can we better articulate such a complex and dynamic set of inter-relationships, in a way that will still allow comparability as to resource-effectiveness? I will briefly outline two areas which the next sections of this book will increasingly connect back and forth to: educational practices and design issues. First, by mapping existing and preferred social and spatial processes and practices of learning in post-compulsory education (rather than functions or activities), we can also engage more directly and transparently with the implications for space and resource effectiveness. For, just as our inability to properly map learning onto space has left architecture and education with only the flawed concept of improving flexibility to enhance learning, so estates planners are 'caught' with having to use space utilisation frameworks which remain problematically open-ended about the distinctive characteristics of learning as a dynamic, transitional and liminal process.

Second, the arguments already made in this book – that space and its occupation are always partially related, contested and changing – can actually open up space planning to more creative and constructive engagements with teaching, learning and research, rather than being an (always failing) attempt to accurately match space and usage through time, simply to get occupancy rates up. Evaluation of learning spaces can move away from a concentration on their mechanical utilisation and towards approaches which understand space as a sustainable and valuable resource. The physical and virtual spaces of a university or college can then be seen less as a cost burden and more as an opportunity (with the associated opportunity costs) for adding value to learners and teachers, to the institution's standing, and to its relationships to the wider community, research and business.

Mapping the patterns of post-compulsory educational practices

What, then, is so particular (or peculiar) about the characteristics of post-compulsory learning spaces? Space use in universities is very variable and dynamic, compared with even many colleges, let alone schools or other related building types. While there are regular and predictable patterns through each day, week, semester and academic year, modulated via the parallel and sequential accumulation of modules or courses, I suggest that there are two distinctive underlying patterns – both of which make efficient space planning harder rather than easier. The first is that modules tend to have a 'standard' sequence of analysis, development, concluding submission and assessment, which affect what types of activity are happening where and when. But this also tends to 'bunch' pressure on particular spaces, for example around introductory sessions and assessment periods, while at other times on-campus teaching spaces may appear relatively empty as students work at home or in the library on their own studies. Second, university lecturers continue to have relative autonomy in designing their own modules and courses, and an in-built tendency for a 'just-in-time' approach. This means both that it is more difficult to predict what spaces they will need, and that space requirements may change at short notice as teaching and learning activities are adapted to on-going students' needs. While enormously frustrating to space planners, who see booked rooms endlessly left un-used (thus preventing other tutors and students from using them), this kind of just-in-time course design in fact precisely mirrors contemporary demands for more informal learning, as against over-structured provision.

Students and academics, then, can be envisaged in an endlessly dynamic dance as they come together in different patterns both within and outside the learning environment, here as large static groupings for a period, there as small groups moving around within a specific setting, and elsewhere as scattered autonomously-working individuals. And throughout these processes, what might be considered 'learning' is forever being blurred with other activities, whether eating, socialising or 'incubating' an idea while appearing to do something else. As one tutor put it:

Learning is such an ambiguous thing. Where does it really happen? There is all that prepared material, so ideally it should happen in the studio but maybe it happens in the corridors. Students discover something, they need it to be reinforced, maybe physically experiencing something [. . .] Learning happens best in the minibus, just driving along, coming home from a visit. There you will find students discussing the course together, without prejudice about strong or weak learners, they don't judge each other, and suddenly understanding something they didn't get before.

(Boys 2009, unpublished interview notes, University of Brighton)

While some of these patterns are recorded in formalised contact hours, many are not. Unlike primary and secondary schooling, which have a clear framework of time-tabled classes, much of what students and academics do is self-directed, making space and resource usage the complex agglomeration of many personal learning trajectories. This process becomes ever more problematic to plan, at least in the UK, as contact hours are reduced (the standard pattern currently in UK HE being around five of a student's own 'learning' hours expected to support one 'contact' hour).

In addition, unlike working in an office or factory, students may not have a 'base', or if they do, may occupy it for much less time than their employed colleagues. Similarly, there is a regularly reoccurring (and accurate perception) among space planners that where academics have their own offices these are so under-occupied, as to be obviously wasteful. Again, the peculiar characteristics of tutoring, with its varied combination of preparation and assessment, research and pastoral care, make it difficult to map straightforwardly onto space – or at least to do so in a transparently effective way. We urgently need to think of more creative and effective ways of embedding both the distinctiveness of learning spaces in post-compulsory education, and their dynamic patterning through time, into estates and resource planning and management. This is a process that is already happening, as estates planners and researchers explore a variety of techniques (Loughborough University 2005):

I agree with the need for more complex space planning models. One that I've used in the past is core/flexi/on-demand. Core tends to be owned by courses, flexi is bookable and on-demand is freely available. What's interesting is that, when the model is introduced, people start overlay-ing the academic year and identifying where each type of space is most needed and, if more is required, how it might be obtained (e.g. temporary use of additional space at key pinch points). What seems to work about the model is that it links activity to space management in a way that feels already familiar to everyone.

(Fiona Duggan 5 May 2010, unpublished email interview)

But such work remains, unfortunately, fragmented and is failing to have the impact it deserves on debates about learning spaces across architecture and education.

Thinking space beyond learning

As part of their SMG-funded report 'Impact on space of future changes in higher education', Barnett and Temple (2006) interviewed many academics and managers in a cross-section of English universities and colleges to find out what kinds of factors were driving space changes. Despite beliefs that new information and communication technologies would eliminate the need for traditional campuses, or make them a more minor element of learning, in fact post-compulsory education has continued as a coherent organisational and physical form, and the demand from students to be based in one place remains an important factor of their studies. As Kilner adds, summarising the work, 'many HEIs derive strength from their highly-integrated nature: from trans-disciplinary contacts, from connections between teaching and research, and between academic and social activity. A coherent physical presence allows these features to operate effectively' (SMG 2006a: 8). For Barnett and Temple a key issue is that space planning does not depend on simple coefficients such as student and staff numbers, or on simple efficiencies of space occupancy, but is driven by 'a set of complex factors related to institutional missions and aspirations' (Barnett and Temple 2006: 11). In the UK these factors include, for example, government plans to increase the participation rate of students aged 18–30 to 50 per cent, and to increasingly focus on research 'impact' and on knowledge transfer and exchange between universities, business and the wider community. Space, then, is not just about its efficient usage for teaching and learning and, Barnett and Temple argue, managing space usage should not be an end in itself; space is one of a number of elements which need to be considered in aiming for, and achieving the intended outcomes of the university or college.

Towards creative mapping, planning and management

I am here suggesting that the very complexity and difficulties of thinking about spaces for learning as always contested and changing, actually opens up estates planning and management to more creative and constructive ideas about how to improve the effectiveness of space as a resource. Currently the standard techniques for improving space efficiency in this context are central room booking and space charging. From an estates management viewpoint, these have been effective:

> Statistical analysis found that there is a clear correlation between HEIs that centrally timetable all their teaching space (both general purpose and specialist) and space performance. On average, and allowing for a range of external drivers affecting institutional size, HEIs with 100 per cent of teaching space centrally timetabled have 17 per cent less space than those which do not.
>
> [. . .] Statistical analysis also found a correlation between space charging and the size of the HE estate. On average, HEIs that charge for space have 12 per cent less net internal non-residential area than those that do not charge. The findings support the National Audit Office's conclusions on the role of space charging in promoting efficiency in space use.
>
> (SMG 2006a: 5)

But what such limited techniques actually show are the tensions between the different understandings of what learning space is for, already outlined. These are not just between individuals or discipline groupings, but built deep into current frameworks for post-compulsory education. So, on the one hand – pedagogically – the shift towards active and informal learning suggests space that can be owned, personalised and is adaptable to different activities. As Temple goes on:

> On the basis that much effective learning takes place as a result of interactions between students, designs need to provide a variety of spaces for them to work and socialise in together (Kuh *et al.* 2005; Kuh and Pike 2006). However, cost-driven pressures in higher education to maximise space utilisation may have the unintended effect of reducing the opportunities for informal learning. For example, improving space utilisation by the central timetabling of space previously 'owned' by departments, where teaching took place and academics worked, reduces the possibility of casual encounters between academics and students (Barnett and Temple 2006: 10).
>
> (Temple 2008: 232)

Similarly central room booking and timetabling can result in loss of a sense of ownership and belonging as students and staff lose subject and department-located home bases and facilities to general use and hot-desking: 'efficiency gains measured in the amount of space per student have been bought, it seems to many, at the price of some diminution in learning and of the student experience more broadly' (Barnett and Temple 2006: 11). Other techniques for increasing space efficiencies, such as timetabling 12-hour teaching days, are similarly likely to have unintended consequences for the quality of teaching and learning.

Space charging also creates as many problems as it solves. The first of these problems is the difficulty of pricing. In conversation with two heads of department at a university where space charging is just being introduced, the key issues were the lack of transparency and sophistication in pricing models, and the issue of considerable differences in quality of space within the same price band (either because of functional characteristics such as location, layout and services, or because of differential space maintenance costs covering, for example, cleaning or re-decorating). The second problem concerns how to allocate space which is inherently various in quality, suitability and historical patterns of usage. It is a limited, relatively inflexible and non-interchangeable resource. This is not just about who gets the 'worse' spaces, it is also about whether the additional costs of new-build should be passed on directly to the departments using them, or spread more widely. The third problem concerns how to manage parity between students whose courses may have very different kinds of costs:

> It would be good to survey the variations in what creative subjects need. How do we cost the space needs of a dance student who wants to

rehearse – alone – in the biggest lecture space on campus, compared to photography or painting students?

(Boys 2009, unpublished interview notes, University
of Brighton)

And the fourth problem raised is how to cost the 'value' of space beyond its occu-pancy, for example, not just in terms of student income but also other forms of income-generation such as research and consultancy, or community or business use. For the academics interviewed, space charging barely began to capture the complexities of their decision-making. Neither did it offer openings for alternative and creative ways of managing space usage. We therefore need to be extending the kinds of possibilities available for thinking about space management beyond such techniques. This might be around such approaches as mapping processes and practices rather than functions; exploring the implications of altering time patterns as much as spatial ones; and the effects of thinking of space/time activi-ties as not necessarily contained within the university or college campus itself. All of these will be explored throughout the rest of this book. While the proposed SMG space assessment model outlined above offers a much better attempt to map these kinds of complexities than the old space norms, it still seems to lack a mechanism for embodying the dynamic inter-relationships of activities, people, space and time.

Interestingly, approaches to new office design – particularly creative offices – already outlined in Chapter 1, are offering a way to make just such a decisive shift away from space utilisation models:

Work is an activity not a place – work is no longer confined to the office environment and we need to support work in different locations and on the move;

The activity and time will vary – work is a mixture of activities which are best suited to different environments and times.

The office is a social experience – we are social animals and at times crave interaction, and off-line interaction may lead to collaboration and innovation.

(Oseland 2008: 15)

Space becomes articulated not through its functions (lecture hall, seminar room, studio) so much as the processes undertaken, for which different kinds of spaces can offer appropriate *conditions*. Here, evaluation is increasingly focusing not on cost but on value:

Property is an asset, not a cost burden – the key purpose of our properties is simply to support the activities that take place within them. We need to design and manage property to maximise the benefits and focus less on just the costs of the property; [. . .] Measure value not just cost – at its most basic, Value equals Quality over Cost ($V = Q/C$), we need to maximise quality and minimise costs, rather than create poor quality low cost (cheap) environments.

(Oseland 2008: 15–16)

Where space is a creative and constructive enabler of relevant activities, particularly those centred around mobility, autonomy and interaction, then 'property managers must shift from focusing on saving space and cost, to creating workplaces that enhance individual creativity and performance, team collaboration and innovation and the productivity and success of the occupying business' (Oseland 2008: 14). Just what this might mean for the planning and resource-effectiveness of the university or college estate remains a problematic and contested issue; definitions of value are just as ambiguous as efficiency or effectiveness (Fig. 3.2).

What matters finally, though, is this. First, estates planners also share with their educational and design colleagues the need for better conceptual frameworks and methods for understanding and evaluating relationships between space and its occupation. Second, what their subject brings to the 'bigger picture' is both that post-compulsory educational space must also be considered *beyond* its occupation for learning and teaching and that we urgently need to find ways of relating the social and spatial practices of education to its value and costs.

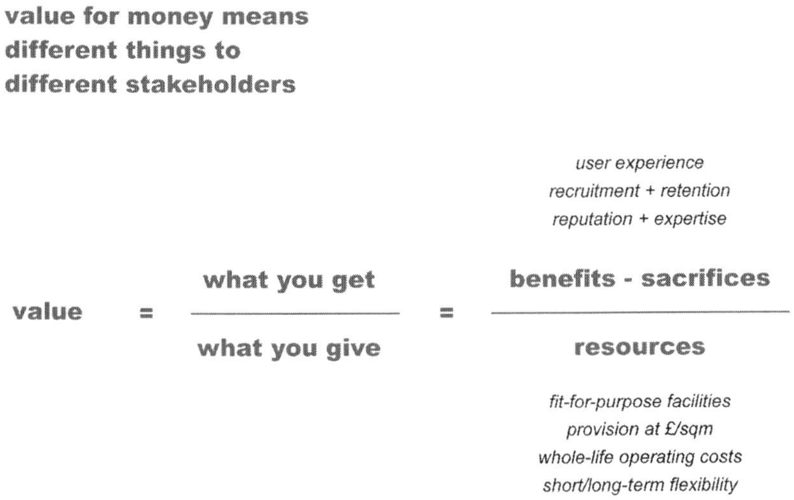

**value for money means
different things to
different stakeholders**

Fig. 3.2
Example of
value equation,
adapted from
Loughborough
University's VALiD
(Value in Design)
project, 2005
(see http://www.
valueindesign.
com/principles/
principles.htm).
Image: Fiona
Duggan.

*user experience
recruitment + retention
reputation + expertise*

$$value = \frac{\textbf{what you get}}{\textbf{what you give}} = \frac{\textbf{benefits - sacrifices}}{\textbf{resources}}$$

*fit-for-purpose facilities
provision at £/sqm
whole-life operating costs
short/long-term flexibility*

Part 2

Mapping the terrain

Chapter 4

Getting beneath the surface

Re-thinking relationships between learning and space

The previous section opened up problems and gaps in our understanding of relationships between learning and space, from the different perspectives that are currently impinging on debates and developments in post-compulsory education. Here, the intention is to go back to basics; to start unravelling what is it that *matters* about learning, in relationship to material spaces. This means examining in greater detail what it is that is distinctive about teaching and learning in post-compulsory education, before developing an alternative conceptual framework for relating learning to the spaces in which it takes place; and then beginning to consider appropriate methodologies for both analysing existing spaces and evaluating 'improved' ones.

I will first suggest that, despite its many problems, the concept of 'communities of practice' does help us engage with learning spaces in productive and creative ways. In addition, rather than articulating space as providing a setting for learning behaviours, more recent approaches from cultural and architectural theory begin to show how learning can be understood as a social and spatial *practice*, which as ethnomethodology describes it is a 'problematic accomplishment' (Turner 1970) which itself has to be learnt. I will also show how some contemporary theories, particularly about the 'location of culture' (Bhabha 1994) can offer a valuable and creative purchase on thinking about the spaces of 'doing learning'.

Re-visiting communities of practice

Some of the uses of, and debates over, the concept of communities of practice have already been explored. Here I want to suggest that, despite its contested and problematic nature, 'communities of practice' does manage to capture some of the key characteristics of teaching and learning in post-compulsory education. In the original book Lave and Wenger actually set out to criticise learning within the academy/ formal learning sector by juxtaposing it to *situated* learning, offered up as a better, because socially engaged, form of learning. They argued that rather than students attending lectures and writing exams, they learn better through participation in an ongoing specialist activity with others who have varying degrees of expertise. As in some forms of apprenticeship, newcomers begin at the periphery of the group and gradually move towards the centre as they become experienced, passing on, in turn, their situated knowledge to other new entrants. This is 'doing but not just doing in and of itself. It is doing in a historical and social context that gives meaning to what we do' (Wenger 1998: 47).

What Lave and Wenger perhaps miss is that within post-compulsory education just such a process is taking place – in bringing new entrants into the community of practice of *knowledge creation and development*. Rather than a simplistic, oppositional divide between 'real' activities in workplace settings and the 'artificial' activity of academy-based learning, here I want to value knowledge creation and development in its own right. For this activity the educational institution *is* the 'situated' location, not just some substitute for a more 'real' place. Learning, in this context, *is a form of doing*. This, of course, is part of the inherent tensions in higher education which separate it from education at primary and secondary levels; it brings learning as a means to develop expertise in a subject discipline which will be used outside the academy together with learning as a means to enable the growth and change of the academy-as-a-centre-of-knowledge itself. Teachers, tutor-practitioners, researchers, research students, teaching assistants, educational development workers and students are all engaged to varying degrees not only in their subject area, but also in the post-compulsory educational community of practice which has historically had knowledge creation and development at its core.

This again underlines the very blurred boundaries between 'formal' and 'informal' education. The practice-based and situated learning methods favoured by Lave and Wenger assume learning as an outward-oriented activity, aimed at increasing application in the real world. Importantly, they do not articulate this mechanically as merely training, but are assiduous in underlining the value of meaning-making to learning: 'practice is about meaning as an experience of everyday life' (Lave and Wenger 1991: 52). However, in setting such processes against 'formal' learning, they ignore the parallel (rather than oppositional) concept of learning for its own sake, for the development of knowledge itself – what could be called 'inward-oriented learning'. This is an activity undertaken both by students and by teachers and researchers. As authors such as Ronald Barnett (2005, 2007a, 2007b) and Maggi Savin-Baden (2008) have shown how this kind of learning in universities is currently under attack, at least in the UK and the USA, Savin-Baden's book argues for the importance of:

> the idea that there are diverse forms of spaces within the life and life world of the academic where opportunities to reflect and critique their own learning position occur. The kinds of spaces I am referring to, while also physical, are largely seen as mental and metaphorical. In such spaces, staff often recognise that their perceptions of learning, teaching, knowledge, and learner identity are being challenged, and realize that they have to make a decision about their own responses to such challenges. Yet these often hidden spaces are invariably not valued by

> university leadership and industrious colleagues nor recognized as being
> important in our media-populated culture.
>
> (Savin-Baden 2008: 1)

She suggests that these kinds of meditative learning spaces are increasingly missing from academic life; that they are a vital part of the academic community which
is thus becoming fragmented and dissolved; and that such learning spaces need to
be valued and re-built for the intellectual health of academia. To her, these spaces
of knowledge reflection and creation are not just spaces of withdrawal, but also of
engaged debate about the nature of teaching, learning and research activities themselves, of value to both staff and students. 'Inward-oriented learning' is thus not
simply 'in-the-mind', nor only about intellectual reflection. It is equally a *situated* form
of learning – for personal development, critical engagement with university or college
as a knowledge sharing and creating community, and through the process of critiqu-
ing the wider context (for example, what constitutes subject knowledge, the status
of particular knowledge, or the location of teaching, learning and research). It also has
its own practices, whether of writing essays, doing experiments or calculations, or
making things, all forms of thinking through doing. And such learning-as-knowledge-
creation is not merely self-centred or of limited value to wider society. In fact, in the
gallery and museums sector, for example, informal learning of this kind is seen as
valuable precisely because it develops qualities of creativity, personal development
and social cohesion:

> The task [. . .] is to provide experiences that invite visitors to make
> meaning through deploying and extending their existing interpretative
> strategies and repertoires, using their prior knowledge and their preferred
> learning styles, and testing their hypotheses against those of others,
> including experts. The task is to produce opportunities for visitors to use
> what they know already to build new knowledge and new confidence in
> themselves as learners and social agents.
>
> (Hooper-Greenhill 2000: 139–40)

Crucially for the argument here, outward and inward-directed learning are neither
oppositional, nor divided by an embodied/cerebral split. Learning occurs through the
negotiation of shared, social meanings, in the *spaces in-between* these forms of collective knowing and our own individual knowing, informed not just by our 'location'
within a community of practice, but also what we bring to it, both from previous
and from parallel experiences elsewhere. Learning then, is always happening at the
intersections of what we know/do and what we don't; and material space is one
of the means through which we engage with and test our cerebral and embodied
experiences, both within ourselves and with others. In fact, part of the resonance of
the concept of legitimate peripheral participation (LPP) is that it captures a version
of this knowing/not-knowing relationship. However, I would suggest it is only one
example of such a moment, and that the practices of post-compulsory education,
rather than lacking such encounters, are actually full of them.

Starting from the interplay of inward and outward-directed participation is centrally important to any study of post-compulsory learning, whether in an adult education class, a museum-based workshop or an undergraduate degree, because of four underlying key characteristics which, I suggest, separate this kind of learning both from the everyday learning of life experience itself and the work-based learning explored by Wenger:

1. Individuals deliberately enter such a 'learning space' to open themselves up to new knowing.
2. This kind of learning emphasises the creative and constructive importance of the 'unstable' space between what that individual already knows and what they are learning about, as the place where new forms of thinking and doing take hold.
3. Within the communities of practice of post-compulsory learning, all participants (teachers, researchers and learners) undertake generative activities related to knowledge creation and development.
4. Processes of post-compulsory learning have the potential not only to change individuals, but also to challenge and alter the communities of practice, both of the subject discipline being studied and of learning itself.

Unlike the tendency to stability in the communities of practice model outlined previously, knowledge creation and development has contestation and instability as the basis of its operations. This is true for all participants, not just new entrants – the 'learners'.

Lave and Wenger, then, offer us a resonant conceptual model for articulating learning as an embodied, meaningful and situated activity, which can give us many clues about its social and spatial practices. But this model also needs to be opened up for critique (by investigating what it doesn't cover as well as what it does) and intersected with other conceptual models and spaces. Second, such a model needs to be problematised internally, so that the tensions, gaps and conflicts it contains for different participants are opened up for view. And, finally, while outlining its distinctive patterns, we need to understand that 'communities of practice' is only a very generic and uncertain term; what is or isn't a community of practice remains always fluid and partial. In addition such groupings come in many various forms, and are not automatically 'good'. Any specific, situated community of practice can be more or less effective for the learning development of its participants. But by decisively shifting debate from learning seen only from the perspective of the teacher/learner dyad to learning as a dynamic and group process, Lave and Wenger are central to the opening up of our understandings of learning as a social and spatial practice.

Opening up the conceptual spaces of communities of practice

The 'communities of practice' model, as developed by Wenger, has come to incorporate at least three ways of engaging with space conceptually (Wenger 1998: 137). The first of these is in the articulation of learning as a journey, a movement, generally from the periphery to the centre (although Lave and Wenger note that this is not inevitable, that participants may place themselves in a variety of ways). Various authors have considered the implications of such a movement on learning; that it requires an initial boundary crossing (Savin-Baden 2008) and is a space of *transition*.

Second, learning as a community of practice demands both a belief in communality of understanding ('mutual engagement') and an increasing responsibility to the total entity and its development ('joint enterprise'). It is a space that must enable motivation and develop involvement through an iterative and relatively systematically organised sequence of encounters, towards the absorption of a specific set of social and spatial practices. This produces a space of increasing *becoming* and *belonging*. The concept of 'legitimate peripheral participation' indicates a particular pattern to learning as a series of jobs with increasing demands and responsibilities, where learning takes place through the combination of increasingly more complicated tasks with the observation of, and engagement with, experts already undertaking those tasks. As Lave and Wenger show, where the processes of the community of practice do not enable such a passing on of knowledge and skills, learning will not take place effectively (in their example, trainee butchers were located such that they could not see – and therefore could not learn from – the methods expert butchers used to produce different cuts of meat).

Third, a community of practice is based on a *repertoire* of events, objects and procedures which do not just come to be consciously recognised by community participants but ultimately are so completely embedded in their shared knowledge and practices as to appear ordinary and 'obvious'. This repertoire is part of ongoing negotiations within and beyond the community of practice, which renews itself precisely through its capability and legitimacy to make and remake these events, objects, procedures and spaces meaningful.

As noted previously, the concept of 'communities of practice' has become an influential one in education, management and social sciences in recent years – 'It is currently one of the most articulated and developed concepts within broader social theories of learning' according to one recent commentary (Barton and Tusting 2005: 1). The research has also generated considerable criticism, as much for what it doesn't cover as for what it does:

> Underlying this social approach to learning is a consensual view on social interaction, where people act to reach a space of shared understanding. [. . .] Practices exist as coherent and established wholes with their 'insides' and their 'outsides', even when sustained over time by continuities and discontinuities that allow them the possibility of change and transformation (Wenger 1998:125). As a consequence the tense, conflicting, ambiguous processes of the discursive and power negotiations implied in the construction of these centres is silenced as if it were a settled process. Who defines the unitary entity, how it is defined and in whose interests it is defined as a whole does not appear.
>
> (Keating 2005: 108)

Educators and researchers working with basic literacy and adult education skills, for example, have commented that where they have used the 'communities of practice' model to shape learning,

> [m]ore confident members may thrive, whilst those less socially able may find their disadvantage continued – or even reinforced and extended; or members committed to the successful outcome of a particular project find their goals conflict with others who are less committed or productive.
>
> (Harris and Sheswell 2005: 166–7)

They thus emphasise the 'unspoken interactions' in such encounters, around issues of, for example, confidence, mutual respect, checks and balances on behaviour, shared goals, etc. For these authors, there are inherently legitimation conflicts around who is included and excluded. These are around what they term expansive or defensive learning (2005: 173–4), which links to ideas of threshold concepts and mimicry explored earlier; to issues of boundaries and barriers (2005: 170–1) and – similarly to other authors already mentioned – to the difficulties of 'boundary crossing', especially in relation to issues individuals bring with them when making an entry into a community of practice.

In these critiques, then, the spaces of any community of practice are seen as contested and complex rather than as (relatively) unproblematic. If the processes of inculcation into a community of practice take place through its repetitive daily routines – its affective encounters, social and spatial practices and repertoires – then these also continually intersect and are challenged/resisted/changed by, on the one side knowledge and skills as framed by the community's experts, and on the other through the adaptations and transformations wrought by the newcomers.

Here, I will suggest that re-framing communities of practice by exploring some contemporary theory, particularly the writings of post-colonial theorist Homi Bhabha, can open up to complexity, contestation and partiality the processes of learning articulated through its characteristics of boundary crossing, centripetal movement, iterative affective encounters and negotiated engagement through a specific repertoire.

The problems of learning as 'outside-in'

Wenger acknowledges that all communities of practice inherently have particular tensions, for him, most importantly, as new generations inevitably take over from previous experts:

> The different ways in which old-timers and newcomers establish and maintain identities can conflict and generate competing viewpoints on the practice and its development. Newcomers are caught in a dilemma. On the one hand, they need to engage in existing practice, which has developed over time: to understand it, to participate in it, and become full members of the community in which it exists. On the other hand,

> they have a stake in its development as they begin to establish their own identity in its future.
>
> (Wenger 1998: 115)

These contradictions are played out through changing power relations, so the community of practice itself is also in motion, but for Wenger, basically stable. For other authors though, the basic act of separation of insides and outsides (insiders and outsiders) which any community of practice implies, indicates patterns of inclusion and exclusion that may not just be occasionally problematic, but are based on an underlying relationship which is *inherently* unstable (Bhabha 1994). A community of practice must always be about reproducing a certain kind of normal, where all 'abnormal' characteristics are split off and located outside the boundaries, at the extremities or margins. In Wenger's writing and consultancy, such boundedness is just a necessary characteristic which enables a 'like-mindedness' within the group. This does not preclude change, but Wenger makes no judgements as to what might constitute 'good' and 'bad' forms of shared knowledge, or the potential inequalities of particular inclusions and exclusions. As he writes:

> In this regard, a community of practice acts as a locally negotiated regime of competence. Within such a regime, knowing is no longer undefined. It can be defined as what would be recognised as competent participation in the practice. That does not mean that one can know only what is already known. A community's regime of competence is not static. Even knowing something entirely new, and therefore even discovering, can be acts of competent participation in a practice.
>
> (Wenger 1998: 137)

Crucially for theorists like Bhabha though, the very common-sense structure through which such a community aims to continue making a separation between those included and those who are not, actually generates rather than prevents instability. This is because a stable group based on inclusion/exclusion is inherently impossible to maintain. A community of practice requires an outside against which to frame itself, yet this doubling undermines the possibility of ever attaining the implied desire for a totally shared stable, transparent and consensual culture, since outsiders are *necessary* for this very notion, are built into its very definition. Second, no social category or identity is pre-given or fixed. Relationships between what is inside and outside are always slippery and subject to change, disruption or re-framing. Finally, framing 'others' as not part of a particular community of practice does not of itself 'make it happen'. In fact, it can – through that very process – place these others in an ambivalent and difficult-to-occupy location, one that *is not of their making and that they do not recognise*. Or it can introduce many ambiguities as to what are or are not the 'proper' competencies for a community of practice. And it can, of course, generate deliberately disruptive or provocative challenges to a community of practice from outside it. Recognising these facts does not negate the concept of communities of practice, it just opens up the potential problems in assuming a smooth(ish) transition from outside to inside, requires an awareness of the inherent tensions and complexities of boundary crossings, and opens up to critique the metaphor of learning as an outside-to-inside movement, visualised as a centripetal spiralling in from edge to middle.

Beyond 'legitimate peripheral participation'

Through the concept of LPP, Lave and Wenger attempt to articulate learning as neither the passive transmission of knowledge, nor the active learning supported by much contemporary educational theory, but as a *negotiated* process, centred on meaningfulness to the various participants. As previously noted, in their articulation, learning is both a type of social practice (instructional education), and a feature of all social practices (becoming/belonging). Lave and Wenger focus on the latter, on the processes through which learning enables membership of a community of practice. They define learning as 'an integral part of generative social practice in the lived-in world' (Lave and Wenger 1991: 35) and argue that 'this social process includes, indeed it subsumes, the learning of knowledgeable skills' (1991: 29). This, then, is a participation not just in a separate and isolated space of 'learning'; but through the integration of doing and thinking. This idea of learning is important because it does not separate out learning as a form of becoming (being a designer, rather than merely doing design, for example), from simply understanding subject content:

> This pivotal emphasis, via LPP, on relations between the production of knowledgeable identities and the production of communities of practice, makes it possible to think of sustained learning as embodying, albeit in transformed ways, the structural characteristics of communities of practice. This in turn raises questions about the socio-cultural organisation of spaces into places of activity and the circulation of knowledgeable skill.
>
> (Lave and Wenger 1991: 55)

This, they argue, is ultimately a theory of learning in general not just specific to work-place-based study:

> There has crept into our analysis, as we have moved away from conventional notions of learning, an expanded scale of time and a more encompassing view of what constitutes learning activity. LPP has led us to emphasise the sustained character of developmental cycles of communities of practice, the gradual process of fashioning relations of identity as a full practitioner, and the enduring strains inherent in the continuity–displacement contradiction. This longer and broader conception of what it means to learn, implied in the concept of LPP, comes closer to embracing the rich significance of learning in human experience.
>
> (Lave and Wenger 1991: 121)

They thus end with a deliberate critique of conventional learning, by re-defining the activity as an engaged and long-term process. But there are two slippages here, in relation to their assumed prioritisation of outward-directed learning, as already outlined. First, they fail to unravel the whole variety of mechanisms for a simultaneously cerebral and embodied thinking through doing; that is, the multiple and iterative affective encounters we have with self, others, language, objects and spaces. By focusing on learning as outward, shared and socially meaningful, they make invisible the contestation and problematic nature of how and what becomes socially meaningful to different individuals and groups; that is, how individuals position themselves in, and are positioned by different communities of practice. There may be a recognition that a space exists *between* the perspectives of individuals (what they bring to a subject, what they take from it, how they challenge or adapt its 'norms') and the beliefs of the community of practice; but this space is not critically examined, except as part of an assumed overall tendency to stability and congruence. The authors therefore ignore the creative and constructive learning and knowledge development embedded not in stability per se, but in the endless shifting backwards and forwards from stability to instability between individual participants and the group, and between the group and other communities of practice. As I have already said, knowledge creation and development as a community of practice *demands* explicit movements of contestation and patterns of constructive difference over ideas and methods, affecting individuals both in their personal academic development and also in their subject discipline contexts; and situated in the spaces in-between both.

Second, Lave and Wenger don't explore the impacts of the wider context, sometimes implying that communities of practice have full agency and are autonomous. The relationships between communities of practice (whether competitive or collaborative or both) are not considered, nor are the external forces that may affect where and how a community of practice can operate, or which may impact on its beliefs and practices. This is highly relevant to post-compulsory education and its core activity of knowledge creation and development, which often does not have strong control over its own boundaries (however hard it tries) but must engage with the wider political, social and economic context, and wider attempts to frame definitions of this particular community of practice which are different from the way it perceives itself.

While recognising the powerful potential of LPP then, it is suggested here that building a picture of the distinctive characteristics of learning in post-compulsory education needs to include many forms of affective encounters. All of these hold to the important underlying points in Lave and Wenger's work; that in learning activities thinking and doing are integral, not separate; that learning involves not just cerebral knowledge but is also always embodied; and that learning is an on-going process which is centrally about social meaning-making in the world.

The problem of the repertoire

Interestingly Wenger does engage directly with the material world in his analysis, in a way that is uncommon in educational theory. Both design and objects/spaces are seen as part of the processes through which communities of practice are developed and maintained. For him, this is also through ordinary social practices of repetition through which common-sense meanings become embedded in concepts, objects and architecture. He calls this 'reification', defined as:

> the process of giving form to our experience by producing objects that congeal that experience into 'thingness'. In so doing, we create points of focus around which the negotiation of meaning becomes organised [. . .] any community of this kind produces abstractions, tools, symbols, stories, terms and concepts that reify something of that practice in a congealed form.
>
> (Wenger 1998: 58–9)

What is more, 'reification' can happen through everything from abstract ideas to bus tickets:

> A wide range of processes that include making, designing, representing, naming, encoding and describing, as well as perceiving, interpreting, using, reusing, decoding and recasting [. . .] from entries in a journal to historical records, from poems to encyclopaedias, from names to classification systems, from dolmens to space probes, from the Constitution to a signature on a credit card slip, from gourmet recipes to medical procedures, from flashy advertisements to census data, from single concepts to entire theories, from the evening news to national archives, from lesson plans to the compilation of text-books, from private address lists to sophisticated credit-reporting databases, from tortuous political speeches to the yellow pages. In all these cases aspects of human experience and practice are congealed into fixed form and given the status of object.
>
> (Wenger 1998: 60)

While for Wenger, reification is a useful and constructive mechanism which helps glue together communities of practice, for many other authors it is a problematic and inequitable process. They ask instead whose 'ordinary' is being congealed and in whose interests. Theorists such as Homi Bhabha, already mentioned, Michel Foucault (1970, 1977) and Pierre Bourdieu (1987) have analysed how the congealing of a particular 'ordinary' is perpetuated through the material fabric of society. Reification here becomes the attempt to make transparent and obvious (by locating it externally in the 'concrete' world) that which is actually a specific enunciation of ideas and practices, and a particular translation of these ideas and practices into things and spaces. In *The Location of Culture* (1994) Homi Bhabha explores how to 'see through' the persistency of this mode of thought in terms of not just its own legitimations but also the anxieties it represents for dominant groups, and how to make visible the positions of those it 'contains' in a specific way. He first proposes how to conceptualise different positions:

> The move away from the singularities of 'class' or 'gender' as primary conceptual and organisational categories has resulted in an awareness of subject positions – of race, gender, generation, institutional location, geopolitical locale, sexual orientation – that inhabit any claim to identity in the modern world. What is therefore theoretically innovative, and politically crucial, is the need to think beyond narratives of originary and initial subjectivities and to focus on those moments or processes that are produced in the articulation of cultural differences. These 'in-between' spaces provide the terrain for elaborating strategies of selfhood – singular or communal – that initiate new signs of identity, and innovative sites of collaboration, and contestation, in the act of defining the idea of society itself.
>
> (Bhabha 1994: 1)

Unlike Wenger, then, Bhabha conceptualises the relationships between ideas and their reification not as a stabilising mechanism for the easy recognition of certainties, but as a much more uneven terrain of hybridity, negotiation and contestation. As he goes on to say, 'the exchange of values, meanings and priorities may not always be collaborative and dialogical, but may be profoundly antagonistic, conflictual and even incommensurable'.

What does such a critique imply for the notion of 'reification', in relation to learning spaces? Not only the lecture theatres, seminar rooms, laboratories and staff offices, but also the timetable, curriculum and modular frameworks, and the essays, exams and other academic protocols, make learning 'concrete' in post-compulsory education. In a specific form, they can become congealed as 'natural' and straight-forward, thus making a particular form of teaching and learning seem transparently obvious and correct. For Wenger this serves a useful purpose. For other theorists it hides the actual contestations over what learning is and how it should take place:

> We must be insistently aware of how space can be made to hide conse-quences from us, how relations of power and discipline are inscribed into the apparently innocent spatiality of social life, how human geographies become filled with politics and ideology.
>
> (Soja 1989: 6)

For Soja, material space is deeply ambiguous because it has the potential to both hide and express social relationships and practices simultaneously. That is to naturalise a specific set of social relationships and practices as the obvious and normal arrange-ment of things, so as to make other possibilities much harder to imagine.

So instead of what often happens, which is that space is seen as directly reflecting the social life that it contains, here material space and its occupation are seen as always potentially in tension, with many complexities, gaps and unintended consequences in relationships between them. It is important to note here that it is not just the spaces or repertoire which appear obvious and yet are always problem-atic; it is also the social and spatial processes towards the reification of particular types and relationships of space (what goes together and what is kept apart) which can seem 'normal' but are really contested and in flux. The ongoing debates over what learning spaces should be like in post-compulsory education, and the range of new built examples produced as a result, only highlights this endless struggle to first challenge existing patterns and then move towards the 'normalisation' of the new. This means that we should not only list the repertoire of a given community of practice at any one time – for example its typical building types – but we must also open up what is being challenged, and how, and the processes through which such 'campaigns' are or are not successful.

Towards a framework for re-thinking relationships between learning and space

In his seminal work *The Production of Space* (1991), Henri Lefebvre famously proposed a spatial triad, as a means of conceptualising relationships between space and the social, which went beyond the simplistic pattern of binary oppositions and the false coherence of space and society reflecting each other transparently through a process of association, analogy or metaphor in an endlessly tautological circle.

The first of Lefebvre's divisions is the spatial practices of a society. Our daily routines are embedded in space and time, through what goes together and what is kept apart. These are the ordinary, unconsidered experiences which I have already outlined, using terms from ethnomethodology, as being about 'nothing much'; and which, although in actuality are 'problematic accomplishments', are only recognised as constituting *work* (i.e. 'doing' learning) when normal social and spatial practices are 'breached'. Second, these everyday social and spatial practices are intersected through what Lefebvre calls 'representations of space', meaning the conceptualised space of planners, scientists and other experts that tends towards a system of verbal signs (Lefebvre 1991: 39), such as maps, plans, models and designs. According to him, representations of space are about the history of ideologies (Lefebvre 1991: 116) because these are attempts to explicitly describe particular coherent patterning of the social in space – concrete guidelines for how 'thought' can become 'action' (Lefebvre 1991: 165; Harvey 2000: 203). Finally, the third part of the triad is representational space, the space of inhabitants and users. It is the space that is or can be altered by ordinary people; where their imaginations seek to appropriate, adapt or transform 'normal' social and spatial arrangements and where change 'from the bottom up' can occur, although often incoherent or partial.

Because Lefebvre writes within a Marxist perspective, and through a period where modernism still held sway, he predominantly articulates representations of space as the abstract space of contemporary capitalism (for which designs built environment professionals and their clients appear as mere 'conduits'); while representational space particularly reveals attempts by individuals and groups to challenge such capitalist patterning, for example in the ideas and practices of the Situationists (Debord 1995).

But I suggest that, if these three aspects are taken as partial and overlapping – and often with gaps, unintended consequences, or contradictory elements – they offer a potentially rich conceptual framework for linking architecture and its occupation. Here, building on Lefebvre's spatial triad, examining the relationships between learning and space requires understandings of – and an analysis of the intersections between – the following three aspects, situated in specific contexts and locations:

- the 'ordinary' routines of existing communities of practice in education (Lefebvre's 'spatial practices' or what I have called 'social and spatial practices');
- attempts at, and impacts of, designed transformations of existing spatial practices (what Lefebvre calls 'representations of space' and Wenger calls 'repertoires');
- participant engagements with, and adaptations of, these social and spatial processes and repertoires (what Lefebvre calls 'representations of space', and I have described as the *spaces in-between*; that is, our own individual positionings in relation both to existing and specific social and spatial practices and the spaces in which these take place).

Instead of a closed oppositional 'backwards-and-forwards' of learning between either its assumed formal/bad and informal/good locations – or even a circular movement from outside to centre, as described by the communities of practice model – perhaps we can envisage such a patterning more as three parallel lines which overlap sometimes, or stretch far apart; sometimes run very close for long periods of time, or moving jerkily; sometimes thick in their intensity, sometimes petering out. Intersections between lines are always dynamic, with changing relationships towards and away from coherence and stability. Where individual lines drift too far apart, then the pattern is likely to be lost and a new pattern forms (Fig. 4.1).

Importantly, such a method offers one means of opening up our understandings to the concepts of gaps, tensions and unintended consequences. That is, the spaces in-between the 'conventional' social and spatial practices of post-compulsory learning, our different interpretations of those social and spatial practices, and actual attempts at manipulating form and space towards particular learning 'ends'. As I have said, these patterns never settle, nor can they be explained

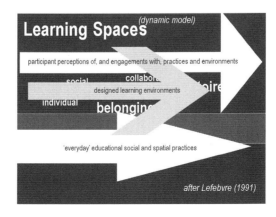

Fig. 4.1
Approach for examining learning space as a pattern of 'and/ and' encounters and practices, based on Lefebvre's spatial triad (1991).

in totality. But such a visualisation suggests that the particular and non-coherent intersections in a specific situation of both individuals and groups can be *illuminated* (Parlett and Hamilton 1972), as can the processes through which change occurs, personally, at the level of communities of practice and across wider social and cultural contexts. I will explore how such a framework might help us understand something about the qualities of spaces at the detailed and immediate level of learning encounters in post-compulsory education, in the next chapter.

This adaptation of Lefebvre's triad also articulates, with some measure of equivalence, the distinctive characteristics of post-compulsory learning that I have begun to outline. Existing practices can be framed via the concepts of communities of practice already discussed. Participant interpretations and their adaptations open up the centrality of what different individuals bring to the processes of negotiation within and across various communities of practice as they learn through developing their own meaning-making, both inwardly and outwardly. And Wenger's idea of 'negotiated repertoires' seems a resonant means of engaging with the *design* of spaces, objects and procedures in its widest sense; that is both the production of space by architects and others and also its interpretation, negotiation and adaptation by those who occupy it.

It is beyond the scope of this book to research in any detail the whole gamut of social and spatial practices that constitute learning in post-compulsory education or their intersecting patterns in different contexts and locations with specific architectural spaces and participant experiences and engagements. But such an outline framework for understanding relationships between learning and space does enable a way of beginning to critically explore our many different experiences of teaching, learning and research in post-compulsory education; and to open up the kinds of questions and debates we should be having to inform the architectural design of our colleges and universities in the future. In Chapter 6, I will begin to explore what this means for the design of educational institutions.

Chapter 5

On the ground

Searching for the student learning experience?

I ended the last chapter by suggesting that an adaptation of Lefebvre's spatial triad could be useful in capturing something of the experiences of learning spaces. At first glance, unravelling the intersections between a particular set of social and spatial practices, the places in which these take place, and what we each bring to the situation may sound unnecessarily complicated. But of course, it is what we actually do all the time, as we continually negotiate our relationships with each other and the world. This chapter begins by examining how student (and other) experiences of learning spaces are usually evaluated, and then goes on to explore the research of Clare Melhuish (2010a, 2010b). She brings to the debate a background in both ethnography and architecture, and therefore suggests one approach for examining both social and spatial practices.

Student-centred?

Much current literature around post-compulsory learning spaces is increasingly – and rightly – focusing on evaluating the student experience, as a way of better understanding the effectiveness of particular spaces for learning. However, reviews of evaluations to date (Barnett and Temple 2006; Temple 2008; Joint Information Systems Committee (JISC) 2009) have demonstrated how these have tended to lack any kind of theoretical framework which explicitly articulates a relationship between learning and space. In addition, very few studies of learning spaces make use of the wide range of potential methodologies which examine the occupation of material space across anthropology, ethnography, ethnomethodology, discourse analysis, phenomenology, behavioural psychology, cultural geography, human–computer interactions, sociology and the like (Cousin 2009). In their 'Study of effective evaluation models and practices for Technology Supported Learning Spaces' funded by JISC in 2009, Ian Pearshouse et al. set out to 'identify and review the methods and tools currently used to evaluate the contribution that technology-supported physical learning spaces make to learning and teaching' (JISC 2009: 3):

> Our initial investigations showed that although institutions were keen

> to advertise new or innovative learning spaces, the practice of evaluating such spaces was not made readily visible and was thus harder to identify or track. A key finding to emerge from the study was that if evaluations were undertaken they occurred as part of an internal institutional process, typically prompted as part of a student satisfaction survey, of which the outputs were not ordinarily deemed to be for external consumption. This has limited the extent to which knowledge-sharing about learning spaces has been promoted across the whole educational community.
>
> (JISC 2009: 3)

Overall, their findings were that evaluations tended to be local, and under-resourced. They were usually initiated by, and conducted within, the home institution by managers or other in-house staff, rather than external evaluators. This had an effect on scope and remit; studies were under-theorised and without a clear methodology, often containing an element of 'justification' and closure, rather than any critical analysis. I have already suggested in previous chapters that the very structure of our assumptions about learning spaces – that we 'obviously' need to move from formal/passive/bad to informal/active/good learning spaces – works against the kind of critical questioning which is central to proper analytical and evaluative study. The current 'common sense' may actually be preventing evaluators from seeing any underlying conceptual problem about how to relate space to learning, or considering methodological issues explicitly. In addition, merely having more space tends to be seen as something that will make a change for the better to learning (which given that any new space involves a valuing of the particular activities it is designed for, is not surprising). Pearshouse *et al.* show how, in some cases, studies of the student experience were perceived as confirming evaluators' expectations that, based on space usage and student satisfaction ratings, learning could be seen to have improved. They note the difficulties in blurring whether a space is liked or not with whether it enhances teaching and learning:

> From these examples, the enabling of new learning and teaching scenarios is implicitly associated with new, 'better' ways of learning, acting as a shorthand for improved pedagogic action. This association of new uses with improved learning is paradoxically often reliant upon indicators of occupancy, usage and scenarios rather than data concerning the socio–cognitive processes of learning, or general assessments of learning. Many evaluators were aware of this tension, and identified learning processes as important, however, only fifty per cent were able to recognise these factors within their evaluations, and in these cases evaluators relied upon self-reported learning.
>
> (JISC 2009: 13)

It is therefore clear that we still lack frameworks and methods for understanding how space can or might impact on learning in post-compulsory education.

Towards better methodologies

The argument in *Towards Creative Learning Spaces* to date has suggested that:

- Learning in a post-compulsory context involves participants making a deliberate commitment to enter a 'learning space' and to become involved in the inherently unstable process of new knowledge development and creation.
- Learning in post-compulsory education can be envisaged as the negotiation of various boundary conditions; the choreography of a series of affective encounters through a transitional and liminal space; and the orchestration of learning via a repertoire of spaces, objects and procedures.
- Learning encounters cannot be simply 'read' off a space. The shape of material space does not align coherently or congruently with the activities that take place in it; learning activities are always about more than the space; and space is always about more than just the activities that go on in it.
- Analysing how learning space is experienced and interpreted by its participants involves mapping the complex, non-overlapping and partial inter-relationships between the 'ordinary' social and spatial processes of existing communities of practice in post-compulsory education; designers and clients' attempts at transformations of existing processes and repertoires; and how different participants engage with, and adapt, to these social and spatial processes and repertoires.

To explore how such a conceptual framework can inform evaluations of the student (and staff) experiences of learning space, I will re-visit some research undertaken by Clare Melhuish (2010a, 2010b) entitled 'Perceptions of three new learning spaces and their impact on the learning and teaching process at the Universities of Sussex and Brighton', which was commissioned by two of the HEFCE-funded Centres for Excellence in Teaching and Learning, one through Design (CETLD) and one in Creativity (InQbate). This pilot study aimed to explore how ethnographic methods might be usefully applied to exploring experiences of learning spaces. Here, Melhuish both worked from a pre-agreed set of spatial/aesthetic characteristics (developed in her own previous PhD and other research (Melhuish 2007)) and adapted this set in response to the interpretations of her interviewees. Such an approach is informed by a close reading of existing research about peoples' interactions with material space, such as Augoyard's study of a housing project in Grenoble, France (1979). This is an attempt to develop a detailed phenomenological enquiry of everyday engagements with the material environment. Following Lefebvre, Augoyard also stressed the difference between the static, planned spaces designed by architects and planners, and the 'lived space' as experienced phenomenologically, through the senses, through physical movement, and through the imagination, by its inhabitants. As with other ethnomethodological studies, already outlined here, the aim was to examine everyday un-noticed social and spatial practices, through for example, study of:

> walking, movement, and the associated process of verbally naming, or describing, different elements of the environment, [which] reveals much about the way different individuals relate to spaces and environments,

and embodies the social dimension which activates and deconstructs the original formal intentions mapped out on the drawing board.

(Melhuish 2010b: 9)

Such an approach, then, is as much about observing what people do, as about what they say, with 'embodied' enactments as well as discursive reflections. Augoyard's analysis was based on detailed observation, mapping and photographic documentation, and led to a quasi-scientific notation of individual movements, based on concepts from linguistics. This concern with developing a structuralist, holistic and objective terminology for relating space and its occupation has been increasingly challenged within anthropology, especially by the Geertzian school. They emphasise the personal and subjective character of all interpretation; Geertz uses the phrase 'thick description' as a way of describing all observation and interpretation as culturally produced, partial and personal (Geertz 1973). As Melhuish goes on to note:

> Geertz's work was not specifically concerned with the intersection of culture and space, but his subjective, interpretative approach parallels that of the environmental and architectural phenomenologists who have promoted an understanding of space as subjectively perceived, through the senses and the imagination, by the individual – such that the same space may be experienced and described by different individuals in quite different ways.
>
> [This] is essentially an empirical method of study, wherein the researcher must remain fundamentally open-minded as to what s/he observes in the field, what responses s/he may elicit from respondents, and what those responses may signify. These are the accepted fundamental principles of any ethnographic research, where the ethnographer, as 'author', must aim to set aside any preconceptions and personal bias when entering the field, to draw out rather than prompt responses from participants, but ultimately acknowledge, through the process of interpreting the data, the ways in which the final analysis is shaped by the inescapable conditions of the author's own background and prior experience.

(Melhuish 2010b: 9)

What is valuable about Melhuish's work is that she uses ethnographic methods to ask detailed questions about the *architectural* properties of the learning spaces investigated, but in a way which remains always integrated with relationships between those spaces and its wider practices and agendas. So, she starts by describing the institutional, physical and social settings of the learning spaces under consideration. Then she asks her participants about their perceptions of each physical setting: its spatial layout and furnishing, lighting, colours, smells, sounds and technology, status and image. She also asks about its social setting: its occupation, uses and interactions, and about her participants' interpretations of both institutional agendas and the impact of space on their learning.

What Melhuish begins to capture in her study is most crucially the sophistication of participant responses. Rather than the simplistic 'likes' and 'dislikes' of functions or material properties that many studies elicit (too light, dark, hot, cold), here both interactions with, and readings of space, are articulated around the underlying social and spatial practices which energise them in specific ways in different contexts. Her interviewees – both staff and students – are easily able to engage with the new learning spaces under study at a variety of levels simultaneously, from the immediate encounters being mediated, to the relationships with other spaces and activities; and to the wider context of the institution. Second, she enables respondents to open up to view the inherent tensions and overlaps in how particular spaces are perceived. They show an awareness of difference, complexity, contradiction and paradox as they consider the intersections (what I have already called the *spaces in-between*) across the social and spatial practices of learning being offered, the design and educational intentions of these new learning spaces, and their own interpretations and experiences.

Here, I will make an extended review based on some of Melhuish's data; not to critique it, but to add another angle of view to her important work, which focuses on aspects of what I have already called the distinctive characteristics of learning in post-compulsory education. These distinctive characteristics are framed in relationship to the three qualities that define communities of practice as proposed by Wenger: i.e. the negotiation of boundary conditions, the choreographing of affective encounters (what I have also called everyday social and spatial practices) and various engagements with the repertoire.

Experiencing boundary conditions

Material space obviously creates a series of physical thresholds – which, as I have emphasised, do not need to align with conceptual 'thresholds'. But both physical and conceptual boundaries do intersect with and therefore affect, and are affected by, our everyday spatial, aesthetic and sensory experiences. These can be described in terms of the relationships between spaces, such as closeness or distance from a point of entry; enable relative ease of access so as to imply particular inclusions and patterns of 'exclusivity'; and can act as a landmark, or express 'front', as against 'back', qualities. But what is most important is not merely the *fact* of such descriptions but also the *meanings* such relationships take on in particular situations to different participants.

In Melhuish's research study respondents all described, in different ways, how the new and innovative learning spaces they were using formed a separate 'bounded' category from the rest of the university's spaces and activities. They were able to articulate the quality of these new learning environments as 'conceptual' spaces and as 'physical' spaces, and to engage with the tensions between the two. First, there was an awareness of a specific spatial context; that these facilities had value due to sheer lack of space-availability elsewhere, and particularly due to the lack of availability of comfortable or appropriate space. As already suggested, this reinforces the 'common-sense' evaluation often given, that merely having the space becomes something that enhances learning. This is important, not just as an obvious conclusion, but in seeing that just providing newly designed or renovated space can open up activities that previously did not exist simply for lack of somewhere for it to happen (Fig. 5.1):

> The CETLD funding enabled the creation of a learning space in a place – the RIBA library – which is implicitly about learning but had no way of imparting it. Just the addition of a simple physical space was transformational: it made it possible to have an ambitious, aspirational programme for Higher Education, which is already having many repercussions.
> (Irena Murray, director British Architectural Library, RIBA,
> (Boys 5 February 2009, unpublished interview notes))

However, such new learning spaces also imply additional operational demands, such as educational support staff. Where the new space and its intended occupation are explicitly 'labelled' as different to the conventional social and spatial practices of post-compulsory learning, this also puts them 'outside', that is, in an ambiguous and potentially problematic relationship to existing university communities of practice. So, rather than seeing a lack of positive take-up of such spaces as indicative of staff and students 'resistance to change' (as is often the case), we should investigate it instead as evidence of the contested and negotiated practices and repertoires of learning in post-compulsory education.

In Melhuish's study, most respondents saw all the three new learning spaces investigated as, for example, a space 'away' from an existing department and/or a cross-boundary space that did not 'belong' to any particular department and as located outside of 'standard' centralised timetabling and booking systems, which meant staff who booked them had to 'be in the know'. Negotiating the means

Fig. 5.1
CETLD Bene Education Room, Royal Institute of British Architects (RIBA), British Architectural Library, London. Photograph: RIBA British Architectural Library Photographs Collection.

of accessing these spaces could give both staff and students a sense of their own 'specialness'. This can make a space simultaneously visible and invisible (Fig. 5.2):

In some way, then, the [CETLD] room is perceived as a high-status venue, which has '*got a purpose*', is '*serious* [. . .] *challenging*' [. . .], and in which users themselves become elevated to a higher status or level of engagement – not only while in the space, but also subsequently, through its stimulating effects: '*this is the only class I've ever done where every week I will go home and I will write up my sketchbook*', comments one student [. . .] This status is reinforced by the fact that it is easily accessible, on the ground floor, near the entrance to the campus, and highly visible through its glazed display cabinet, giving a view onto red, white and black items of furniture inside, which are '*obviously meant to be examples of good and innovative design*' [. . .], putting out a specific message.

But, at the same time, and paradoxically, it is not highly visible. As Tutor 2 points out, the name means nothing to most students, and many of them don't know what its purpose is or whether they are permitted access to it or not: '*most students don't know what it is* [. . .] *it's surprising*' [. . .]. The display of magazines inside suggests free access and browsing, but in fact there is a perception that it can only be booked for use, and you cannot just wander in and out: '*you couldn't do that*' [. . .] – even though there is a notice clearly displayed by the door which says there is free access on Mondays and Fridays. There is a sense that it has '*the potential to be more heavily used*' [. . .], but the booking

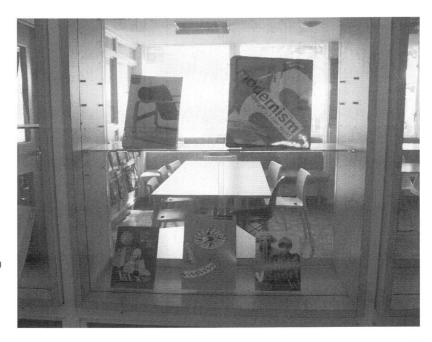

Fig. 5.2
View into CETLD learning space, University of Brighton, 2009. Photograph: Clare Melhuish.

> system establishes clear boundaries around its use which effectively gives the facility invisibility except to those in the know about how the system works. The problem, as perceived by Tutor 1, is that if such spaces '*become too visible, you'd need lots and lots of them*', because everybody would want to use them. Hence the system works well '*in this transition phase*', but could break down under pressure of demand.
>
> (Melhuish 2010a: 47)

The participants in the study expressed the felt contradictory nature of a space which sits between a recognisably known and an unknown setting, especially where its physical and aesthetic boundaries gave out ambiguous cues about what is 'normal' in terms of educational space. Here boundary crossing both indicates a difficulty and a benefit, and is thus recognised as inherently problematic – good for the staff and students who use it, but 'reduced' if the facility is more generally available.

The other spaces investigated – the InQbate Creativity Zone at the University of Sussex and the Creativity Centre at the University of Brighton – are differently located, towards the back of buildings, reached by a journey through several corridors (Fig. 5.3). Both students and staff articulated an awareness that this location helps to keep it 'separate', while also indicating that using the space implies a special kind of commitment by, and benefit to, its participants.

As with the CETLD room, but through a different spatial configuration, the Creativity Zone simultaneously signals both availability and exclusivity and makes itself difficult to 'recognise' in relation to conventional learning spaces. Melhuish also found that her respondents were aware that two of the three spaces studied were perceived as having a tension between 'insider' and 'outsider' communities of practice, that is, between university and external business use:

> One of the implications of this is, as at Space B, that it is being increasingly hired to outside companies – 'because they [the university] can't afford to have it, apparently' [. . .]. There is a general perception that the expense of running the place may jeopardise students' and staff's access to it, which is regarded as a serious drawback. Tutor 4 says 'it would be tragic' if she couldn't use it next year, because it is 'an excellent resource'. She says that use of the space has not been guaranteed for next year, and this would make it very difficult for her to teach her course in its present form. This sense of uncertainty and mild resentment seems quite pervasive. 'We're not timetabled in there', comments one student: 'it's a booking thing. Because when we go in there, they don't get any money' [. . .].
>
> (Melhuish 2010a: 32)

But as she also notes, the attractiveness of these spaces to outside users is also enjoyed by those 'inside' the institution because it provides students with the opportunity to engage with professionals within the university context and that of their course. Experiencing each of the spaces, then, is informed not just by its immediate material qualities, but also by awareness of wider social and institutional agendas and

Fig. 5.3
Entry to InQbate
Creativity Centre,
University of
Brighton, 2009.
Photograph:
Clare Melhuish.

contexts; and engaging with the various boundary conditions/crossings of learning spaces is not merely a physical act, but a complex negotiation of meanings.

The choreography of affective encounters

I have already suggested, based on the 'communities of practice' model, that we can understand post-compulsory learning as a series of iterative affective encounters, moving towards increased becoming and belonging, through something which is experienced as an uncertain, liminal space. The material environment and its associated objects and procedures (repertoires) are one mechanism through which such encounters are mediated. To begin to open up how such mediations might be explored, I want to examine how respondents in Melhuish's research interpreted and interacted with their chairs and tables in the new learning spaces studied.

As already noted, the CETLD seminar space is set out café-style with a number of small square tables and examples of modern designer chairs. Tables can be also pulled together to form a larger surface. According to Melhuish:

> Within the CETLD space, the layout and furniture are perceived as not only inviting, but also as creating an informal and relaxed atmosphere which is not immediately associated with a teaching venue: '*When I first saw the space my impression was it looked like a café or something because of the tables and the mix and the funny chairs, and I thought, that's a bit strange. But [. . .] it does actually encourage you to relax*'. Another student describes it as '*a lot less formal*' [. . .]. On the other hand, it is not necessarily that comfortable. Tutor 3 maintains the chairs are '*quite uncomfortable*', though less so than '*those awful chairs with the little fold-down table [. . .] which are really uncomfortable and isolating for students*'.
>
> (Melhuish 2010a: 42–3)

Again, then, the furniture is interpreted in relation to conventional provision, and 'read' in terms of the meanings that are associated with the new variation, here to do with a contemporary, informal and creative feel (Fig. 5.4):

> The drawback of furniture that clearly looks 'designed', and possibly more appropriate to another sort of environment, is that it may be intimidating

Fig. 5.4
Examples of furniture, CETLD room, University of Brighton, 2009. Photograph: Clare Melhuish.

to some users, in terms of the aspirations which it symbolises. Although one describes it as stimulating – '*so modern [. . .] I want to come up with innovative ideas here*' – it also raises the bar of expectations: '*it seems more modern here, not just the interior, but also the way of working here seems more millennium-ish*'. For one History of Art student, that is perceived as somewhat daunting: '*because of the design, chairs and the colours and the tables and the fabric on the sofas, it seems very sort of modern and creative and innovative [. . .] I sometimes feel slightly pressured into being creative and I'm not really*' [. . .].

(Melhuish 2010a: 43)

Generally, the setting of café-style tables is interpreted as an effective alternative to the traditional seminar room, where sitting around a large table affects whether students feel capable of making a worthwhile contribution to the general discussion 'either because of the feeling of being under a spotlight, with all eyes directed at one point, or because of the difficulty of waiting for a gap in the conversation – 'like crossing a busy street'. As Melhuish continues:

In the CETLD room, the fact that 'there are chairs facing away from you and facing in different directions', means there are multiple focal points, which eases up the flow of conversation – 'with small tables you're sure to have your opinion heard [. . .] everybody does have respect for other people's ideas. It's quite a sort of comfortable feeling'. It is not 'like a ring around you', as in the (conventional) seminar room, where 'there are about 14 of us around this huge table and it does go very, very quiet at times' [. . .].

(Melhuish 2010a: 43)

In addition, the potential mobility of table and chair layouts seems to make it easier for students and staff to stand up and move around during a class. Melhuish suggests that the importance of these particular tables is not so much about working with books or drawing, as it is about creating interchangeable focal points for group interactions. It should also be noted, however, that in this process of patterning and re-patterning during a class, the rectangular room shape retains a 'front' and a 'back':

with the body of students and staff generally clustered around the screen at one end, whether or not it is in use, leaving the rest of the space free. Tutor 2 sees this as beneficial, in that it allows students to graduate towards the back or side of the space if they feel like taking a back seat. It also allows the teacher to withdraw from the class at points. Like looking out of the window, this can accommodate the natural rhythms of teaching sessions in a flexible way. 'The set-up of the room makes you concentrate so much on the work because you're so deeply discussing with other people' [. . .], but at the same time it is possible to take breaks and let your mind wander, which is relaxing, and allows the teacher also to feel that s/he is not under a permanent spotlight at the front of the class.

(Melhuish 2010a: 43–4)

The precise details of spatial arrangements are here articulated in relation to particular learning activities, enabling the generalities of 'flexibility', so often used, to be opened up as a distinctive and specific set of social and spatial learning practices.

Both the other two studied spaces use mainly beanbags for seating (Fig. 5.5). Here the cues offered by such seating are potentially more ambiguous:

> Although beanbags [. . .] seem to prompt more spontaneous and playful behaviour during teaching sessions, perhaps because of the smooth floor surface, perhaps because of the makeup of the student group in question – 'almost not grown-up enough to use the beanbags', with a 'macho dynamic' [. . .] – they do not attract the same level of comment or evaluation from students or staff [as the CETLD furniture]. They clearly facilitate group working at the whiteboards around the perimeter of the space, and there is comment on the comfort which they offer, although it is somewhat qualified: 'it's nice to sit in beanbags, but [. . .] that just induces sleep if it's not interesting [. . .] if you're sat on a chair, you're forced to sit up', says one [. . .]. While another suggests that it's better to be bored and asleep rather than uncomfortable: 'much better being relaxed than in a lecture hall where you're also not listening, but you sit there really uncomfortably'.

(Melhuish 2010a: 28)

As with the CETLD room, tutors can choose to orchestrate how beanbags or 'ordinary' chairs are used in the space to indicate different degrees of formality and

Fig. 5.5
Examples of furniture, InQbate Creativity Zone, University of Sussex, 2009. Photograph: Clare Melhuish.

informality. The furniture is read for the clues/cues it gives about the learning encounters taking place. It is experienced as a space and set of objects which are interacted with by each participant so as to continually 'locate' themselves in relationship to the learning taking place, whether by 'mucking about' or being 'serious' students. This is always within what is available, and concerns both how they are positioned, and how they position themselves, in relation to the social and spatial practices of learning being undertaken and to the larger group and context. Within the same setting there will always be a variety of experiences and interpretations.

Thus, we can 'pin down' some of the precise characteristics of space that can impact on the learning encounter at this detailed and immediate level. From the above, these can be seen to include insides/outsides, boundary conditions, backs/fronts, spatial and social configurations of tables and chairs, patterns of focus and 'distraction' through visual and environmental conditions, and the 'language' of seating and setting. At the same time, though, there can never be a single correct solution because there is no one-to-one, coherent or obvious relationship between how the space is 'choreographed' (whether by designer, client, estates manager, tutor or student) and the range of individual embodied encounters experienced within it. These are not completely relative, that is, they are not so various as to be closed to analysis or evaluation. What we each bring differently to our learning encounters in particular spaces and contexts means that we cannot expect to find a consensus beyond the gaps, partialities, contradictions and paradoxes as indicated by the participants talking here. Within such a conceptual framework, architecture and design is always only about offering up a 'best guess' through mapping, re-thinking and then translating into material form a particular set of social and spatial practices.

Negotiating a repertoire: the impact of new technologies

Most environments for post-compulsory education seem to be made up of generic components, or following Wenger, to have been reified into a particular repertoire. Besides the kinds of furnishings already mentioned, such as seminar tables and chairs, this includes: rooms such as lecture theatres, seminar rooms, design studios and computer laboratories; the lecture, tutorial, experiment, essay and presentation; the learning 'module' with its associated learning outcome and assessment criteria; the curriculum and academic timetable; the academic year cycle; patterns of taught and self-directed study; sequenced levels of achievement with controlled entry and progression points across a number of years; methods of research funding, development and assessment; relationships to stakeholders and associated facilities such as library, student support services, staff offices, administrative support facilities, canteens and cafés, students' union, sports facilities and rental accommodation. These elements are also intersected with the specific characteristics of particular institutions (campus, town-based, university/ex-polytechnic, further education college, elite/research-based/teaching-based) and of various academic disciplines, which give shape to a variety of – linked – communities of practice, both in how learning is differently articulated and in how subject specialisms are framed.

To recap: Wenger treats these repertoires as tending towards stability and 'obviousness' – making concrete and 'true' the arrangement of things in a particular form and set of relationships rather than any other – which is useful in focusing on what makes the common sense of 'doing' learning, the everyday social and spatial practices in post-compulsory education. What it obscures is the extent to which this is a 'problematic accomplishment' where some potential participants cannot be 'ordinary' learners and where particular repertoires may be ignored, misunderstood or challenged by insiders to a community of practice; or how it may be undermined or redefined by outsiders. Most importantly for the study of learning space design, analysing what makes communities of practice a basically stable structure prevents us from understanding how repertoires change – i.e. how any specific reified component comes to lose its obviousness and therefore its power; or from unravelling the dynamic processes through which learning repertoires are more or less settled or contested through time and in different situations.

In Melhuish's research, the key element that the different spaces studied share, is their concern with embedding the potential of new technologies for learning within existing educational repertoires, either as an addition to existing elements, or as a deliberate and major challenge to them. However, as has already been argued, this attempt to 'shift the repertoire' cannot be taken as straightforward and obvious. Because such as approach is framed by a 'deficit' model of teaching and learning, which defines existing educational processes and practices as the problem, it sets up complicated and ambiguous relationships between supposed insiders and outsiders. Those who argue for the centrality of new communication and information technologies as an 'obvious' mode for re-thinking learning define themselves as within the community of practice which is post-compulsory education. Simultaneously, of course, they frame those who do not agree as 'outside' such a community, that is, as 'improper' members. Meanwhile, many academics consider the educational developers and other teachers who adopt new technologies in this way as the outsiders, as relatively irrelevant to the 'real' and normal practices of teaching and learning.

I have already outlined how Bhabha (1994) shows that this patterning of binary oppositions between inside and outside – which are then linked associatively through the mechanism of either/or to superior/inferior and right/wrong – is inherently conceptually flawed. It merely offers a tautological and closed circle with its own internal (and unprovable) logic. How, then, can we think about repertoires in a way that breaks out of this patterning, informed by the kind of contemporary cultural theory outlined in Chapter 1?

Rather than seeing the new technologically-rich spaces as obviously good or bad, negotiating the repertoire here comes up against underlying issues of power and control. Thus arguments over repertoire affect not just the usability of spaces and things, but are a key mechanism through which individuals and groups within a particular community of practice offer up a new and supposedly 'improved' version of themselves. Here space can provide an opportunity to *make concrete* one particular model of the repertoire and to enable – through an ongoing process of accumulation of examples – the slow shift towards a different pattern of reification, together with its associated 'better' community of practice. But these contested attempts to define what elements should be 'in' rather than 'out', central rather than marginal, and drivers rather than mere effects, result in many ambiguities and complexities.

This is particularly so where such attempts to shape the world through simplistic binary oppositions come up against the multiple understandings, experiences and interpretations that individuals bring to any situation.

Technology-rich spaces for example, tend to simultaneously highlight ICT as very visible and important to learning, and at the same time want to emphasise its obviousness, normality and ubiquity. This also means that participants in these spaces are often articulated as requiring 'special' support in developing/changing their teaching and learning practices and yet also *already capable* of using such additional elements of the teaching and learning repertoire, as a 'natural' and unproblematic development of what they already do. As Melhuish shows, on the whole her respondents neither located new technologies as central to their learning and teaching nor separated it out from the whole milieu of social and spatial practices in which they were operating. What they articulate most clearly are the experiences of being located in the *spaces in-between*, on the one hand, a recognisable 'push' towards more technologically-rich learning methods in the learning environments being studied and, on the other, their everyday experiences of learning and teaching:

> Both the CETLD room and café spaces are equipped with sockets and internet access, inviting use of individual laptops in addition to the integrated system. They indicate that you can come and 'just hook up' [. . .]. 'If there are that many power sockets then they're expecting people to have laptops' [. . .]: however, as the focus group points out, there is only one student on the course in question who actually uses one: 'I'm the only one'. They suggest that personal technology does not play such a big role in the learning experience as might be imagined, and they point out a number of reasons why many students may not wish, or be able, to use a personal laptop computer; notably because of the cost, lack of a printer at home, slow typing speed, noisiness of typing in the classroom, and anxiety about losing or damaging portable equipment and its contents while on the move.
>
> (Melhuish 2010a: 45)

While a tutor did note that students brought in memory sticks and mobile phones for presenting and recording work (and that the facilities are there to use them), when Melhuish observed a typical session, the tutor used a flipchart rather than the smartboard and almost all students engaged in traditional paper-based note-taking. The teacher seemed to want to exploit the physical and interactive qualities of writing manually, but also admitted to preferring 'a simpler form of technology that I know how to use and is reliable', than a more complicated system that requires technician support; even where, as in this case, that support was immediately accessible and within close physical proximity' (Melhuish 2010a: 45). In fact in all the spaces studied, while the technology was no more complicated than in a standard modern lecture theatre, it usually required help to set up and use, because of the different configurations and added functionality available (Fig. 5.6). The research also showed that some students quite explicitly contested any emphasis on ICT:

Fig. 5.6
Innovative
new learning
technologies at
InQbate Creativity
Centre, University
of Brighton.
Photograph:
Clare Melhuish.

Surprisingly, there seemed to be some resistance, amongst the particular student group interviewed, to the principle of technology; something which may be partly attributable to the fact that they were all History of Art students and considered themselves to be essentially more orientated towards textual than visual material. 'I get the feeling that technology is being used for the sake of it [. . .] they've bought all this technology and they have to use it [. . .] I don't like the feeling of technology being forced upon us', says one. Another suggests that tutors' use of pre-prepared PowerPoint presentations effectively structures lessons much more tightly, whereas, without it, 'discussions kind of evolve' and become more free-flowing: 'you're never quite sure where it's going to go and where you're going to end up [. . .] it does feel a lot freer' [. . .].

(Melhuish 2010a: 45)

At both the other two learning spaces studied, specialist staff were available, not only to help with equipment but also to work with tutors on their design of teaching and learning sessions, and to suggest creative ways of using the available space. On one of these sites the technology was deliberately cutting-edge, enabling immersive environments through 360-degree images, and with considerable control on space size, shape and colour. While this offered considerable opportunities, the complexity of the provision meant 'that neither staff nor students are really allowed to interact with the technology themselves, and that this can make using it "extra stressful"' (Melhuish 2010a: 31). Students are also well aware of how expensive and complicated the technology here is, which also generates a sense:

that they are not trusted enough, and therefore not given sufficient responsibility, to be allowed to interact with the resources in the way they would like: 'the lecturer decides if they want to do something. That takes away the fun and greatness of it [. . .] it's really controlled in there. We're not allowed to use the light patch [. . .] to move the walls [. . .] so it makes it not flexible at all. We are adults [. . .] I'm sure we can manage that' [. . .]. On the other hand, the sense of frustration seems more acute on the part of female respondents, while, amongst the males, there is a fear that they may, indeed, be lacking in sufficient maturity to engage with the space in a more responsible way: 'I don't know, always people mess around in that kind of space [. . .]'

There seems, then, to be a level of uncertainty within the group about how much responsibility they feel able to assume, and, further, an acute awareness of the cost of equipment and the potential risk of causing accidental damage to it, which is inhibiting in their overall engagement with the space.

(Melhuish 2010a: 31).

The technology here is neither simply good nor bad, rather it was designed with specific intentions which could only partially be fulfilled, and is experienced not just 'as it is', but also in relationship to much wider agendas about the idea of technology, the complexity of its current positioning within post-compulsory education, and differences between individuals' encounters with it. I will return in greater detail to the impacts on space of new information and communication technologies in Chapter 8.

Illuminating experiences of learning spaces

The experiences of learning spaces explored by Melhuish begin to suggest how the boundaries, affective encounters and repertoires which together give shape to a 'community of practice' of post-compulsory education can be explored as complex, partial and contradictory conditions. In this chapter, I have tried to draw out some threads and offer some directions for mapping and evaluating students (and other) experiences of learning spaces, which starts from just such a perspective and opens it up for investigation. Such a conceptual framework and method does not result in either design 'solutions' or guidance on how to design the architecture of post-compulsory education. In their influential paper Parlett and Hamilton (1972) argue that the primary concern of evaluative research 'is description and interpretation rather than measurement and prediction' (10–11), so as 'to contribute to decision-making'. As they go on to write:

Each group or constituency will look to the (research) report for help in making different decisions. [. . .] A decision based on one group's evaluative criteria would, almost certainly, be disputed by other groups with different priorities. A 'mastery of fundamentals' for one group is, for another, a 'stifling of creativity.' [. . .]

> Illuminative evaluation thus concentrates on the information-gathering rather than the decision-making component of evaluation. The task is to provide a comprehensive understanding of the complex reality (or realities) surrounding the program: in short, to illuminate. In (their research), therefore, the evaluator aims to sharpen discussion, disentangle complexities, isolate the significant from the trivial, and to raise the sophistication of the debate.
>
> (Parlett and Hamilton 1972: 31–2)

Melhuish's study already suggests some of the kinds of issues and questions that architects, their clients and users, should be addressing and debating in the design of post-compulsory learning spaces. Her approach works directly with the properties of architecture at the immediate level of encounter – its spatial layout and furnishing, lighting colours, smells, sounds and technology, and status and image – so as to illuminate the complex and problematic relationships between these and everyday social practices. At the same time, she is able to begin to unpick how our understandings and experiences of a particular educational and social setting, and of wider institutional and societal agendas about learning (what Parlett and Hamilton call the 'learning milieu') impacts on our experiences in, and interpretations of, particular material spaces. In the next chapter, my aim is to extend the outline conceptual framework and methodological approach being offered here so as to also unravel aspects of learning beyond learning encounters; that is, at the level of communities of practice and the wider educational and societal relationships and contexts within and across which these operate. I will begin to explore how different communities of practice attempt to 'frame' themselves as definable and distinctive, through what is located inside and what is outside; via forms of boundary construction and maintenance; in the choreographing of particular practices and through the reification of those practices into repertoires. I will consider how material space can be one of the mechanisms through which these framings are orchestrated and made concrete. This means also examining how different communities of practice overlap or conflict, their patterns of similarity and difference, and their relative weaknesses and strengths through time. Finally, it enables us to think about how things *change*, about how new social and spatial practices of learning can and do shift, either incrementally or (occasionally) dramatically.

Chapter 6

Shaping learning

(Re)designing the institution

In the last chapter I looked at teaching and learning encounters and began to map their complex and partial relationships to the physical space in which they take place. This revealed that, while the activities and the spaces in which they occur have only a partial relationship with each other and are always situated and specific, some key questions and issues for design can be discovered through close observational and other investigations of particular learning spaces. Next, though, I want to 'go up a level' to examine the social and spatial practices of the educational institution, and the 'shape' of post-compulsory education providers.

This initially involves challenging two conventional assumptions: first, that to develop new and innovative designs we need improved participation and collaboration; and second, that design at the level of the educational institution can be explained as 'representing' some aspect of the learning 'entity'. Instead, I will suggest that we need to re-think the architecture of universities and colleges around what *matters* about the design of space for the social and spatial *practices* it orchestrates. This involves returning to the concept of 'communities of practice' and exploring the complexities, conflicts, gaps and unintended consequences where such communities intersect. It is about organisational cultures, the roles and relationships of an institution, and how sets of activities are articulated, bounded, enforced and contested as a particular obvious and 'natural' pattern rather than another. It is also about the learning context – the wider understandings of how different communities of practice, individuals and organisations are categorised and 'located' politically, economically, culturally and socially, and the processes through which new links are forged or undone between and across groups and space. These issues are neither new to, nor unconsidered by, architects. Here, though, I am particularly interested in how we can build an understanding of the non-congruence and partial translation between intentions, representation in form, and lived experiences, into the core of design approaches.

The problem with participation

Much of the literature concerned with improving the design of learning spaces at the level of the institution focuses on the importance of participation (JISC 2009; Harrison and Cairns 2009; Neary *et al.* 2010). Doing this 'properly' is assumed to enable a better integration of different perspectives, and therefore lead to both consensus and 'ownership' of the resulting space. This ideal of a shared engagement is itself seen as a key means of improving the social and spatial practices of post-compulsory education:

> Bickford (2002) sees a way forward in the fundamental re-orientation of the institutional culture of the university. He says improved learning spaces requires the development of a collaborative culture, to overcome a structure previously based on silos of expertise, with the long-term goal being the creation of a learning organisation capable of drawing on its collective and evolving expertise.
>
> (Jamieson 2008: 26)

However, setting up effective collaborations as part of the design process is also articulated as being difficult for a number of reasons. First, teachers do not tend to think explicitly about space:

> [There is] a lack of concern shown by most academics for the classrooms in which they operate. Few academics give much thought to how the physical environment of the classroom setting influences their approach to teaching or how it impacts on the quality of the student learning experience. This is hardly surprising when the majority of academic staff are not formally trained in teaching practice, and professional development is infrequent and often optional. Also, due to the formal demarcation of professional responsibilities and authority within institutions, even the most capable and motivated university teacher generally has no opportunity to participate in the design of those learning environments where they conduct their own teaching.
>
> (Jamieson 2008: 25)

Nor do students seem to be any more interested than staff:

> Other work in higher education suggests that students are not overly concerned about the spaces in which they work: 'it is clear', reports one recent study, 'that many of the physical aspects of the University services are not important with regards to student satisfaction' [. . .]. Other studies [. . .] have similarly found that most students place emphasis on the teaching abilities and subject expertise of the staff, tutorial support, library and information technology facilities, and other matters directly related in students' minds to teaching and learning, rather than on physical facilities.
>
> (Temple 2008: 237–8)

Second, as mentioned, the conventional divisions between disciplines involved with space-use, management, design and use, mean that conflicting priorities and differences in language and perspective make collaboration problematic. This is also connected to a perceived resistance to change, and a lack of commitment to involvement in innovation:

> We should note, though, that similar ideas on new learning spaces have been under discussion for several decades: Hickman (1965) welcomed experimentation in the design of teaching rooms, noting the creation of novel horseshoe-shaped lecture theatres, special visual-aid class-rooms and other innovations. We may speculate on why innovations of these types have been so slow in taking root. An academic attachment to traditional pedagogic practices may be part of the story: 'old self-understandings and sets of values live within the new' (Barnett 2000, 28). A lack of clear evidence as to the learning benefits of these new approaches may be another part of the story.
>
> (Temple 2008: 235)

What is more, students, staff and others seem to find it hard to imagine other scenarios, or worry that any alternative may offer a threat rather than an improvement:

> Students (and teachers) are not always willing or able to speculate on the nature of a new and possibly more radical learning environment. Understandably, students may not favour situations of change where they perceive that the adoption of new teaching practices may jeopardise their own learning experiences and/or grades.
>
> (Jamieson 2008: 30)

Thus the spaces of learning are not much thought about, and any suggestions for change (a process with its own long history) seem difficult to conceptualise. Third, and as also already outlined, methods for evaluating whether changes to learning spaces are effective or not are very underdeveloped. This leads to claims about success which are either too obvious or too vague to inform or improve methods for collaborative design development:

> The conclusion from the literature points to the link between space design and learning outcomes being weak at best, and it may often easily be masked by a number of other factors. A high proportion of the literature makes unsupported, or anecdotal claims about the benefits of new designs or new configurations of existing space. Where they are presented, empirical findings are usually flawed, as they either tend to report changed student attitudes (rather than learning outcomes), or where learning outcomes are reported, they fail to take account of observer effects of various kinds.
>
> (Temple 2008: 237)

Much contemporary activity aims to resolve these ongoing difficulties through the repeated calls for 'better' forms of collaboration and participation, and by attempts to invent improved methods and tools that can somehow finally 'solve' the issue. But while working towards improved participation and collaboration in learning space design *is* important, reliance on it as *the* method for enabling change obscures more than it reveals. As I have already suggested, this is because of the underlying problem – a lack of understanding about relationships between space and what goes on in it.

The focus on participation can, in fact, make invisible the lack of a better conceptual framework and/or research for mapping and analysing the distinctive characteristics of teaching and learning encounters, relationships and contexts. Instead it relies on the mere accumulation of individual opinions and approaches to subject specialisms and spaces. This has three inherent difficulties that any participation and collaboration method needs to address explicitly. First, individual views are, of course, informed by considerable expertise, but they can also tend to repeat generalities about architecture (that spaces need to function properly, be comfortable and flexible), tend to blur conceptual and metaphorical descriptions of space with material ones, and tend to assume that design intentions will translate transparently and coherently into lived experience. It is therefore based on a common-sense approach rather than a theorised framework for linking learning and space.

Second, and just as crucially, the very structure of communities of practice – of how we make sense of and survive in the world – means that individuals and groups are deeply embedded in the 'reification' of their own subject, whether as a teacher, learner, manager or estates manager – and of academic life itself (exactly what immersion in a community of practice is meant to do), such that they may find it hard to articulate explicitly the underlying 'ordinary' social and spatial practices and repertoires of their university or college, to think about alternatives or to agree that changing existing patterns and procedures is necessary. Third, membership in a community of practice involves both collaborative and competing engagements with other groups. There is no 'natural' universal consensus to achieve, because each grouping is *inherently* bounded around their particular view of the world. But while we cannot expect communities of practice to merge seamlessly into each other through consensus, they can forge strong and long-term alliances where particular ideas and/or practices come to resonate positively across many participants in specific situations (Cockburn 1991, 1998).

When communities of practice intersect

As already outlined, a major critique of Lave and Wenger's work is that it plays down the difficult, complex and often conflicting processes that underpin the construction and ongoing maintenance of any community of practice in a particular form. Rather than existing as relatively unproblematic unitary entities, then, we need to critically examine how specific groups define themselves (and are defined by others). We need to explore in whose interests such definitions are articulated, and where, when how and by whom these are recognised. And we need to understand particular boundary definitions and relationships, specific social and spatial practices and group repertoires, not as obvious and normal 'reifications' of a community of practice but as partial (and partially successful) attempts to make concrete one view of the world rather than another. Again, following Bhabha, it is inherent in communities of practice to attempt to use 'thingness' to both obscure and normalise power relationships through making them appear transparent in language and objects, and thus to externalise (reify) our everyday encounters and practices. This is because specific acts of articulation and translation are justified through a call to their obviousness, to an assumed 'natural' consensus and coherence, which is offered up as both simply achievable and inherently good (Bhabha 1994).

Attempts to make particular spatial or aesthetic changes are clearly one of the mechanisms in these processes, through which various participants both collaborate and compete over what is the 'proper' repertoire for a particular situation and community. Thus, both the development and design of new learning spaces and their various 'translations' through occupation are not so much represented by, or reflected in, the design; they are integral to, but only one specific mechanism in, competing attempts to define particular communities of practice. These processes may tend to more or less stability, but will also be uneven and dynamic.

As many critics have noted, analysis is made more difficult by the fact that Lave and Wenger's framing of what precisely constitutes a community of practice is itself deliberately vague and ambiguous. We can envisage post-compulsory learning in the UK as one; or separate it out into individual educational institutions (for example, by seeing an ex-polytechnic and the University of Cambridge as very different entities); or divide up different departments or subjects within a university or college; or group together academics as different from academic librarians or other learning-support or administrative staff. Here, though, I want to suggest that the ambiguities are actually *useful* precisely because they reflect our ways of being in the world, as individuals constantly negotiating its ordinary complexities. Rather than attempt to define communities of practice as congruent and clearly bounded, we can see them as we experience them – as internally partial, richly complicated and layered; and as having amorphous, ambiguous and awkward interstices, one to another. Swales, for example, offers a detailed account of the 'discourse' communities – what he calls a textography – of three departments that occupy one university building, both through a careful critique of the communities of practice literature, and through the kinds of situated 'thick description' and careful observation and listening already outlined:

> In terms of findings, this inquiry into textual ways of life at the close of the 20th century complicates a number of widely held current perceptions. At least within its own localised context, many simple and stereotyping dichotomies are undone. The detached nature of scholarship, and of the scholar is subverted, as is the detached nature of scholarly writing [. . .].
>
> Beyond these floor-level generalities and communalities, there are a few observations that pertain to the building as a whole. As we have seen, one concerns its service role, or rather the somewhat different service roles of each of its three floors. And connected to this is [. . .] its partial disarticulation from the academic year 'clock' that so dominates

life in traditional departments. Meanwhile, behind these floor level generalities and communalities, tucked away in the interstices of these communal matrixes, are the particularities of individual textual ways of life that a textography can at least aspire to bring to life. There is much colour and pattern here.

(Swales 1998: 192)

These kinds of detailed analysis of educational groupings also intersects with the type of conceptual framework, informed by the writings of theorists such as Baurillard, Deleuze, Foucault and Lyotard, and being considered in contemporary architectural theory. Just as Lefebvre's spatial triad was examined in the last chapter as a means of exploring the unevenness, non-congruence and contradiction of everyday social and spatial experiences, so here, we need to consider how to better examine the uneven shapes, connections, overlaps and gaps in and between communities of practice at different scales and granularity that can open up to view what currently constitutes the social and spatial relationships and contexts of post-compulsory education. This can also help us examine how and where change is or should be happening. To deeply over-simplify (and potentially misuse) the philosophical and post-structural geographies of Deleuze and Guattari (2000), if an individual's embodied encounters with social and spatial learning practices have already been envisaged as lines which are sometimes thick or thin, are far away or close together, and are running slower or faster, then communities of practice can be imagined as dynamic 3-dimensional terrains where these myriad trajectories coalesce into intensities, or fold back onto themselves. Marcus Doel offers the image of origami:

Everything that presents itself as a whole One is a special effect of a certain regulated display of folding. It suffices to refold this figure in order to produce another. [. . .] Or rather, since the whole One *can* be refolded, and insofar it is *nothing but* the relative stabilisation of its own refolding, its apparent integrity and self-sufficiency is illusory. Indeed, the folds of space are never *around* the figure, they are *in* the figure.

(Doel 1999: 27)

Crucially, as before, it is not so much the various entities (what a community of practice 'is') as the differential relationships, the intervals, or *spaces in-between* and the movements between and across them, which requires a 'philosophy of passage, and not of ground or of territory' (Nancy 1996: 112).

To that extent it is futile to isolate discrete theoretical-practices – each with its own system of ideas, conceptual apparatus, phrase regime, frame of reference, proscribed territory, and logic of internal development – and to position each over and against the others. For each is endlessly other: it is not a whole being but a multiple becoming. Each theoretical-practice is a multiplicity without unity since it is always open to

> difference, deferral, iteration, transformation, and perversion. Hereinafter, there are nothing but open systems that are always already everywhere, shot through with vectors of disjointure, disadjustment and dislocation.
>
> (Doel 1999: 32)

Again, such a conceptualisation focuses on practices and trajectories, not on entities or appearances. And change comes through adaptations of, or disruptions to, these dynamic patterns of resonance or dissonance. To Cynthia Cockburn (1991, 1998) for example, change occurs either where the intersections between lived experience and its representation and practices becomes so problematic or contradictory that a new perspective is inevitable; or where offered alternatives resonate strongly enough with existing beliefs and concerns to enable alliances to be formed or to deepen.

What then, are the implications for architectural design practices?

Educational architecture: representation and practices

Most studies of educational architecture still tend to 'map' the meaning of university and college buildings onto, and read from, the material space itself. As Mitchell writes, 'When colleges and universities build, they don't just add to their inventories of floor space. They reveal – sometimes unwittingly – their prevailing values, aspirations and preoccupations. Campuses are evolving, continually-contested representations of the communities they house' (Mitchell 2007: vi).

Yet, as Temple (2008) notes, specialist architectural books on campus planning (Dober 1992; Edwards 2000; Strange and Banning 2001) have tended to focus on how the design of universities and colleges at this level operates as a representation of the 'mission of (the) university in built form' (Edwards 2000: 3) – that is as a stable and unproblematic unitary entity. Temple is rightly critical of this emphasis in the literature on 'the signals that both campus design and the architecture of individual university buildings might send' (Temple 2008: 231). As he says:

> [W]hat is meant when claims are made about epistemologies being 'found' in building designs? What is presumably to be understood here is that designers of university buildings may aim to reflect their own understandings of a building's purpose in its outward form. This form is then interpreted by observers in the light of their own understandings of the building's purpose, or through their skills in de-coding the socially-constructed meaning of neo-classicism, say. If this is so, it must cast doubt on the sweeping claims writers such as Edwards make on behalf of university architecture: a university building is no more distinctive in this respect than, say, a Victorian town hall. This seems to be the view taken by Dober (1992: 5) in his study of the (mainly, American) campus, when he notes that university 'landmark' buildings 'are cultural currency [. . .] charged with allegorical significance and perceptual connotations and meaning'.
>
> (Temple 2008: 231)

Temple cites examples from the 1960s of the master plans of the universities of York and Kent in the UK, which were based on ideas about teaching and learning being enhanced by the spatial integration of academics, and of making spaces for informal communal encounters across disciplines – 'not obviously supported by any evidence, incidentally' (2008: 230). Of course those 1960s campus designs are now seen rather differently:

> There is some limited evidence on the role of campus design, as well as the design of individual buildings, in supporting student learning. As learning is a social activity, campus designs are needed that create welcoming, informal spaces for people to meet and talk, and perhaps to work in small groups. The windswept, charmless plazas which are a feature of some 1960s UK universities – 'a preoccupation with imagery [which] led to architectural indulgence' (Darley 1991: 356), presumably designed with the aim of creating social spaces – are not what is needed.
>
> (Temple 2008: 236)

Three interconnected points here, then: university and college architecture is perceived as having been predominantly designed and interpreted around representational qualities; the assumed connection between representation and its assumed interpretation is not supported by any kind of clear theoretical framework; and – on occasions at least – this intended match between 'image' and resulting occupation has been shown to be deeply incongruent in reality. As I have already outlined, what is crucial here is to separate out the role architecture invariably has (although unevenly and problematically) in 'representing' the activities it contains from that of 'choreographing' everyday teaching, learning and other practices as a dynamic patterning of uneven and variable conjunctures (Doel 1999). In fact, 'reading' university architecture predominantly as a symbolic representation results in many more problems than it answers. As Temple goes on to write, while most universities and colleges want, for example, to create a sense of community,

> [h]ow do ideas of community and participatory governance in higher education relate to teaching and learning, and to space? This is an under-researched, but potentially important, field. It has been proposed that the physical form of the university is important in supporting its integrated nature, intellectually and socially, and that it is 'the preservation and development of this integrated form, with its dense network of connections, that provides many of the management and planning challenges in higher education' and which supports institutional effectiveness (Temple and Barnett 2007: 7).
>
> (Temple 2008: 232)

But how does a particular appearance and arrangement of spaces 'translate' into either the 'feeling' or the 'reality' of community? Kathryn Moore (2009) suggests that, while ideas about creating a 'sense of place' (Temple 2010) are often used to connect particular aesthetic and spatial representations with human scale, social belonging and connectedness, these are actually both philosophically flawed and closed to effective investigation or evaluation. She argues that buildings and land-scapes should not be treated as some mysterious, elemental, shared, non-verbal form of communicating meaning which somehow just 'happens' through the senses, but pragmatically, as a series of situated, interpretative experiences framed by what we each already know:

> This has dramatic consequences for our understanding of aesthetics. As with any other kind of human experience, the aesthetic occurs in response to our interaction with the physical world about us, in all its multifaceted, cultural, social and complex sensuality, marked indelibly by memories, associations and preconceptions. We react and respond holistically, to 'the environment that is human as well as physical, that includes the materials of tradition and institutions as well as local sur-roundings' (Dewey 1934: 246). The response is inevitably influenced by knowledge, mood and context. This locates us, not as cool observers of the world 'out there', but as an indispensable part of that world.
>
> (Moore 2009: 65)

Following the pragmatist philosophy of Richard Rorty (2008), she argues that design representations do not contain the kind of 'true' meanings that architects, critics and even clients may wish for, that can be simply and obviously read off a building or interior, but are rather partial, complex and negotiated. 'Rorty describes this as a movement away from "an attempt to correspond to the intrinsic nature of reality" towards "an attempt to serve transitory purposes and solve transitory problems"' (Rorty 2000: xxii, quoted in Moore 2009: 61).

In the late 1990s, the Massachusetts Institute of Technology (MIT) undertook a major building redevelopment programme, which included five build-ings by world-renowned architects Kevin Roche, Steven Holl, Frank Gehry, Charles Correa and Fumihiko Maki. As Mitchell writes (from his position at the time as both dean of the MIT School of Architecture and Planning, and as architectural adviser to MIT's president):

> The process of campus reconstruction confronted MIT and its architects with the need to reflect critically on the very idea of a campus for the twenty-first century research university, to engage a vigorous ongoing debate about principles of campus design, and to re-think the constitu-ent building types.
>
> (Mitchell 2007: vi)

To Mitchell, architecture does not reflect a university's characteristics directly, but the chaotic, contested and uneven process itself through which such buildings are realised. As he writes:

> Designing a building is a messy, informally-structured generate-and-test process: it is framed by the cultural conditions of the moment, the architect's wide-ranging imagination processes, whilst some combination of institutional and economic imperatives, emerging exigencies, and sheer accident disposes. It is the social exploration of a complex, shifting solution space. The construction of today's MIT campus has actualised just one politically and economically contingent path through a maze of might-have-beens, and the paths projected, but then not taken, are as interesting and revealing as those that were.
>
> (Mitchell 2007: viii)

What does that mean for our understanding of what (and how) buildings come to express some kind of shared representational meaning? For Mitchell, the final form in some way embodies the complexities and conflicts of the underlying processes. The Ray and Maria Stata Center (Fig. 6.1), for example, designed by Frank Gehry,

> arose from the growth to prominence of a research area – information science and technology – that had not even been imagined when the campus was initially planned [. . .] As the project evolved, its program snowballed – a process that continued right up to the addition of two levels of underground parking at the end of the design development phase. [. . .] there was a process much like that of tacking amendments onto a bill passing through Congress. As the project gathered momentum, deans, provosts and others realised that it would provide their best opportunity to get various things that were important to them done, so they manoeuvred to get elements added to the program.
>
> (Mitchell 2007: 62–5)

At the same time, Gehry's design was explicitly based on the expression of dynamic juxtapositions and interconnections across and between the hybrid people and activities it contained. As he said:

> The main problem that I was given was that there were seven separate departments that never talked to each other. And when they did talk to each other, if they got together, they would synergise and make things and it was gangbusters [. . .] So they asked me to make places where people could bump into each other, so we made these two C-shaped buildings and in the bottom put a street and the communal stuff and created a little village.
>
> (Gehry quoted in Mitchell 2007: 72)

Thus, for Mitchell, the building can be read at two different levels – as an expression of an uneven and contested process, and as an architectural design 'device' aimed at a particular social and spatial outcome. However, both of these understandings have the same conceptual flaw: that is, that intentions (however muddled) can be

Fig. 6.1
Exterior view of
Ray and Maria
Stata Center,
Massachusetts
Institute of
Technology (MIT),
Cambridge (Gehry
Partners, 2004).
Photograph:
Jos Boys.

'read' transparently, directly and obviously from the shape of a space itself. I have already outlined in the last chapter a different framework: that interpretations of space necessarily occur *between* its design, its everyday social and spatial practices, and what the individual observer brings to it (through both seeing and 'being', that is, their embodied responses). The informal and layered qualities of the Ray and

Fig. 6.2
Interior view of
Ray and Maria
Stata Center,
Massachusetts
Institute of
Technology (MIT),
Cambridge (Gehry
Partners, 2004).
Photograph:
Jos Boys.

Maria Stata Center may reinforce the feeling of being part of a community for some occupants, while making others feel exposed and threatened (Fig. 6.2). The building continues to produce often competing, non-congruent interpretations and reported experiences. This is not just in terms of its particular, immediate encounters but also at the institutional level as a variety of problems with the building are being negotiated by the different players involved (Mitchell 2007). And as I have already noted, the idea that physical proximity can, of itself, generate constructive interactions, without supporting brokers (what Etienne Wenger (2009) has called in some of his most recent work, 'learning citizens' and 'social artists'), is deeply flawed.

Thus, just as previously argued about the experiences of particular learning spaces, how we 'read' their appearance and layout at the level of the institution always depends on where we each locate ourselves (and are located) in the spaces in-between, on the one hand, a particular architectural/campus design and, on the other, the social and spatial practices of that institution within its wider context. Buildings cannot have a single 'reading'; they do not represent 'something': they are just one means through which multiple and various communities of practice attempt to describe (and 'stabilise') themselves *as having the appearance of* recognisable entities.

Thus, the continuing emphasis on representational 'meaning' at the institutional level of the university or college in fact prevents a more productive (if equally complex) debate. This debate should be about how to design for the social and spatial practices of education, while accepting their uneven, dynamic, multiple and amorphous character. What is actually happening in a process (such as the development, design and occupation of the Stata Center) is a series of contested, overlapping and partial attempts to shift what is conventional common sense (usually so 'normal' as to go unnoticed) about which activities are to be combined, which kept apart, and about which 'categories' have associated repertoires in both space and time. Crucially, this is not a process that is represented/expressed directly by the building's appearance or layout. It cannot be read off the surface, or off any spatial/ aesthetic relationships, but it is embedded in both the made design relationships and their missing 'pieces'; that is, both in what is made concrete, and what is not. And its meanings are constructed as the ongoing intersections and negotiations with individual perceptions and the social and spatial practices of the communities that occupy it.

What is needed then, are richer, more sophisticated and comparative (but also situated) methods for mapping, describing and analysing the complex interstices between and across different communities of practice and their repertoires. This is about unpicking the conventional categorisation of activities within an educational institution – not just how it organises learning, but what else is associated with this activity – and how learning is intersected with all the other operations of a university or college, from its accommodation, catering, maintenance and cleaning services through to administrative and management processes. How then, can we elucidate these processes, most particularly their differences and gaps – in more detail?

The space of the institution

In Chapter 4, I proposed that whatever the problems with the 'communities of practice' model, investigating its characteristic qualities of boundedness, of cho- reographing iterative and affective encounters, of a negotiated repertoire, and of movement through a liminal space towards increased becoming and belonging, was invaluable in improving our understanding of the social and spatial practices of learning. If Chapter 5 explored the implications of this for the learning and teaching encounter, the aim here is to centre on the institutional scale. This is about what activities a specific university, college or other educational service houses within its boundaries and how these are related, conceptually, physically and virtually. I call this the space of the teaching and learning relationship, because it is about the sets of connections and disconnections that any participant has with all the activities of that institution. For a student this will range across, for example, peers, student services, canteen staff, cleaners, academics, administrators and researchers. These relationships are also mapped – inaccurately and inadequately – into the space of the institution. Both physical and virtual spaces are attempts to delineate particular categories, boundaries, relationships and exclusions (with varying degrees of con- sciousness and success). Only by understanding these relationships can we get a clearer picture of what constitutes the many journeys that are made through the space of the institution.

Roland Barnett has reflected on this ongoing 'shaping' of the university when he considers how research is being 'located' in relation to teaching and learn- ing across different subjects and institutions:

> Not only do universities exhibit diversity between themselves with their contrasting missions and internal characteristics, but they are supremely dynamic organisations. They move, they shape changes

as – for instance – their disciplinary base shifts, or their interventions with the wider society take on new forms, or their priorities alter, and, in the process, the balance of their activities may even be changed.

A related matter is that of space. If the key activities of the university – research, teaching, management – may be considered as so many shapes forming patterns, different possibilities present themselves as far as space is concerned. It may be said that the history of the university has been the successive introduction of new spaces.

(Barnett 2005: 2–3)

In Chapter 2, I argued that post-compulsory education has particular characteristics that combine the teaching, learning and research of particular subject disciplines with the practices of knowledge creation and development. Again Barnett asks some key questions:

[I]f we conceive of research and teaching as occupying the spaces of the university then we can ask questions of the following kinds: What are the spaces that these activities occupy? How are they shaped? How do these spaces stand in relation to each other? What is their configuration? Are there spaces for other activities? Are the spaces genuinely open or are they actually closed in some way (by virtue of the ideologies they represent or the resources they demand for their occupation)? Do the actors in these spaces feel that the spaces are theirs to a certain extent? Can new spaces open up within the activities themselves?

(Barnett 2005: 2–3)

Importantly, he also asks what is left out, what 'is occluded or distorted, submerged, indistinct or contentious, blurred', both within the university and between the university and the outside world. I have insisted throughout this book that we cannot merely 'read' university practices off its spaces, but must always assume a partial and uneven relationship, which will inevitably lead to gaps, inconsistencies, contradictions and unintended consequences. Material space may set up particular categories of activity and be part of their 'naming' as having a specific character and value. It can organise how spaces are bounded and related to each other (what is together, what is apart, what does not exist). It can 'speak' to a wider identity. But, it is also occupied through a mixture of social and spatial practices which change through time and accumulate as much by tradition and practice as by design. One university, attempting to unravel its existing practices, used a process review exercise to not only map out what had already happened, but also as a means of articulating and then getting shared agreement about a more resource-effective (and student-centred) set of processes (Patel, Powell and Boys 2006). Although in this case the outcomes were never implemented, the project is a useful example of how to unravel the processes – rather than just the functions – of a university (Table 6.1).

These kinds of review bring people from across an educational institution together to map all the different tasks that make up existing processes, through

Table 6.1 Core processes definitions as part of a UK university's process review exercise, adapted from Boys and Ford (2006).

Post-compulsory education: Core processes	Roles across core processes		
Managing the student experience	Careers, welfare, counselling	Personal tutors	Academics
Facilitating learning and curriculum development	Subject leaders, educational development teams		
Undertaking research	Research centres		
Providing consultancy services	Business and community engagement groups		
Managing support processes	Information managers		
	Finance managers		
	Human resources		
	Estates management		
	Quality managers		
	Strategic planners		
	Senior managers		

methods which allow conflict and difference to be explicit and which build in mechanisms for validating proposals for change across participants at various stages. What is important about such a method is that it starts from *difference* and *conflicts*, and that its main aim is to reveal gaps in, and unintended consequences of, existing social and spatial practices. So, for example, one activity involved passing around a piece of paper to act out what a student needed to do in order to enrol at the university. At one stage, the paper went backwards and forwards between two participants, due to an uncertainty about what should be the next stage in the process, and led to an argument about how enrolment worked, which powerfully showed the process's underlying problems. The particular process re-engineering method used here also did not demand – as is so often the case – a commitment to a shared consensus or institutional culture; all it aimed at was agreement about how to improve the processes through which the university operates. What is more, this was not just around learning and teaching, but all the other aspects of the university, for example how it orchestrates new student entry and induction:

> This university's review team then focused on one process in particular – student entry – itself understood as a sub-component of the core process called 'managing the student experience'. Their student entry process was then defined as 'a comprehensive and continuous process designed to help the [u]niversity achieve and maintain the optimum recruitment and retention rates of students'. In redesign terms, the process was seen as starting as soon as a potential student became aware of the university and only ended at the point where they became

fully established as a student. Within these boundaries, five supporting sub-processes were identified – 'attract applicants'; 'process enquiries'; 'process applications'; 'register students'; and 'orientate students'. These processes were conceived of as parallel rather than sequential processes and continuous, developmental processes rather than 'events', and also as highly interdependent.

(Patel, Powell and Boys 2006: 117)

Here, then, was a means through which the various communities of practice could come together, from a position of equality, to negotiate their preferred repertoires. In this case, the group proposed, described and agreed a number of core processes, and then broke each of these down into the associated tasks. By discussing what these tasks were, what they needed to be performed appropriately, and where they would happen, such an approach was able to re-think social and spatial practices simultaneously so that, for example, a one-stop shop (literally like a shop-front, centrally located and easily accessible on the university campus) was introduced to handle new student enquiries as well as related recruitment aspects.

On location, scale and distinctiveness

This kind of approach demands that we start from quite basic philosophical questions. What kinds of educational services should a particular educational institution be offering, and what are the spatial and design implications (if any)? If process re-engineering focuses on the activities of an institution, others are exploring the repertoires themselves.

Lorcan Dempsey, for example, has explored how to re-think the location, scale and content of library services, particularly in response to the impact of new technologies (Dempsey 2009). He argues that different information and communication technologies have their own appropriate 'scales' of operation, and associated transaction and interaction costs. This is equally true for a book or an online service; by examining information in this way, it becomes possible to both analyse the social-spatial characteristics of such technologies and to make comparable judgements about 'what best happens where'. To illustrate his point, he outlined the range of services that libraries in universities and colleges conventionally deliver. They offer study and social spaces; interpret and support students' and staff teaching, learning and research needs; provide personalised research assistance; undertake marketing and other promotional activities; and enable the discovery, management and preservation of artefacts and collections. To do this, they need to constantly acquire, update and develop information resources and the related services that can support evolving research and learning activities. So what scale does each activity best work at?

Dempsey suggested that the key axes here are, on the one hand, the relative uniqueness of an artefact; and on the other the means of its 'stewardship'. Thus Google or Facebook work as an open facility with generic qualities, while a rare book collection is unique and is in particular ownership and care. The discovery, management and preservation are necessarily at the local level. So, he suggests that individual educational institutions think about what is the distinctive scope of their library services; look at how to develop what is unique to them, while rescaling the uniform and conventional so as to not merely expensively replicate what can be offered easily elsewhere or at a different, more generic scale. For example, outputs of research and learning as well as institutional level promotion and record-keeping through websites, databases, etc., can be seen as of high uniqueness to a university, but needing low stewardship – that is, they do not need to be 'contained' within the institution. Here, he suggests there is often 'multi-scalar confusion', which prevents effective and creative use of available information and communication technologies. So research is not automatically disseminated (through, for example, cross-institutional digital repositories), and university-wide resources, record-keeping and information management remain in their separate silos, without taking advantage of holistic systems or multi-media.

To Dempsey, we need to move beyond an assumption that post-compulsory education is centrally campus-based, where the appropriate scale for most of its services is at the institutional level. As he notes, infrastructures are increasingly collaborative, national, international and/or externally sourced. This increasing overlap and interchange between what happens 'at' university level and what happens beyond it are becoming a central part of the debate over learning spaces, as post-compulsory educational institutions have increasingly explored outsourcing or other forms of collaboration for the delivery of activities such as catering, cleaning, accommodation, financial services, and assessment and validation procedures (Boys and Ford 2006). They are also exploring more flexible modes of space management, such as differentiating between core spaces and those which could be held on short leases or rented only briefly (Neary *et al.* 2010: 6).

Re-shaping spaces for post-compulsory education

The argument here is that only by unpacking the multiple, layered and dynamic components and relationships through which learning and space intersect backwards and forwards across the different scales of learning encounters, institutional relationships and societal and cultural contexts, can we develop the appropriate tools and tactics for improving the architecture of post-compulsory education. In terms of learning encounters, changes might just involve small-scale alterations of teaching and learning approaches, curriculum or spatial arrangements; or could be part of a wider institutional engagement with the quality and type of learning encounters being offered. Engaging at the scale of the university or college is mainly about strategic institutional change, because it involves changing the locations, relationships, scale and distinctiveness of practices; even if the resulting impacts are felt most at the small-scale and/or local level. Then, there is considerable potential to re-think learning spaces at the scale of the pedagogic model; this can be realised by exploring not only how museum, workplace and other spaces could be linked to campus-based education, but also how educational involvement in community and work-related activities can constructively blur some of the conventional boundaries between what learning in higher education is and where it happens.

Instead, we need to find ways to open up communities of practice across post-compulsory education to enable richer debate and more informed theory and practice that can move beyond the simple arguments about shifting from formal to informal learning spaces. This means opening up new 'discursive spaces' where educators from across its various locations can engage in constructive and creative debate – not necessarily aiming at 'consensus', but valuing differences so as to fully explore the complexities of teaching, learning and research. It means re-viewing institutional divides, so as to shift boundaries and remove the obstacles that conventionally separate the knowledge and experiences of museum, gallery, library, HE and other educators. And it proposes that educators act together in building a strong community of practice around the shared contemporary concerns over the status of authority, knowledge and inclusion in post-compulsory education. I will explore the implications of this for design in more detail in the next section. In this, architecture's role is not to offer the 'sticking plaster' of an assumed consensus through participation, or the reflective imagery of a design metaphor, but to listen to how the shape of post-compulsory education is being articulated as particular patterns of social and spatial practices, and to understand, and creatively imagine and communicate the design implications.

Part 3

Shifting the boundaries

Chapter 7

Designing learning as a transitional space

The main argument in this book so far has been that, rather than 'thinking' learning space around the binary formal/informal divide, we should examine both the distinctive characteristics of learning (and teaching, research, student-support, etc.) in post-compulsory education, and also what it is that matters about space. It has been shown that learning is articulated in contemporary educational theory as a transitional and liminal space, where participants negotiate their way via particular boundary conditions and specific social and spatial practices and repertoires. It has been suggested that space is not so much a metaphorical expression or setting for learning, as one of the (many) mechanisms through which contested ideas about what learning is or should be are articulated – both in offering up 'pictures' of potential new repertoires, and in 'making concrete' the preferred repertoires of particular communities of practice.

In this final section, I will begin to explore some different aspects of what this means for the design process. This chapter will again focus on learning encounters, so as to simultaneously develop a more nuanced view of how learning in post-compulsory education can be articulated and debated, and to suggest how this intersects with architectural design. As I have said before, because both the 'distinctiveness' of post-compulsory learning – and what matters about space in relationship to it – are always situated, there are no correct solutions. The chapter is therefore concerned with offering examples of how architectural designers (and their clients and co-professionals) can ask the right sorts of *questions*.

In taking this viewpoint, I am again arguing that we accept the deep ambiguity of architectural space, understood as neither determinist 'controller' nor merely neutral 'container', but as always in partial interaction with the practices that take place in it, and never separate from the perceptions and experiences of its occupiers. It is necessary to see that space is not central to the social and spatial practices of everyday life, but does have a role of varying relevance dependent on the situation. It can ameliorate or exaggerate aspects of those practices, and intersect with their resonances and tensions. This is particularly true where multiple, overlapping, contested and unclear social and spatial practices and/or communities of practice are in processes of collision for whatever reason. Then, it is likely that repertoires (including building types and the design vocabulary of different elements) are destabilised, become more fluid or momentarily become central to debates over future social and spatial practices.

The spaces of creative learning

In her book on learning space design, *In Sync* (2004), Leonie Scott-Webber begins by suggesting that building and interior designers are not very good at making use of existing research, mainly because of the differences in vocabularies used by various specialists involved in the built environment. She therefore offers her work as a 'translation' of her subject area – environmental behaviour research – particularly focusing on the form and manipulation of material space concerning 'the situations we find ourselves in when we need to share information (knowledge sharing)' (Scott-Webber 2004: 1). What is interesting here is her articulation of knowledge exchange as central to learning spaces, and her attempts to articulate different levels of knowledge sharing, development and creation, framed by five archetypes (Table 7.1).

Table 7.1 Adapted from 'Archetypal Attributes for Knowledge Environments' in Scott-Webber, 2004, (p. 42 and Table 2, p. 44).

Learning environment	*Process steps*	*Protocol attributes*
Environments for *Delivering* Knowledge (EDK) • information is imparted via a formal method so that others may learn	• prepare and generate presentation • deliver to an audience presentation • assess understanding	• a formal presentation • instructor controls presentation • focus is on presentation • passive learning
Environments for *Applying* Knowledge (EAK) • places where an organisation puts knowledge into practice	• knowledge transferred via demonstration • practice by recipient • understanding achieved	• controlled observation • one-to-one • master and apprentice alternate control • informal • active learning
Environments for *Creating* Knowledge (ECK) • where organisations create, innovate, and implement new ideas	• research • recognise need • divergent thinking • incubate • interpret into product/ innovation	• multiple disciplines • leaderless • egalitarian • distributed attention • privacy • casual • active learning
Environments for *Communicating* Knowledge (ECmK) • where people exchange information, formally and informally, verbally and non verbally	• organise information • deliver • receive and interpret • confirm	• knowledge is dispersed • impromptu delivery • casual • active learning
Environments where Knowledge is used for *Decision-making* (EDM) • the place where information is distilled and judgements are made and acted upon	• review data • generate strategy • plan • implement one course of action	• knowledge is dispersed • information is shared • leader sets final direction • situation is protected • semi-formal to formal • passive/active learning

While Scott-Webber begins her argument from the psychological and physiological aspects of behaviour (such as territorial instincts), she soon opens up socio-cultural practices, particularly by referring to the importance of the communities of practice literature and to Nonaka and Konno's (1998) research on the relationship between explicit and tacit knowledge:

> Explicit knowledge is impersonal (i.e. quantitative), and therefore is more easily shared in objective forms like data files or furniture specifications. By contrast, tacit knowledge includes not only skills but also intangible cognitive dimensions from life experiences that define our world view (i.e. qualitative). Tacit knowledge (things you just know) is exchanged in a social, experiential setting. Nonaka and Konno go on to say that both explicit and tacit knowledge areas are employed to convert the knowledge of an individual or collective into a source of creation.
>
> (Scott-Webber 2004: 36)

Learning therefore requires an integration of explicit with implicit – unspoken – engagements; that is, it is both about knowledge content and also its social modes of exchange. Her archetypes start from what might be considered as the conventional lecture theatre type (environments for delivering knowledge, or EDK). But – most crucially from the point of view of the arguments being made here – is her careful unpicking of the similarities and differences between environments for *applying* knowledge (EAK) and environments for *creating* knowledge (ECK):

> The EAK archetype advocates the application of knowledge in a learner-centred space. The basic premise is that the learner needs to own his or her own knowledge. Even though knowledge may be presented in a delivery setting, learners should be given opportunities to experiment and move knowledge from a level of awareness to one of understanding. Examples of a learner-centred setting may include a design studio, research laboratory, shoulder-to-shoulder presentation, or computer tutorial. Size requirements can vary widely from two people sitting side-by-side overlooking a laptop presentation, to a training centre with hands-on learning. In all cases, learners have opportunities for giving meaning to information. The process of discovery is important in these settings.
>
> (Scott-Webber 2004: 53)

For Scott-Webber, such 'knowledge-applying' spaces are a hybrid between formal and informal learning. They involve hands-on relationships between a master and a learner, often supported by a prior demonstration, and enable 'an immediate transfer of knowledge from the "master" to the learner through discovery and practice' (Scott-Webber 2004: 53). Here learners can increasingly develop expertise, through participation in the practices of the subject discipline. But for Scott-Webber, spaces which enable knowledge creation are different and even more complex than this:

> Creating knowledge means we move through a highly creative, often messy, repetitive process that culminates in an innovation (a product of some sort). Trial and error and keeping the process transparent and open to others in the team is critical (information persistence). In knowledge-creating, collaborative settings, employees'/learners' individual tools and specific expertise form an integrated network of expertise.
>
> (Scott-Webber 2004: 58)

Crucially, this is a form of learning that completely integrates thinking with doing, intuition with conscious reflection. In addition, the learning dynamic requires not just teachers but also learners to have control over the physical adaptation, flexibility and transformation of their immediate environments. This is something that seems to often arise as a key difference in thinking learning spaces between the creative disciplines and other subjects. While most learning and teaching emphasises collaboration and participation, art and design tutors often want students to be able to adapt and customise the very fabric of their learning spaces:

> The exchange among collaborators is seen as interaction rather than feedback, because they equally participate in the construction of shared knowledge. Knowledge is neither located in, nor owned by, single individuals, but distributed in the network. [. . .] The cognitive processes in their group depend on the total knowledge distributed across the group, its environment and artefacts, resulting in what in the literature is referred to as 'distributed cognition' (Darrouzet *et al.* 1994).
>
> (Scott-Webber 2004: 58)

Scott-Webber outlines her take on the multiple aspects of this kind of knowledge creation space:

- Research to become knowledgeable about the problem under study;
- Define the innovation opportunity or problem;
- Generate options and recognise the need for a new solution;
- Incubate – let the job rest and distil over time in order to process and digest information; and
- Select an option and interpret into a product idea.

> (Scott-Webber 2004: 59)

She suggests that this involves two distinct areas which 'must be included and yet interrelated: (1) a place of refuge to think and incubate, and (2) a place to collaborate and share information'. (Scott-Webber 2004: 59) This kind of learning then, needs to enable both individual and group activities, personal and interactive engagement; to provide a variety of degrees of privacy/protection and proximity/collaboration/ social engagement; together with exposure to 'parts, pieces, artefacts [. . .] for the group to use, remember, and stay stimulated (information persistence)' and the possibility of 'thoughtful reflection or mindless activity (e.g., a ping-pong table area)' (Scott-Webber 2004: 59).

Such a close and careful mapping is very useful in helping us to articulate learning (and particularly affective and creative learning encounters with spaces, objects and others). What is valuable about Scott-Webber's work is that she simultaneously captures something of Laurillard's social constructivist 'conversations', of Lave and Wenger's notions of legitimate peripheral participation (LPP), and of Savin-Baden's concerns for more private, meditative engagements as well as public, collaborative ones. However, as a behavioural and environmental psychologist, Scott-Webber offers such sets of relationships as 'archetypes'; that is, as somehow delineating an 'essence' of learning. Here, I suggest that such observations in fact reveal aspects of detailed everyday – routinised but culturally generated – social and spatial practices of learning in the creative disciplines. These are not so much 'inherent' in our psyches as negotiated personally, socially and culturally as part of the making and re-making of various communities of practice. What we need to add here, then, is an examination of how best to critically *intersect* the particular teaching and learning practices she outlines with, first, other competing and/or connected ones; second, the experiences, engagements and negotiations of various participants in these practices; and, third, how design works as an act of translation in creating new spaces for learning encounters. Each of these will be briefly explored in turn.

The social and spatial practices of creative learning

What is important about Scott-Webber's approach to learning encounters is that it offers a rigorous, observational description of a sequence of activities – of particular recognisable enactments with their associated repertoires. And rather than focus on the representational (what things look like) it deals with relationships and characteristics – with the social and spatial *practices* of learning. However, rather than articulating these as 'natural' and 'generic' behaviours, I have already suggested we should be understanding them as part of the contested processes through which different communities of practice across education (both within and outside the academy) attempt to both frame and negotiate what learning *is*. And there are very real (but often invisible and sometimes contested) differences across, for example, universities and community colleges, Ivy League and equivalent institutions and their less elite alternatives; across different geographical locations and through time; and across and between different subject disciplines. How, then, does the space of learning encounters act as one means through which these contested positions and understandings are played out? How can we inform design through a better understanding of these similarities and differences in articulating learning 'on the ground'?

To take an example: in some places in the contemporary period, educationalists and policy makers are arguing that as societies move to a 'knowledge' rather than a manufacturing economy, the skills and attitudes required globally are shifting, demanding an increasing emphasis on creativity, flexibility and responsiveness (Leitch Review 2006; Office for Economic Co-operation and Development (OECD) 2007). At the same time the story goes, university and college education is not adequately developing these abilities. There is some evidence to support such a position. Kolb and Kolb (2005), for instance, undertook a comparative research study across higher education business and arts courses, examining the distribution of student learning styles across three US courses: the Case Weatherhead School of Management MBA programme, the Cleveland Institute of Art undergraduate programme, and the Case Western Reserve University undergraduate programme. They conclude that the learning frameworks for business management and art students were very different:

> Management education was almost entirely organised around texts that deliver an authoritative scientific discourse. The scientific basis of the management curriculum was established in 1959 by an influential Carnegie Foundation report that sought to improve the intellectual respectability of management education by grounding it in three scientific disciplines: economics, mathematics, and behavioural science. The text-driven approach of management education contrasts with the experiential learning process of demonstration–practice–production–critique that is used in most art classes. This process is repeated recursively in art education, while management education is primarily discursive, with each topic covered in a linear sequence with little recursive repetition. Management education focuses on telling; art education emphasises showing. Management education tends to emphasise theory; art education emphasises integration of theory and practice. Art education focuses on the learners' inside-out expression; management education on outside-in impression. Most time in management classes is spent conveying information with relatively little time spent on student performance, most of which occurs on tests and papers. In art classes, the majority of the time is spent on student expression of ideas and skills. Art education tends to be individualised, with small classes and individual attention, while management education is organised into large classes with limited individualised attention.
>
> (Kolb and Kolb 2005: 202–3)

While their research therefore indicated a good 'match' between the different learning styles demanded by different subjects and the learning environments in which they take place, for Kolb and Kolb, contemporary education requires a holistic approach; that is, it develops abilities across the whole learning 'region' (Fig. 7.1), not just a specialised part:

> [T]o learn skills outside of their home region, learners need to move to other regions and the learning process for any skill requires the ability to move through the experiencing, reflecting, thinking, and acting cycle. To fully develop the whole person requires an educational culture that promotes diverse learning spaces and locomotion among them. The enhancement of experiential learning in higher education can be achieved through the creation of learning spaces that promote growth-producing experiences for learners.
>
> (Kolb and Kolb 2005: 205)

Fig. 7.1
'The nine-region'
learning style
grid, adapted
from Kolb and
Kolb (2005).

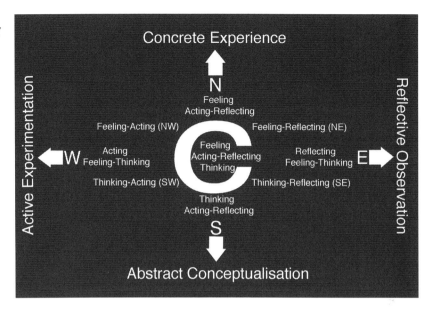

Similarly, but from the point of view of the community of practice/subject area rather than students' particular learning styles, Robertson and Bond (2005) differentiate different framings of knowledge, research, teaching and learning across various disciplines in higher education from the 'transmissive' relation in subjects such as chemistry and economics to those with 'hybrid', 'symbiotic' or 'integrated' relations (Table 7.2).

While the various disciplines overlap categories here (and may, in fact, vary from tutor to tutor/learner to learner), creative subjects such as art, media and design clearly fall into the more 'questioning' categories; not just interested in positioning new knowledge in the context of a wider picture, but in seeing things in a different way, in challenging and transforming the existing. This raises the question of how relevant these capabilities are across all subjects at post-compulsory level.

Importantly, as before in this book, what such studies offer is the potential to open up debate, to expose and constructively negotiate tensions and contradictions, rather than to merely recommend a particular division of activities, way of operating or preferred 'solution' to architectural designers. It concerns questions about the extent to which new learning spaces should 'match' the perceived differences between communities of practice/disciplines, or move all subjects towards the kind of knowledge creation model offered by Scott-Webber. It may even enable a richer critique around how creativity is defined and where it happens. The articulation of post-compulsory learning as simultaneously involving both 'a place of refuge to think and incubate' and 'a place to collaborate and share information' – which links it firmly to the activity of *research* understood in the widest sense – seems to me to cover many subjects and activities from essay writing to scientific experiments to computer programming to the kind of role-play that is common in nursing and social-work courses. Could it be that because the qualities of incubation/collaboration are

Table 7.2 Outline of differences between academic disciplines, adapted from Robertson and Bond, 'Being in University', in Ronald Barnett (2005: 85–6).

View by discipline	View of knowledge	View of teaching	View of learning
Transmissive (chemistry, economics)	An understanding of the world we live in; the sum of the pieces; the bigger picture	Imparting knowledge and enthusiasm; distilling essentials; presenting information clearly; conveying how ideas are developed	Memorising; acquiring skills; linking new information to current knowledge; positioning new knowledge in the context of the bigger picture
Hybrid (art history, geography)	Shared system of concepts and beliefs; no longer absolute; can be contested	Passing on research knowledge and skills modelling; encouraging students to become independent thinkers; induction into process of knowledge creation	Asking and answering questions; knowing more; understanding; interpreting; seeing something in a different way
Symbiotic (classics, philosophy)	Understanding; constructed in relationship with others; contested; perspectival	Working alongside; developing critical thinking and lifelong learning skills; bringing people and ideas together; bridging	A process of exploration in company of teacher and other learners; generating and 'owning' knowledge
Integrated (French, history)	A journey; a community construction; an act of engagement with the world; power	Engaging (with) students in research processes of interpretation; de/constructive critique and inquiry; challenging ways of thinking and seeing the world	Understanding; engaging with the world; thinking differently; changing as a person; transformation

central, explicit and therefore highly *visible* in creative subjects, they are 'seen' by researchers there, but go unnoticed in other subjects where incubation, for example, may be invisible and implicit, because it takes place in private or outside the university or college setting? Could it also suggest that a focus at post-compulsory level on learning 'researching' is a distinctive, but sometimes ignored, characteristic of post-compulsory education which could also open up different routes for learning space design? At the same time, others are arguing that while a 'research-led' environment is increasingly being offered as the best way to frame post-compulsory teaching and learning, the evidence is:

> that many students now 'drift' into HE as something that is considered normal. Given this, it seems likely that for many students the research-led environment is of marginal importance and that they may be largely unaware of their institution's research culture in the absence of activities to engage them.
>
> (Taylor and Wilding 2009: 2)

These authors suggest that this turns the issue into one which is less about learning as research per se and more about how to enable meaningful student engagement, that is, 'to re-create the notion of an inclusive academic community where learners, teachers and researchers are all seen as scholars and collaborators in the common pursuit of knowledge' (p. 3).

Designing the spaces between comfort and risk

If one layer of complexity involves the intersections of communities of practice across a variety of scales and locations from subject disciplines through to governmental strategies, another is at the immediate level of personal and group perceptions and experiences of learning. As I have already said, understanding these must integrate not only the activities that Scott-Webber outlines, but also what participants bring to both the learning situation and its physical (and/or virtual) spaces. Occupation is always an encounter, whether with objects, spaces or others. We always bring to it what we already know about space (our expectations of what it will or should be like) in relation to the activity we are undertaking, and the context in which it takes place. As I have already noted in Chapter 5, for some participants, beanbags may imply informality, for others childishness. For a student who has had bad experiences of education before, the conventions of the lecture theatre may feel safer than the 'unknown' of an unrecognisable learning space; or an informal space might be preferred because it helps to relieve previous anxieties. This is further complicated by the fact that we don't just encounter space, we also interact directly with it. We can adapt and shape it, from moving furniture, to repainting surfaces, to making new openings or adding/removing walls. We can do this temporarily or permanently; and in different situations we will have more or less control. But having a flexible space with moveable furniture does not automatically mean that students will feel empowered or that equipment will be moved. Again, it depends on the conventions and assumptions – the ordinary social and spatial practices – that participants bring to a space, the activity and the context. I will repeat: we cannot separate out the participants, the activities and the contexts in analysing how space works; to do so is to over-simplify and potentially misunderstand.

Thus, while Scott-Webber offers a cogent and recognisable repertoire for creative learning, providing the elements she outlines in an architectural design will not, of itself, mean that such learning takes place. The necessary activities can be defined, but what about the 'liminality' that learning (at least in its early stages) produces? Participants are initially likely to feel uncertain about what is being asked of them and will need to be motivated, to develop an understanding of how the creative process works, and to be enabled to become increasingly confident, self-directed and self-critical in their creativity. If we follow Wenger, then learning is also always a process of actively becoming and belonging as part of a community of practice around a subject discipline. How, then, can we think harder about the culturally specific and affective complexity of individual engagements with spaces for learning such as these? Developing such an understanding will not tell us how to design (or how to teach or how to learn) but it will help to elucidate – illuminate – what already happens, so as to enable critical responses concerning how to do it better. In Chapter 5, I offered some examples of how methods from ethnography and ethnomethodology can help us to better map the embodied experiences of occupying specific learning spaces. Here, I want to look briefly at how designers and design teachers have used a variety of – particularly visual rather than verbal – methods to 'get at' what creative learning is like as such a transitional space.

There has been much recent work on using visual as well as or instead of verbal/written modes of enquiry and analysis, such as Pink on visual ethnography (2006) and Gaver *et al.*'s (2004) exploration of 'cultural probes' as a research method. In addition, some of the UK HEFCE-funded Centres for Excellence in Teaching and Learning (2005–10) and other recent initiatives have undertaken research which tries to unravel some of the unspoken aspects of creative learning (Austerlitz 2008; Lyon forthcoming) or explored ways of developing creativity in subjects where it is under-developed, such as InQbate (see http://www.inqbate.co.uk/) and the South East region of the UK's Creative Campus Initiative (CCI). In 2009–10, Ike Rust, senior menswear tutor and Teaching Fellow at the Royal College of Art, London (RCA), was funded by the Centre for Excellence in Teaching and Learning through Design (CETLD) to make a digital video entitled *Halycon Daze* (Rust 2009), with the specific intention of 'undertak[ing] a visual investigation of the physical, intellectual and emotional space in which my students learn fashion menswear'. As Rust continues:

> I wanted to define the interaction between student and tutor. How we share creation, meaning and purpose, and integrate the emotional experiences of desire, excitement, anxiety and doubt into a physical mastery of skill and technique.
>
> Design students learn to design by behaving like designers – through the experience of repetition, mistake-making and experimentation. In pedagogy this is referred to as 'doing'. It is learning through physical activity. However, this 'doing' doesn't take into account desire, or the longing

that drives designers and artists to create. [. . .] The film is a true account of how my students learn, while also attempting to establish – through showing – a language of designing that encompasses the unspeakable, intangible and difficult to express.

(Rust 2009)

Rust argues, following Archer (1979), that 'there exists a designedly way of thinking and communicating that is both different from scientific and scholarly ways of thinking and communicating, and as powerful as scientific and scholarly methods'. He suggests that design is learnt through a process of osmosis that completely integrates the embodied and the intellectual, 'evidenced in the spoken word, through repetitive comforting gestures, hands drawing ideas into open space, as frustration, silent appreciation, excitement, tiredness and desperation'. In the film students both show and report the difficulties, challenges and pleasures of learning design, as they learn to 'delve into' and expose themselves and their ideas; to integrate intuition and reflection and to find ways of translating their ideas and feelings into physical artefacts (Fig. 7.2). As Rust puts it:

In art and design our teaching practice is often described as occurring 'by osmosis' rather than by pedagogy. This learning – by observation or absorption – is difficult to express because our craft becomes tacit, deeply buried in our process and not separate from who we are.

(Rust 2009)

Thus, the creative learning practices – research, innovation opportunity or problem, options generation, incubation, selection and interpretation – outlined by Scott-Webber

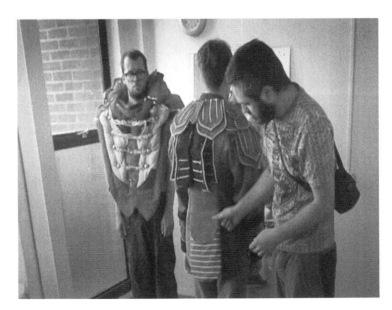

Fig. 7.2
Still from *Halycon Daze* (Rust 2009) showing tutorial, MA Menswear Design, Royal College of Art, London.

are shown to be not just activities but embodied interactions which happen in complex, multiple and uneven ways. And effectiveness comes to reside not merely in the availability of a particular type of space, but in the capacity of ongoing learning encounters (with other students, tutors, objects and spaces) and the student's 'journey' (into a community of practice) to enable this increasing absorption and, what has already been outlined in an earlier chapter as 'flow' (Fig. 7.3); that is, to come to literally *embody* an understanding of, and engagement with, one's subject.

As with the work of Wenger and others, such rich interpretations and analyses help to illuminate learning as a form of transitional space, with boundary crossings or 'thresholds' en route to not just a new kind of knowing but also to becoming a new kind of *person*. Initial boundary conditions orchestrate how both cerebral and embodied 'rules of the game' are disclosed to potential new entrants as they negotiate the various processes of joining the communities of practice of post-compulsory education. Once on or across such borders, these communities offer frameworks of varying kinds (to particular people) for enabling increasing belonging as well as safe-enough conditions to enable risks to be taken and expertise (becoming) to be developed. Importantly, the learning process takes *time* as existing knowledge is challenged and alternative approaches and attitudes are 'incubated'. Learning, then, is more a series of iterative, repetitive and often confusing encounters than a step-by-step, outcome-by-outcome accumulation of knowledge and skills. The journey leads – in the right conditions – to a step change in understanding, a crossing of thresholds. It is about both 'getting it' and becoming embedded in a subject, so embedded that the frameworks and repertoire of the community of practice become increasingly common sense and unnoticed as expertise is developed – that is, as ideas and practices to be thought/enacted with rather than thought *about*. As I have already noted in Chapter 2, some participants may deliberately refuse to engage

Fig. 7.3
Still from *Halycon Daze* (Rust 2009) showing 'flow' during studio design process, MA Menswear Design, Royal College of Art, London. The student is standing at a large worktable, in a small crowded studio. She is both looking around and at something in front of her, all the while dancing absent-mindedly to some music, lifting her hands and arms up in time. Then, at a certain point you can see that she has suddenly become completely absorbed in her own work – that something is flowing between her hands, eyes and thought. The studio and her surroundings just cease to exist.

in the preferred ways of practice, may not be able to 'get' what is going on, or find out that they cannot just 'be' ordinary members of a particular community (Sacks 1984) because of the exclusions built into its everyday social and spatial practices.

In this process, material space may have a relatively minor role, or be relevant only in specific ways. The Royal College of Art offers the 'prestigious space' of an internationally renowned and respected institution, and the achievement of a place on one of its masters courses sets the context for, and expectations of, both hard work and (potentially) anxious pressure for students. Learning on the menswear design course here, for example, is undertaken in a studio that provides just enough space to support the particular repertoire of the subject, together with a few additional multi-purpose rooms. What is most important about this physical space, perhaps, is that it concentrates most of the social and spatial practices through which students both become and belong *as* menswear designers into a relatively small area; it thus forms an *intense* site for learning.

At the University of Brighton, Alma Boyes and Cynthia Cousens also used CETLD funding to investigate how aspects of craft practice are taught in workshops through practical demonstration. As with Rust's project, there was no separation assumed between learning 'skills' and accumulating experience of *practice* as embodied knowledge:

> Demonstrations, where a student is physically shown how to do a process, technique or how to use a piece of equipment, are the chief way technical knowledge is acquired and therefore hold a central place in the delivery of a 3D materials practice course.
>
> Reading a demonstration, identifying what is critical to enable emulation and then applying the information is a complex process for students. Techniques, equipment and processes can be sophisticated, they are often used in combination, and employing them involves the whole body and all its senses.
>
> (Boyes *et al.* 2008: 4)

What is valuable about this research is how it examined the importance of *performance* in the process of enabling both full bodily engagement and absorption. They explored how demonstrators use the full tactile and sensory repertoire of their subject (including introducing its specialist language), to develop spoken and gestural languages, as well as timing, rhythm and pace of delivery to support their teaching; and show how student 'novices' take their first steps in emulating, practising and then creatively developing the actions they are being shown. They note that it was the patterning of 'mistakes and corrections (which) acted as bridges between the student and expert, creating learning paths for the student' (Boyes *et al.* 2008: 31). Thus, opportunities to *fail*, are articulated as constructive, and the struggles with what Meyer and Land call threshold concepts or 'sticking places' are themselves a central part of development. Again the key issue is about how students can translate what is being viewed and heard into their own embedded absorption of, and creative flow with, the manipulation of particular materials through newly learnt actions.

Here, at the most basic level, the physical space mattered where it inhibited visibility (although some spaces had built-in CCTV to help) or was acoustically poor; characteristics that were equally dependent on the size and scale of the craft being demonstrated as on the number of students and staff involved. In addition, the researchers suggest that space and activity should allow students to regularly move around – 'the quickest way to activate the brain is to move' (Boyes *et al.* 2008: 22). At the same time, the researchers began to explore how the 'ethos' of workshop-based practice, and the different characteristics of its various forms – for example the excitement and engagement generated by the more risky environment of raku firing for ceramics, the more detailed nuances and control of small-scale work in jewellery or the strong physicality and spatiality of learning dance. While in creative subjects such as these the body is clearly not separate from the mind in developing learning, what it suggests is that all subjects at a post-compulsory level in some way have embodied repertoires of specific languages, movements and associated body-related devices.

How then, can architectural designers work with such an understanding of learning as comprising liminal and embodied encounters? For Savin-Baden, the key issue becomes the centrality of uncertainty itself. She offers up Burbules in support:

> We must move from the idea of translation to the idea of an aporetic encounter – finding our way through a labyrinth with no clear lines to follow. Uncertainty, difficulty and discomfort in such an encounter are intrinsic. And because the failure of translation in practical contexts of communication is related to the inability to act or coordinate action, such difficulties are *moral* difficulties as well. The challenge of moral responsiveness in the face of radical difference is as much a part of the feeling of aporia (note: puzzle, impasse) as are epistemic or linguistic limits. Here even the possibility of communication, let alone translation, is put at risk.
>
> (Burbules 1997: 5, quoted in Savin-Baden 2008: 11)

Here, though, I want to suggest that rather than focusing on the concept of uncertainty itself, we can define our 'location' more precisely. Designers in fact operate – like learners – in the *spaces in-between* what we already know, and what is not yet known. And while this may *feel* like 'finding our way through a labyrinth with no clear lines to follow', such a space actually offers much communicative potential. While design requires an act of translation which can neither transparently nor directly reflect particular learning practices, it can both build on and constructively alter what we already know and do; or it can deliberately disrupt existing assumptions and conditions. How, then, can designers explore such potential?

On the minimum conditions for creativity

Virginia Woolf famously suggested in 'A Room of One's Own' (1929) that the minimum conditions for creativity were to have a private and un-interrupted space in which to work. However, in a series of projects with new students into architecture and interior design (Fig. 7.4), it became clear that their response to this question was much more varied. Students at two institutions (Access and Foundation students at London Metropolitan University and first-year undergraduate students at the British Higher School of Art and Design, Moscow) were each asked to design and make temporary installations expressing what kind of 'basic' space they needed for creative learning. While there were examples that explored creativity as a solitary and meditative activity, there were many more that played with, for example, ideas of risk, and which communicated a complex engagement with privacy and public exposure. One student, for example, marked out a zone on the floor, and blindfolded,

Fig. 7.4
Student
installations for
project entitled
'The Minimum
Conditions
for Creativity',
London
Metropolitan
University (2005)
and British
Higher School of
Art and Design,
Moscow (2009).
Photographs:
Jos Boys

asked other students to place 'unknown' objects in the zone. Another set himself up on a sofa in a public corridor, so as to almost block general movement; and yet, at the same time, used the device of traffic cones and tape to mark out his territory as 'out-of-bounds'. One student made herself a series of 'hoods' that she could wear to communicate the kind of attention she wished to attract. There was also a box to hide and 'recover' in, a swing to 'incubate' ideas, enabling both slow meditative thought and energetic distraction; and a 'philosopher's barrel'.

I suggest such articulations of creative learning resonate with the work of Scott-Webber, while simultaneously offering design 'ideas' about its social and spatial practices that begin to operate in a field beyond simplistic representational metaphors of formal or informal spaces, or the identification of learning encounters just with the activity of social collaboration. A project designed and developed as part of the 'Creative Campus' at the University of Kent (Fig. 7.5) also takes the spaces and time of meditative and thoughtful learning, through its Labyrinth project. While the idea of the labyrinth clearly has metaphorical associations, it is exploited here in an 'unexpected' way for learning:

> Labyrinths have existed for thousands of years; they appear in many faith and cultural traditions and in many parts of the world, from Ecuador to Iceland, from Arizona to Turkey. [. . .] A labyrinth is not a maze; mazes have many paths (multi-cursal) and dead ends, designed to confuse. Labyrinths have a single, convoluted path to the centre and back again; if you are walking a labyrinth, you can usually see the whole design, though concentration is needed to follow the path.
>
> Walking a labyrinth is a peaceful experience. We don't know how labyrinths were used in ancient times, but there has been a modern resurgence of interest. People walk labyrinths for many reasons; for relaxation, stress and anger management, for a quiet meditative break in the middle of a busy day, for spiritual development, or simply to relax and

Fig. 7.5
Labyrinth
in winter,
University of Kent
(constructed by
Andrew Wiggins,
The Labyrinth
Builders,
Canterbury).
Photograph:
Jim Higham.

enjoy the walk with time for oneself. At the University of Kent, we have introduced the labyrinth as an opportunity for quiet, reflective time and space; as a work of art; and as a creative resource for teaching.

(http://www.kent.ac.uk/uelt/ced/themes/labyrinth/index.html)

Each of these ideas reveals aspects of existing social and spatial practices of creative learning, hopefully making visible aspects that are often obscured or ignored. They literally bring *into view* aspects of teaching and learning that the functional labelling of spaces as seminar rooms, studios and workshops does not.

On breaching: learning spaces and deliberate disruption

As a final example of this more lateral and partial design 'opening up' of learning encounters – informed both by learning as an affective experience and by the partiality and non-congruence of space with occupation – I want to briefly consider the value of techniques for 'disrupting' the conventional social and spatial practices of learning. In ethnomethodology, for example, Garfinkel has suggested that the most effective way to make such commonplace situations visible is by 'breaching':

> Procedurally it is my preference to start with familiar scenes and ask what can be done to make trouble. The operations that one would have to perform in order to multiply the senseless features of perceived environments, to produce and sustain bewilderment, consternation and confusion; to produce the socially constructed affects of anxiety, shame, guilt and indignation and to produce disorganised interaction should tell us something about how the structures of everyday activities are ordinarily and routinely produced and maintained.
>
> (Garfinkel 1967: 37–8)

Garfinkel developed a series of breaching experiments where he asked students to deliberately perform in unexpected ways, and monitored the results. (Garfinkel 1967: 42):

> The breaching experiments were quite simple but turned out to be hugely telling. He asked students to act as though they were lodgers in their own households. And he asked people to ask for clarification of commonplace remarks. Students reported such responses as that they were being too nice and were obviously after something. When they asked if they could have a bite to eat from the fridge a parent noted that this was behaviour that had been going on for a long time and wondered why they had suddenly decided to ask. One parent thought the student was being hostile to his mother and suggested that he leave the house.
>
> (Boys and Shakespeare 2009: 44)

In 2008, Annette Krauss used similar approaches with students to explore 'the unintended and unrecognised forms of knowledge, values and beliefs that are part of learning processes and daily life within high schools' (Krauss 2008: 5). This project argues that a considerable amount of students' time is spent creatively finding 'tricks and tactics to cope with the requirements they face within their education' (2008: 5), that is, to enable them to 'work around' the explicit demands made on them by teachers, and she suggests that these are also valid types of knowledge development. While this work was done specifically with 15–17-year-olds (in two schools in Utrecht, the Netherlands), its idea – that learning can also be looked at beyond its 'official' processes – has the potential to offer an interesting alternative take on learning encounters in post-compulsory education. Rather than merely seeing students as 'failing to get' aspects of their studies (as the threshold concepts model frames it, for example) we can investigate more how students creatively and critically navigate the limitations of the institutional structures and learning frameworks offered to them. The 'Hidden Curriculum' project used workshops to ask students to examine their own tactics and then transfer what they had learnt to other creative ends, through photographs, video and performance: 'Often activating situations that went beyond common sense or secure behaviour, the students reflected on the legitimacy of specific social contexts – such as the school, and areas of public space – and developed critical stances towards their own actions' (Krauss 2008: 5).

Students were asked to bring in a chair, and then to interact with it in a way that 'breached' conventional norms. This was followed by a similar exercise on the scale of the whole building, to investigate non-used, hidden or other 'abnormal' spaces; and then to connect this with, and comment on their own 'hidden' actions. This led to student-led research projects, for example, in investigating how other students used 'tricks', or finding out how people in authority interpreted such actions. Finally students made some sorts of performances that 'transgressed' the standard social and spatial practices both within the school and outside of it, in public.

Simultaneously, for the length of the project, a temporary space was constructed (by Celine Conderelli), called *Show and Tell*, aiming to provide conditions for students to frame a variety of public and private relationships:

> This consisted of curtains, a series of tables, a cabinet and some benches. The arrangement evolved with the project, both reflecting and producing the actions and investigations of the students who attended the workshops. Three large curtains circled into the centre of the room, running on parallel tracks. These were made from red and green translucent plastic, wool blankets, and hessian, offering varying levels of weight and transparency. These could be easily moved in order to quickly alter the space. And could be gathered at either end of the rail, in clumps or in parts, or overlaid in different combinations of opacity. By muffling sounds to different degrees, enclosing or opening up areas, they lent varying degrees of openness and privacy. These elements enabled students to decide how public certain moments and parts of the project should be, and what should be hidden, when and from whom.
>
> (Conderelli in Krauss 2008: 23)

This project offers an illustration of a particular kind of contemporary architectural strategy, also evidenced for example in the work of Helen Stratford and Diana Wesser of Urban (Col)laboratory, on the invisible processes of cleaning and maintenance in continually returning spaces to a particular form of 'untouchedness' (2009). One project involved a series of performative walks of Murray Edwards College and New Hall Cambridge Phases 1 and 2 (designed in 1964 by architects Chamberlain, Powell and Bon) to accommodate a third women's college of Cambridge University, which 'focused specifically on people working at the edges of the college':

> Urban (Col)laboratory spent a week talking to porters, gardeners, administrative staff, caterers, chefs, librarians and maintenance staff to review the college as a stage for everyday performances, rituals and routines from the perspective of those whose functions are academically marginally located, yet whose daily repetition is central to the functioning of the college. The three performative walks took place during the evening routines of the college and focused on the position of the audience who became both participants and performers through the locations they were invited to take up in relation to the physical spaces of the college.
>
> (Stratford and Wesser 2009: 3)

Here, then, I am again suggesting that debates around, and approaches to learning spaces in post-compulsory education can benefit from an engagement beyond the 'usual' commercial consultancy expertise in educational architecture; opening up questions by working with a wider range of creative, and lateral rather than literal approaches. The projects mentioned here offer an indication of how the shifts in architectural theory and practice outlined in Chapter 2 are already impacting on both attitudes and tactics, particularly for architects working in the voluntary and community sector. Such approaches offer a means of creatively examining ordinary social and spatial practices, while accepting the situatedness, partiality and limitations of any interpretation, analysis or design response. Here I am proposing a shift towards design development methods that have the ability to handle the spaces in-between what we know and what we don't know, that is, *ambiguity* (Empson 1930). As Harding and Hale write:

> Some accounts stress the emotional (and professional) consequences of not being able to hold two simultaneous ideas in suspension long enough to solve particular problems. In tolerating ambiguity, it is necessary to withstand the uncertainty and chaos that result when the problem is not clearly defined or when it is unclear how the pieces of the solution are going to come together. [. . .] Sternberg and Lubart point out that 'relationships in transition are ambiguous [. . .] fumbling rather than working according to plan. Ambiguity is uncomfortable and anxiety provoking' (Sternberg and Lubart, 1995). In order to optimise creative potential, there is a need to tolerate the discomfort of an ambiguous

situation long enough so that what is produced is the best possible solution.

(Harding and Hale 2007: 3)

It is precisely this willingness to find both conceptual frameworks and methods that make ambiguity central (rather than the endlessly unsatisfactory result of attempts to 'pin-down' the correct design solution) that has informed the argument of this book (Fig. 7.6). In the final two chapters, then, I will first examine how bringing such a conceptual framework to current debates about new technologies can help us better understand both virtual and material space; and end by examining how to rethink the architecture of post-compulsory education not just at the level of the campus, but also beyond it.

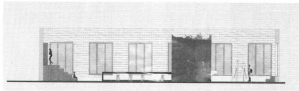

Fig. 7.6
Examples of first-year students' designs for new art and design learning space, drawing on Scott-Webber (2004), BA (Hons) Interior and Spatial Design, British Higher School of Art and Design (BHSAD), Moscow, 2010.

Chapter 8

Hybrid spaces and the impact of new technologies

The recent concern with post-compulsory learning and teaching methods has been partly driven by a frustration with the perceived lack of impact of computing and networking on universities' and colleges' ways of working. A newish discipline – 'learning technologies' – has developed to better understand how changing information and communication technologies can support learning, based mainly on a social constructivist understanding of learning (Laurillard 2001; Conole and Oliver 2007; Beetham and Sharpe 2007) but this remains an under-resourced and often marginalised area in the post-compulsory education sector. Of course learning technologies have a longer history than just the recent exponential growth of personal computing, mobile devices and the internet. In the UK, for example, the Open University has built up a considerable expertise in distance learning design over the last 40 years, based first on a mixture of course books and study guides supported by video and audio tapes, and TV programmes; and then pre and early web-based computer-based conference (CMC) capabilities such as First Class, which enabled online tutorial and seminar conversations, 'e-moderated' by a tutor (Salmon 2000).

Since then, organisations already mentioned here, such as JISC in the UK and Educause in America, have been undertaking research and producing guidance aimed at helping universities and colleges embed the new information and communication technologies, not only in their teaching and learning practices but also in their management and other systems. For these organisations new technologies have an 'obvious' value for education, which should straightforwardly lead to their enthusiastic take-up. But, as I outlined in the last section of Chapter 5, new technologies are in fact part of struggles across many educational communities of practice around what the preferred repertoire of teaching and learning should *be*.

Like material space, these developing technologies are another one of the mechanisms through which attempts are made to shift and 'reify' particular social and spatial practices of learning. In fact, there are many reasons why these kinds of media have not just automatically taken hold or at least been added to the more traditional media of, for example, chalk and blackboard, books and exams. First, they are fast-changing and demand new kinds of specialist expertise, which are perceived as being time-consuming to learn for teachers and/or inappropriate to their understanding of themselves as educators, and which are not being 'programmed in' to existing educational social and spatial practices. I will return to this point about the 'hidden' work of new technologies for teaching and learning. Second, there is a lack of certainty about what kinds of *spaces* they offer, and what benefits these might enable, over and above conventional pedagogic methods. Third – and perhaps most importantly – I suggest that the very framework through which arguments are being made can limit rather than enhance take-up of new technologies in universities and colleges. As I outlined in the Introduction, these start from a 'deficit model' of teaching and learning and from an either/or good/bad opposition between using or not using new technologies, which tends to only resonate with those already converted and therefore perhaps has had the unintended outcome of closing down, rather than opening up debate.

Here, I want to consider new technologies from this other viewpoint: as one element in struggles over the future shape of educational social and spatial practices. But I also want to focus specifically on what it is that these new media are 'capable of'; that is, to critically engage with the concept of affordances (Gibson 1977, 1979; Norman 1988, 1990). Starting from the analysis of what constitutes the specific and potential properties of an object, medium or space is often central to learning technologists (developed from the discipline of human–computer interactions, or HCI) but almost never used by architects. While building designers are deeply interested in the properties of things, they also tend to start from existing problematic situations and contexts. Interface and product designers more often begin from what 'could be', based on characteristics of materials and objects themselves as well as possible uses.

This is an appropriate angle here for two reasons. First, it opens up an aspect of the repertoire not considered by Wenger; that is, that the spaces, objects, media and procedures that come to form (reify or make concrete) a community of practice have their own characteristic properties that will affect what can be and is done with them. And, second, because new technologies are potentially creating types of learning spaces that have not existed before, and for which 'everyday' social and spatial practices or a reified repertoire have not yet congealed, an engagement with the potentialities of things, media and spaces can open up not just issues with online or virtual learning, but also inform 'back' to material spaces and practices as well. I will suggest that, rather than seeing new technologies as being automatically a 'good' development for education, we need to unravel their specific impacts in relationship to the existing practices and repertoires of post-compulsory teaching, learning and research. Here, again, the aim is not to offer answers but to open up key areas of tension, contradiction and contestation.

Affordances and learning

The concept of affordances is used across a range of disciplines, for example, cognitive psychology, environmental and behavioural psychology, industrial design, HCI, interaction design and artificial intelligence. Affordances are defined as the qualities of an object, medium or space that enable people to undertake particular tasks.

From a strictly behaviourist standpoint, the design of an object or space should both 'signpost' and functionally support the 'afforded' action as a direct match; that is, there is a stimuli–response, cause-and-effect relationship between the thing and its use. But the idea of affordances also tends to include the idea of a range of possibilities that an object, medium or space can make available to a user, rather than just a single one. This means that affordances are not just what is functionally possible as a property of the thing, but also depend on the 'signals' it can give, through its design, to make people aware of these wider possibilities.

Through his writings, Donald Norman (1988, 1990, see http://www.jnd. org) has been central in increasingly linking the idea of affordances not just to the properties of an object, medium or space but also to individuals' perceptions and previous experiences; that is, to what we each bring to our engagement with things. Here, the user becomes central, both in what they perceive as actionable possibilities and in what is actually realisable. Thus, a computer screen is always 'touchable' and a cursor always affords clicking, but it is only relevant to the user if they come to know that clicking in a particular place means something and will have the required effect. Learning technologists and some other designers are thus interested in affordances as a means both to analyse the potential properties of an object or space, and to explore how they can influence human behaviour in the direction intended by the designer. Norman has also become increasingly interested in the intersections between real physical constraints (what something is 'capable of') which will affect affordances, and the 'cultural conventions'; that is, where particular actions have, through time, congealed into a generally understood arrangement or norm. Thus, for example, the concept of 'homepage' as a means to separate out the originating location of a website from the page previously viewed is not inherent in how the devices or design of the internet 'afford' that particular action; rather it is one that has become 'obvious' and ubiquitous, through increasingly conventional usage as the World Wide Web has developed.

For Norman, then, in good design desired actions should be perceived and easily understood from the device/setting. It also helps that intended actions can be 'discovered' easily, and that the things we already know apply; that is, that the designed object or space fits with 'the conventions shared by a social group' (http://jnd.org/dn.mss/affordance_conventions_and_design_part_2.html). Here, then, the concept of affordances becomes about the intersections of the inherent properties of an object, medium or space with societal and group 'conventions'; that is, with what I have called existing everyday social and spatial practices.

Translating affordances into practice

Where the concept of affordances is informing the design of technology-rich teaching and learning spaces in post-compulsory education, the tendency has been – as with many newly designed physical spaces – to emphasise flexibility. Analysing affordances, then, becomes about the enabling potential of objects, networks and spaces to open up learning and teaching practices to ways of working that have not been thought of before, or have been unrealisable due to the lack of affordances in existing spaces and facilities. For example, this might apply where an existing lecture theatre with all seats facing a single speaker restricts the potential of collaborative work between students 'across' the room. At InQbate, the Centre for Excellence in Teaching and Learning in Creativity, a collaboration of the universities of Sussex and Brighton (Fig. 8.1), for example, the spaces have been deliberately designed with the aim of:

- Freeing teachers and learners from the constraints of the traditional classroom. New spaces allow new behaviours and dynamics, and support the move away from classic, didactic 'chalk'n'talk-style' teaching to a more facilitative approach.
- Providing teachers with effective tools to engage modern learners. The availability of a comprehensive range of cutting-edge technologies within a flexible space empowers teachers to construct compelling learning experiences and tailor these appropriately to changing needs.
- Enabling teachers to enrich learning opportunities. Teachers will be able to extend the learning experience flexibly according to need through the effective use of layered learning resources where learning items are hyperlinked to deeper levels of information, further rich media resources and relevant individuals and online communities.

(http://www.inqbate.co.uk/content/view/20/41/)

While such spaces offer flexibility as a means of creatively disrupting existing teaching and learning practices, they are not so focused on examining questions of just what the potential *is* of new information and communication technologies, but of

Fig. 8.1
InQbate learning space, Centre for Excellence in Teaching and Learning in Creativity, University of Sussex. Photograph: Clare Melhuish.

what it is capable of in different contexts. For Temple, for example, the opportunities seem relatively limited:

> New media make it easy to incorporate multiple communication modes (image, audio, video), and these modes are 'governed by distinct log-ics [which] change not only the deeper meanings of textual forms but also the structures of ideas, of conceptual arrangements, and of the structures of our knowledge' (Kress 2003: 16). If this is correct, then technology may be seen as changing the conception of learning itself, though the implications for learning spaces appear, again, to be limited. This does, though, lead to ideas of 'blending learning', based on a mix-ture of modes of learning, and requiring 'blended environments', with technology-enabled classrooms.
>
> (Temple 2008: 235)

Here, I want to suggest that rather than seeing technologies simplistically as *either* a threat *or* an obvious development of education (which academics just seem inca-pable of understanding, and resistant to using), we should be much more precise about where and what kinds of media and methods can enhance or restrict learning at the post-compulsory level, by *always* investigating these in the context of exist-ing as well as possible social and spatial practices and repertoires of learning. To consider what such an approach implies, I will next explore just some aspects of learning technologies: the book; online learning resources; and social networking. In each case I am interested in both the properties of the media themselves, and in the social and spatial practices within which they are embedded. This is to help us find out the kinds of questions we need to ask, not just about online learning, but also about the future design of the whole repertoire for teaching, learning and research in post-compulsory education across both virtual and material spaces.

Re-visiting the book

Books remain a central part of academic life. The objects themselves, their col-lection into places called libraries or resource centres, and the particular practices they incorporate – a sustained sequential written argument, building on and citing previous research work – continually consolidates, reinforces and develops both different specialist communities of practice and the idea of the university or college as a central site of knowledge creation within society. Post-compulsory teaching, learning and research assumes reading and writing (in particular ways) as one of its core modes of operation. This is an ongoing and contested process both in defining how and what to read/write as part of the educational and research process (Savin-Baden 2008), and where particular texts, communities, subjects and perspectives come to dominance while others are ignored or fall away (Derrida 2001). Historically the production and consumption of academic books has been integrated into, but separated from, education – it is located instead as part of the free market. In most countries, academic publishing (even when universities have had their own academic presses) has been organised as a parallel but different process of competition, review and circulation, where performance and status is judged both through sales and citations.

What has this to do with new information and communication technologies? At the practical level, in the initial stages of computer-based text, screens did not 'afford' reading very satisfactorily compared to the page. Only small amounts could be seen at one time and were difficult to read. At the same time, computers and networks enabled written text to be linked together in multiple ways (hypertext) rather than just sequentially; and, increasingly, to be integrated with other audio, visual and animated media. Texts could now be made available electronically, enabling multiple on-demand copies and reducing storage demands. The internet not only had the potential to increase the accessibility of texts, but also to widen participation in their creation, re-appropriation and review, most famously through the 'crowd-sourcing' of Wikipedia and the peer-review sharing of Amazon.

Such shifts as these are often framed as indicating an inevitable and/ or necessary shift from previously modernist 'spaces of enclosure' (Edwards and Usher 2008: 54) where the authority and status of knowledge had remained bounded within the academy, to a new, more open, fluid and hybrid environment centred on the multi-connected, student-centred and democratic sharing of knowledge:

> There is a questioning of underlying assumptions about the fixity and stability of the word, the linear text and the teacher as the authoritative bearer of meaning. This opens up the possibility for learning to be more diverse, purpose driven, self-imposed and self-monitored than is normally found in current mainstream education. The claim is that cyberspace creates an environment where the distinction between readers and writers becomes blurred and where, consequently textual production and interpretation becomes less bounded. In cyberspace practices, there are no authoritative meanings waiting to be found by the suitably trained mind. [. . .] Hence this is a possible situation where learners do not simply interpret meanings but actively collaborate in creating meanings, and thus are more able to determine their own paths of learning.
>
> (Edwards and Usher 2008: 54)

Thus, the logic of the academic book as a sequential and sustained argument is seen both to represent and reinforce the authority of the expert, and to be undermined by the more 'democratic' affordances of computer-based networks. Such a view also intersects with its opposite; that precisely this hybrid, easy access to information means that students do not, or can not read 'properly' anymore. Birketts, for example, argues that the fragmented sense of time, speed and lack of duration and effort of current information and communication technologies means the loss of the 'depth phenomenon we associate with reverie, reduced attention span and a general impatience with sustained enquiry' (Birketts 1994: 27, quoted in Edwards and Usher 2008: 56). Birketts also suggests a 'shattered faith in institutions and in the explanatory narratives that formerly gave shape to subject experience' means a decreasing legitimacy for expert knowledge, and an undermining of teachers in relationship to learners.

What is at stake then is nothing less than contestations over the ownership, authority and status of knowledge and information. Even here, though, we need to be careful not to merely elide ease of access *either* with surface understanding and dumbing-down *or* with personalisation and egalitarianism. As Edwards and Usher put it:

> Of course, as always, words of caution are necessary since there are binaries at play in this scenario which it is necessary to question. First there is the binary of enclosure–openness which confers an emancipatory value to learning in cyberspace. It may well be that in both historical and contemporary classroom practices a pedagogy of transmission remains to the fore, but the learning within those spaces may draw on experiences beyond the walls of the institution. Cyberspace may intensify and highlight ways in which learning is not confined to the classroom; but whether it is necessarily more open and egalitarian is another matter.
>
> (Edwards and Usher 2008: 55–6)

At another level, that of the academic repertoire itself, we also need to be careful about both the either/or structure of debate, and of direct analogies between media and practices. It is not a simple choice between books or the web, but about the location, appropriate scale and distinctiveness of each medium for specific practices (which takes into account both the different properties of those media, and the ways in which they are produced and consumed). I have already outlined such an approach briefly in Chapter 6, based on Dempsey's work on re-thinking libraries and collections. And in fact, the recent development of electronic book readers indicates that rather than the book being superseded by the web, new technologies have caught up with their previous lack of affordances around enabling the act of sustained and sequential reading, in an easily portable format. The key question here then, is not the book versus the website, but concerns the relevance and use of both sustained forms of writing and shorter, more interactive ones for learning (and also the relationship of writing to other media) – a debate that could result in changes to, for example, what constitutes an 'academic' book, what a 'blog' should be like, a critique of existing patterns of citation and reference, types of frameworks and business models for electronic academic books and online teaching and learning resources, and new kinds of library space, constructed around the electronic book.

The 'place' and 'shape' of learning resources

If the book retains its power in academic life as a marker of individual subject expertise, as an indicator of the developing knowledge bases of different communities of practice, and as an expression of the university as a central site of knowledge creation, then the location and role of online learning resources remains much more 'in development', contested and unstable. While, as already outlined, this tends to be framed as being a problem – with academics refusing to shift their practices, we might more constructively investigate the 'place' of all the various learning and teaching materials and methods within post-compulsory education at institutional and societal levels, whether paper-based, electronic or a hybrid mixture.

In the UK, for example, the structure of the Research Assessment Exercise (RAE) and the more recent Research Excellence Framework (REF) has in fact reinforced the validity of the academic book as a marker of achievement within post-compulsory education, while failing to either explicitly recognise or provide support for the development of teaching and learning resources (whether online or not). And while making much of the necessity of a shift from formal to informal learning methods, the associated shift in types of workloads and resource support has also been mainly ignored. In fact, the 'work' of – and skills for – designing course material has, in many cases, been blurred together with the delivery of teaching, becoming invisible and now forced into less and less time, as academics are also asked to do more research, teaching and assessment. It remains central to the post-compulsory educational community of practice within UK higher education (but not so much further education) to have a relatively high degree of individual academic autonomy in what and how a subject is taught. Thus, while various governmental attempts to make post-compulsory learning more 'generic', through agreed course and module specifications based on explicit learning outcomes and evaluation criteria, these continue to be resisted by academics and educational institutions in a variety of ways.

Thus, organisations such as JISC (who have been funding online teaching and learning materials development in the UK for many years) have been continually frustrated by difficulties in persuading the post-compulsory educational sector to either develop educational resources which are transferable and reusable, or to use materials developed by others. This is also a problem about the affordances of new technologies for learning. There remains a lack of knowledge of what makes the best scale or type of resource for easy transfer, with much experimentation across, for example, what constitutes reusable learning objects (see http://www.rlo-cetl.ac.uk/), courseware 'shells' or what Laurillard (2002) terms generic learning activity models (GLAMs), virtual learning environments (VLEs) and other types of resource-based learning packages and tools. In addition, new applications from *outside* of education such as Facebook or Second Life (Fig. 8.2) continually throw up new issues as to their transferability and relevance to teaching and learning.

Institutions, meanwhile, are developing their engagements with online learning in a variety of ways through, for example, their own versions of VLEs, managed learning environments (MLE) – which also incorporate some administrative functions – information portals or gateways, and digital repositories for the sharing of research and other information. Again, there are key issues about the type, accessibility and design of online learning resources. There is also an increasing interest in open educational resources (OER): 'putting educational resources – lectures, tests, podcasts, seminar notes, ideas and reading lists and so on, online for free'. As Clarke writes:

> It began with the decision by the Massachusetts Institute of Technology (MIT) in the late 1990s (with huge financial help from the Andrew W

Fig. 8.2
Project exploring
Second Life
as a teaching
and learning
environment for
museum visitors,
by Lars Weineke
presentation
at ReLIVE 08
conference,
Open University,
21–22 November).
Photograph:
Jos Boys.

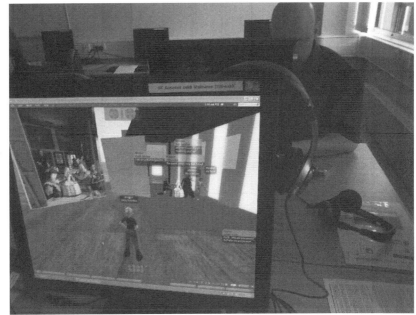

Mellon foundation, The William and Flora Hewlett Foundation – who are now also significant funders of the Open University's OER project – and the Ab Initio Software Corporation) to make all of their undergraduate and postgraduate teaching materials available for anyone with a computer to access. [. . .]

Consequently, the phenomenon of OER requires us to re-think what it means to be a student, the politics of knowledge and the 'business' of education.

(Clarke 2009: 20)

Here, though, two ideas are conflated: the first that universities should share their teaching and learning materials more widely; and second, that these should be free rather than commercially bought and sold, 'in the "commons" and commonly available to all' (Clarke 2009: 20). Through its Open Courseware project, for example, MIT and several international partners have a strategy of putting their course materials publicly on the web, not just to support the idea of the 'commons' but also to represent the added value of face-to-face contact and studying their courses on campus. In fact, what the online materials *mainly* do is show what potential students are missing, in terms of high-quality academic teachers, study support and accreditation.

The UK Open University has a similar site called Open Learn, which both provides free learning resources and acts as a 'taster' for formal, accredited study. This is currently a new and contested field, as different organisations compete to be recognised as *the* place for online resources. It includes commercial organisations such as Wikiversity, Google, and also new manifestations such as the School of Everything (schoolofeverything.com), each attempting to achieve some combination of cultural capital (Bourdieu 1987) and/or economic advantage, while negotiating issues such as intellectual property and uptake. But, as with thinking about the changing role of the book (whether paper or electronic), here the key issues are about analysing both the affordances of different media in specific situations and also critically examining the particular processes and practices through which these are being realised. For example, when the Open University in the UK developed distance learning, it defined new relationships between the course team, separating out the design of course (which could be re-used for several years), from the part-time tutors who just delivered these materials. When they developed online discussion, Open University researchers carefully explored what the 'rules' should be for this kind of learning interaction; for example, how newcomers should behave, and how debates were moderated, and by whom. Educational developers were also employed to help write clear and understandable study packs. At the University of Phoenix in the US, which pioneered e-learning without any face-to-face support, the whole teaching and learning process was re-designed to concentrate tutorial and pastoral support 24/7 at the end of a phone line.

In both of these cases the *amount of work* involved in learning and teaching resource design is recognised, and the relationships between resources and their modes of delivery are critically considered and re-framed. Here, then, the key problem is not paper *or* electronic, it is how learning resources are best designed, developed and delivered in different situations, and where and how this work is done.

Learning and the growth in social networking

One of the key current interests for education around new technologies has been the growth of so-called Web 2.0 applications. These are applications that enable interactive information sharing and collaboration, interoperability across devices and networks, and user-centred design; where content can be added to, changed or re-purposed. Most immediately, social networking sites such as Facebook, Flickr, YouTube, other digital file-sharing sites and personal blogs allow participants to upload and share their own resources via the web. Other groups have taken this potential to offer new kinds of collaborative services. CouchSurfing, for example, call themselves 'a volunteer-based worldwide network connecting travellers with members of local communities, who offer free accommodation and/or advice' (see http://www.couchsurfing.com), providing not just temporary accommodation in different cities across the world but also access to information about events and jobs. Geocaching (www.geocaching.com) is a worldwide game where people hide and find 'treasure', and tell each other about their experiences. Livemocha (www.livemocha.com) provides free language learning resources, supported by participants who not only learn languages themselves but also offering tutoring support to others. And Horsesmouth (www.horsesmouth.co.uk) facilitates collaborative mentoring. Thus many new networks and activities are developing *beyond* the university, which provide information sharing but also can involve learning, and knowledge exchange and creation. As with the development of electronic books, the many providers of these recent versions of educational resources, which build on the affordances of the web, are still struggling with both appropriate formats and business models; such that no general conventions for *learning* can be said to have yet solidified into everyday practices.

At the same time, there has been considerable interest in attempting to exploit the energy and mass take-up of social networking and other Web 2.0-type sites like these for teaching and learning at the post-compulsory level. But as before, there are still key questions to be asked about what constitutes the distinctiveness of learning in universities and colleges, and what the relationships are between such virtual spaces and the social and spatial practices of education as a community of practice. In addition we need to look carefully at the affordances of social networking and similar sites. To what extent, for example, do they (or can they) provide the kinds of spaces for creative learning I have already outlined in Chapter 7, based on Scott-Webber's work? Part of the reason these questions are not being asked, I suggest, is that sometimes debates over the perceived importance of informal learning collude in the idea that education needs to be made more fun, that students need to be 'seduced' into learning (Heppell 2009), and that social networking, for instance, offers just such an inviting space. The common-sense oppositions between fun/exciting/playful and boring/dull/serious make any criticism of the frameworks and templates for social networking sites as currently inappropriate for post-compulsory education, seeming to imply a preference for the supposed alternative – boring, formal lecturing and passive transmission of facts. Instead, we need to engage with the virtual spaces of social networking differently, by critically and creatively examining their detailed intersections with the existing social and spatial practices of learning and teaching.

The Spotlight project led by Chris Mitchell, learning and teaching coordinator of the Royal College of Art (RCA), aimed to explore the potential of their existing virtual learning environment (Moodle) to support creative debate between students from different disciplines at the RCA, something that students had been asking for (Fig. 8.3). An online forum was set up and student volunteers recruited, as well as staff facilitators. Most crucially, an evaluation process was built into the project

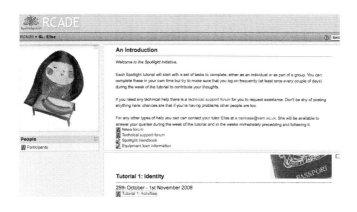

Fig. 8.3
Home page for
Spotlight online
learning project,
Royal College of
Art, London, 2007.

throughout. Mitchell found that students were very affected by how (and how much) their peers responded, and were relatively self-conscious and cautious about their writing, partly because they were not sure what was the right tone, but also had uncertainty about the authority of the online material as a written record and its longer-term permanence. This 'seemed to stifle the dynamism of some debates', he notes:

> I find using [the VLE] acts as a barrier. I find it restricts what I want to say as once I have posted the comment it is on display and so it makes you feel self-conscious about your opinion in a way a vocal tutorial would not (Spotlight student)

> I would like to be a bit more spontaneous and more at ease when answering these questions (Spotlight student)

> My feelings were that [students] found it difficult to 'let go' of their contributions – especially their visual material, although those pieces of work actually posted were very interesting. (Spotlight tutor)
>
> (Mitchell 2007a: 5)

So although overall students reported that the online debate helped development of their ideas and practice they also experienced it as creating additional time pressures, meaning that debate was difficult to sustain to the end of the academic year when studio-based study took precedence. In a comparison with two other online forums, Mitchell (2007b) considers what aspects can enable a momentum to be developed and maintained; and also emphasises the importance of setting up explicit conventions:

> It is important that students get the opportunity to negotiate with their tutors and peers over how they wish to conduct themselves at the outset. If it is a requirement of the course for students to work collaboratively then it is reasonable to allow them to establish how they might go about doing this, particularly in the case of online learning when conventions and cues aren't always apparent. However, it would be a mistake to assume that in a face-to-face environment conventions are always well understood. Although people may be generally better versed in interpreting meaning that is expressed in voice intonation, gesture and body language, different settings – be they cultural, social or educational – bring with them different expectations.
>
> (Mitchell 2007b: 12)

Here, the focus on concepts such as 'momentum' and 'conventions' relates very closely to what I have been calling everyday social and spatial practices, and to the underlying structure of the 'communities of practice' model. Thus, I suggest, just as we need to better examine the boundaries, practices and repertoires of material learning spaces, so we can use similar frameworks and methods to explore the impact and effectiveness of virtual learning spaces.

When we undertook an Arts Council-funded interior architecture project at the University of Brighton (Fig. 8.4) called Making Discursive Spaces – which aimed to explore issues of disability and architecture through the involvement of several disabled artists as tutors – the online blog was the most unsuccessful part of the collaboration, for precisely the reasons outlined by Mitchell. Both tutors and students were concerned about what was appropriate content and 'tone'; and were anxious about the status and authority of the blog site. But just as interestingly, the intention to open up a learning space for thinking differently about disability was, in fact, constrained by the very educational social and spatial practices which framed it. I have written elsewhere about the complexities produced in, and by, this project in its attempts to create a transitional space – that is, one that was both risk-taking and supportive (Boys 2008). In fact, both artists and students welcomed the 'known' of studio-based tutorial practices, while bringing to it and taking from it, different expectations and outcomes. In addition, by deliberately involving disabled artists as tutors, rather than passive 'users' of architectural services, these participants found themselves in complicated positions, in relation to both student achievement and existing course systems:

> The artists viewed themselves variously as practitioners, clients, mentors, collaborators and tutors. It was sometimes unclear how much they were responsible for the student's overall academic development, for example, or for insisting on changes to a student's work.
>
> In addition, they ended up being (due to circumstances beyond our control) very much an additive element to the design project, brought in when students were close to completing their design. This was unsatisfactory for everyone and raised questions about roles and responsibilities more generally.
>
> Finally, project design and co-ordination was done by the in-house design studio team. There were many tensions on access to, and control over, both content and organisation. For the artists this led to questions

Fig. 8.4
Web page from Making Discursive Spaces design project, BA (Hons) in Interior Architecture with Architecture-nSideOut, University of Brighton, 2007.

about what terms of reference they would want for future project like this.

(Boys 2007)

Studying such engagements, then, can help us critically unravel how the distinctive practices and repertoires of post-compulsory learning are played out across both physical and virtual spaces in different situations. This is both about what works (because it seems ordinary and obvious) and what doesn't (because it fails to 'fit' with our assumptions about what teaching and learning is). This is not just about designing more effective online learning resources, environments and methods which better match existing practices, it is also about critically challenging the assumptions and 'normal' social and spatial practices through which educational communities of practice reproduce themselves.

Architecture and new technologies

What is clear is that certain aspects of new information and communication technologies are already firmly embedded and ubiquitous in post-compulsory education, both in the teaching and learning of computer-based skills and in the areas of information searching, sharing and presentation (Google, WebCT or an equivalent VLE, PowerPoint, etc.). Most of these applications, I suggest, have tended to extend, or integrate easily with, the current repertoires and social and spatial practices of universities and colleges. At the same time, attempts to re-shape university systems holistically through integrated technologies (Watson 2006), or to develop materials or networks that aim to shift the nature of teaching and learning towards more task-based or resource-based techniques – whether paper-based, online or in virtual worlds such as Second Life – have had much less resonance or take-up. I have already said that this is centrally a matter of how educational communities of practice *work*. But there is also one final point, about the affordances of various new technologies and how these are themselves changing.

For architects and designers perhaps the most relevant issue is the increasing physicality and spatiality being incorporated into new technologies. This is not just at the level of hand-held mobile devices, touch screens and shake control – as exemplified by the iPod – or new forms of interaction between bodily movement and screen action as with the Nintendo Wii, but also in web-based activities and tools that enable locational and physical interactions with spaces, objects and other people. The development of Global Positioning Systems (GPS), Radio Frequency Identification (RFID) and other 'augmented' realities, such as MIT Media Lab's work with wearable computing, are all shifting the simple divide between 'material' and 'virtual' spaces; and potentially offer alternative material spaces to the serried ranks of computer screens that have become so common in universities and colleges.

In addition, just as sites like Wikipedia aim to support free and collaborative information sharing, there are now many organisations interested in developing what has been called 'distributed creativity'. These, too, are explicitly concerned with re-defining where knowledge and power reside though 'crowd-sourcing', but in these cases, combine sharing information in virtual space with material *actions* undertaken in the real world. Groups such as the Institute of Infinitely Small Things, Proboscis and SFZero all used task-based, often game-playing-related, techniques for collaborative interactions which take place across both virtual and physical worlds. San Francisco-based SFZero for example, describes itself as 'a Collaborative Production Game. Players build characters by completing tasks for their groups and increasing their Score. The goals of play include meeting new people, exploring the city, and participating in non-consumer leisure activities' (see http://sf0.org). As with online gaming more generally, activities are structured around tasks and puzzles, rewarded with points accumulation and movement through levels. In the urban design field, for example, these kinds of resources that connect learning materials with networked activities and physical action (as well as an intention to make potential improvements to the built environment) are becoming more common. Examples include the Urban Design London Learning Space (see http://www.urbandesignlondon.com/learning-space/), Madrid Design Net (see http://madriddesignnet.com/) and the British Council Creative Cities project (see http://creativecities.britishcouncil.org/).

Thus the affordances – what these new media are 'capable of' – are changing in ways that offer opportunities to support learning as knowledge creation as well as information sharing. However, as with Facebook and the like, these spaces do not 'automatically' translate into appropriate or effective learning and teaching practices; the potential intersections remain in need of much more exploration. It is such investigative and creative engagements with the potentialities of things, media and spaces that can open up not just issues with online or virtual learning, but also learning spaces and their social and spatial practices as a whole.

Chapter 9

Creative learning spaces

Towards the porous campus?

Throughout this book I have been exploring how we can investigate what is distinctive about teaching and learning in post-compulsory education, and what it is that *matters* about the design of its material (and virtual) spaces. I have suggested that universities and colleges are complex and contested communities of practice, continually bringing new entrants into processes of knowledge creation and development across different disciplines; and that this has in-built tensions in combining learning, teaching and research as a means to develop subject and practitioner expertise (for use beyond the academy), and as a means to enable the growth and change of the academy-as-a-centre-of-knowledge itself. In this final chapter I want to return again to the level of the educational institution to explore how accepting and engaging creatively and constructively with these tensions can help us re-think the architectural design of post-compulsory education.

Lord Dearing's National Committee of Inquiry into Higher Education (1997) in the UK 'defined the unique role of the university [. . .] as being "to enable society to maintain an independent understanding of itself and its world"' (Laurillard 2002: 18). This was broken down into four main purposes:

1. Inspiring and enabling individuals to develop their capacities to the highest levels.
2. Increasing knowledge and understanding.
3. Serving the needs of the economy.
4. Shaping a democratic and civilised society.

(Laurillard 2002: 18)

Diana Laurillard, in reviewing the impact of these aims on current post-compulsory learning and teaching practices, also notes the underlying tensions for universities and colleges in providing both specialist knowledge and practitioner knowledge. She asks the bigger question – what is the value of a degree course, or a university-based education, which can enable it to remain the dominant means for the supply and certification of particular forms of knowledge, compared to, for example, work-based training?

> Whenever senior academics are rattled by the pretensions of the private
> upstarts in the corporate education business, they incline to the view that
> the degree-awarding powers of universities protect the uniqueness of
> their institutions. At present, this is perhaps true, but governments have
> the ability to change that power if universities are not seen to provide
> something valued and something distinctive from the increasing offers
> of the private sector.
>
> (Laurillard 2002: 18–19)

For Laurillard, the problem remains that academics in universities centrally define
themselves as practitioners and researchers rather than teachers (an understanding
which, as I have already noted, is deeply embedded across most existing educational
social and spatial practices from institutional organisation through to government
regulation). She quotes from Donald A. Schön (1987) to suggest that universities
need to re-think the learning and teaching of practitioner knowledge as a means of
becoming 'better placed' in the competition for post-compulsory education provision within the private sector. Schön also argues that students need to learn to
know 'creatively' and be able to deal with ambiguity, 'to be able to go beyond the
rules – devising new methods of reasoning, strategies of action, and ways of framing problems' (Laurillard 2002: 20). This requires a particular set of social and spatial
practices for learning and teaching, which from Laurillard's point of view, is not yet
in place in universities and colleges:

> Designing, in the broader sense in which all professional practice is design-
> like, must be learned by doing. A design-like practice is learnable, but not
> teachable by classroom methods [. . .] the interventions most useful to
> students are more like coaching than teaching, as in a reflective practicum.
> [. . .] The reflective practicum demands intensity and duration far beyond
> the normal requirements of a course. [. . .] Students do not so much
> attend these events as live them. And the work takes time [. . .] time to
> live through the learning cycles involved in any design-like task; and time
> to shift repeatedly back and forth between reflection on and in action.
>
> (Schön 1987: 157, 311, quoted in Laurillard 2002: 20)

Laurillard's proposed solution, though, is predominantly at the level of changing
individual teaching and learning practices within universities – particularly in making
better use of the new communication technologies of the type outlined in the previous chapter. This is problematic on three counts. First, she continues to blur the
sheer amount of additional knowledge and work required of academics to translate
their existing methods and materials into new forms of project-based and electronic
resources; this in an institutional context where such activities are neither supported
nor valued. Second, by remaining only at the level of the university-centred teacher/
student dyad and her social constructivist 'conversational framework', Laurillard
can appear to 'solve' the problem of a simple binary opposition – practitioner *versus*
expert knowledge, rather than accepting and opening up for view the tensions and

complexities between learning, teaching, research and practice, which I would suggest are *inherent* in the four main university purposes, as defined by the Dearing Report. This is as much about the strategic, locational and boundary conditions of the educational institution as a whole (what goes together and what is kept apart) as it is about particular learning encounters. Third, she offers only a generic answer to what is, in fact, a deeply situated issue, both in relationship to various academic subjects and to the very different experiences of learning and teaching in, for example, an ex-polytechnic, a further education college, a museum and gallery education unit, an adult education service or an international education franchise. These places are unlikely to match the 'typical' research-focused university that Laurillard takes as the norm.

This final chapter, then, aims to open up to view some of these tensions, complexities and particularities. It begins by exploring how to think about what learning space in post-compulsory education might become in the future. To do this requires an initial exploration of some relevant spaces beyond the university, as well as of some new kinds of spaces within it. As previously, these examples are not offered as 'how to do it' guides, but as a means to help us think harder about what a university or college *is*. The built environments offered here do not simplistically reflect their occupation, but are one aspect of how the boundary conditions, social and spatial practices and repertoires of learning are being re-thought in specific situations, across workplace, educational and other public provision. What it does reflect is an increasing interest – from governments, educational providers, business and academics – in thinking of universities and colleges as more 'porous' organisations, where both practitioner learning and knowledge creation can happen across many locations, potentially producing new intersections between work, leisure, study and research. The chapter finishes with suggestions as to what kinds of *conceptual* spaces for research and debate urgently need to be created, in order to both expand upon (and critique) the theoretical frameworks and methodologies outlined in this book, and to enable wider public engagement with the nature, role and locations of specialist expertise and knowledge creation in twenty-first-century societies.

The space(s) of the university estate

Estate planners already know that designing, developing and maintaining their campuses involves a process – partly opportunistic and partly strategic – of keeping, removing, adapting and transforming the buildings and open spaces they have, which will have both patterns of relative stability and variation/dynamism. They understand the 'material' they work with as having recognisable typologies and repertoires that have accumulated through time into specific settings. As outlined in Chapter 1, in the current period in the UK, new and adapted designs have tended to centre on new high-quality 'hybrid' research spaces, including graduate centres (Fig. 9.1), and on informal learning spaces (usually connected to libraries and/or student support services). In addition, one could add examples of new high-quality 'hybrid' research spaces, including graduate centres (Fig. 9.1), and new residential and/or conference facilities.

The motivations for these developments are many and varied. They may be simply to make a university or college more 'attractive' to potential students, or

Fig. 9.1
Exterior view of
Lock-Keeper's
Graduate Centre,
Queen Mary's,
University of
London (Surface
Architects, 2005).
Photograph:
Jos Boys.

to bring in and hold high-quality researchers, especially in competitive subject areas. They may aim to 'express' the distinctiveness of one institution as compared to another. They may be to provide additional facilities that do not yet exist, for example, where new subjects are developed or integrated, or where space is needed for additional student numbers. They may be to explore new kinds of learning environments, or to add technologically-rich ones. They may be to realise cost or other resource savings through building 'swaps', mergers or re-allocations. How, then, do such processes fit with the kinds of re-thinking suggested in this book?

Well, first, many difficulties remain because of the continuing lack of developed theory, analysis or evaluation about learning and space; that is, the ongoing inability of post-compulsory education to research *itself*. Even a small pilot study, such as that undertaken by Melhuish and explored in Chapter 5, shows the level of awareness and sophistication respondents can have of the ways institutional agendas intersect with space, when asked the right questions. Yet almost no data of this kind exists to help assess the effectiveness of the new and adapted buildings currently being constructed across universities and colleges. Second, while there is considerable research and debate about what Mike Neary *et al.* (2010) call 'the Idea of the University', this material often either ignores space or operates only at a common-sense metaphoric and 'reflective' level, and is anyway not much referred to as a way of informing architectural practice and design for post-compulsory education. Finally, we are not much used to exploring the similarities and differences in post-compulsory education across its different providers. Although there has been some research exploring relationships between academic and other types of workplaces (University of Strathclyde and DEGW 2008), there has been very little, for example, about the relationships between universities and museum education (Cook, Reynolds and Speight 2010). Here, I want to focus on this last aspect, as a potentially constructive means of examining existing boundaries between different educational communities of practice at the post-compulsory level, to consider how and where these might creatively and usefully blur and change.

Learning spaces beyond the university

I have already suggested that educational institutions are complex mixes of communities of practice that work in varying degrees of contestation and collaboration; and that the key questions for architectural design are less about attempting to define the specific 'shape' of (and similarities and differences between) each, and more about developing a rich and creative engagement with their *ambiguous* relationships, both across different groupings and at various levels and scales of operation. Here, I want to see how this might be developed by briefly exploring the various articulations of different communities of practice through the underlying characteristics they share; that is, their boundary conditions, specific social and spatial practices and particular repertoires. I suggest we can enhance our understanding through going beyond the university, both to other forms of adult education, and to other building 'types', while also thinking about how to bring this outside world 'in' to post-compulsory education.

Post-compulsory education (in the UK at least) is currently undergoing many changes, in a climate of fierce financial limitations. Regulatory bodies are increasingly imposing resource constraints and examining ways of monitoring efficiency and effectiveness; and also asking universities and colleges to improve sustainability and health and well-being, and to develop areas such as project-based learning, research and consultancy, income generation and business and community engagement. Barnett and Temple (2006) have shown one impact of these shifts, in the increasing promotion of connections between higher education institutions and their regional business communities by a wide range of agencies. As Neary summarises:

> These relationships are associated with new forms of knowledge production, which have an impact on the type of space needed on campus and a blurring of the ways in which facilities are used across teaching, research and third stream activities with business and the community. (Barnett and Temple) also conclude that given the academic drivers behind space demand, institutions are unlikely to experience a significant reduction in overall space needs, as reductions in one area are offset by new demands elsewhere.
>
> (Neary 2010)

Barnett and Temple predict that the underlying infrastructure of university campuses will remain at about the same size; combining an increased learning space demand around provision for student-led and blended learning environments, a relatively limited impact of distance e-learning and a minor increase in research activities, concentrated primarily in a small number of institutions; with work-based and itinerant learning this will lead to some reductions in space needs. How, then, can we move beyond a tendency to merely 'add' new types of educational provision to existing services, and instead re-think holistically what it is that a university or college should provide? I have written elsewhere (Boys and Ford 2006) about this tendency to the merely additive in relationship to the adoption of new technologies by post-compulsory education. Many universities and colleges have themselves already explored such issues, for example by outsourcing catering, accommodation and cleaning; or even financial and assessment services (such as the management of students' professional development plans or other achievement records). Others have extended the services they provide themselves (either directly or through franchising) by building internet cafés and the like. Some of these shifts have been creative about services as much as about space. At the University of Glasgow, for example, a pizza delivery service is provided right across the campus, to support students' informal studying 'everywhere' and retain it on site.

Here, I want to begin to engage with the issues of *what* should happen *where* at a more holistic level, by briefly reviewing projects that challenge or overlap with the assumed boundaries, practices and repertoires of the university campus. First, are two examples of libraries in London. This is because some of the arguments in favour of informal learning space seem to imply a reduced importance to in-depth and 'studied' learning compared with shared, more playful, 'fun' spaces which can 'attract the attention' and 'seduce' students into what is otherwise framed as a dull and un-engaging experience (Heppell 2009). As with considerations of the book, in the previous chapter, I want again to emphasise the importance of understanding post-compulsory learning as an absorbing, time-taking activity, which offers pleas-ures in the *difficulties* of serious study, as well as in the enjoyment of collaboration and sharing. In the UK, at least, this is a key territory across which the 'idea' and role of education is currently being negotiated.

Second, I will briefly consider a public art gallery, as an example of how business, community and artistic communities are already being deeply intertwined. Third, I will examine a 'cross-over' space in a university which re-orchestrates relationships between creative learning and creative businesses. And finally, I will consider a university project which engages with sustainability as part of its learning and teaching agenda. While none of these examples sets out to completely re-think the idea of the university, each, in its way, challenges some of the assumptions we have of what a post-compulsory educational institution is like. Each remains prob-lematic because, without rich and relevant evaluation data about the effectiveness of the spaces considered, their 'stories' can only rely on what this book has consistently critiqued – the expressed intentions of clients and designers.

Beyond the boundaries: Idea Stores and Tower Hamlets College, London

The five Idea Stores, developed by the London Borough of Tower Hamlets in col-laboration with the local Further Education College redefined the nature of the local city library. Research showed that local people were not using the existing libraries, which were often difficult to get to and were becoming quite dated. The Idea Stores therefore combine traditional library and information services, with classrooms for adult education (supported by courses supplied on site by Tower Hamlets College), a local history archive and a variety of reading and study spaces. The five-storey Idea Store in Whitechapel was designed by architects Adjaye Associates in 2005 (Fig. 9.2). It sits on a busy main road next to a tube station and a street market. It originally had multiple entries to both actually and visually enhance accessibility – at ground level and at two other levels by an escalator suspended above the pavement – but only the ground-floor entrance remains open:

> The building is conceived as a simple stack of flexible floor plates wrapped in a unified facade that combines transparency with colour. A curtain wall consisting of a repeating pattern of coloured glass, clear glass, and glass faced aluminum panels encloses all four facades.
>
> Each floor is arranged like a promenade that reveals the services and facilities being offered while affording arresting views of the surrounding area. [. . .] The café is placed on the top floor to draw people past the various facilities and rewards them with panoramic views of the city of London.
>
> (http://www.adjaye.com/)

Through the relatively simple device of 'wrapping' library shelves and spaces around the central circulation core, the Whitechapel building provides a variety of study spaces for individuals, pairs and groups (Fig. 9.3). In doing this Adjaye in fact

Fig. 9.2
Exterior view
of Idea Store,
Whitechapel,
London (Adjaye
Associates, 2005).
Photograph:
Jos Boys.

Fig. 9.3
Interior view
of Idea Store,
Whitechapel,
London (Adjaye
Associates, 2005).
Photograph:
Jos Boys.

reverses the increasingly ubiquitous atrium motif of recent university informal learning spaces, so that people look out to the city, rather than into the building. What is most interesting in the context of this book is the completely public (and popular) aspect of the space, without any of the entry requirements (boundary conditions) of the traditional university. The availability of relatively quiet, unpretentious study spaces beyond both the home – where many people may not have the privilege of a 'room of one's own' – and the additional educational provision – a simple series of seminar rooms – is in many ways truly radical, considering how adult education based on short courses has been severely reduced in the UK over the last few years. This links back to organisations such as the Workers Educational Association (WEA), as well as connecting to other providers of adult education such as the Mary Ward Centre, also in London. Through its Idea Stores project Tower Hamlets aimed to double the use of library and adult education facilities across the borough within five years, and in fact exceeded this target. In addition, the local further education college gained access to another site and facility, so as to extend its 'offer' beyond the existing campus, this being particularly relevant to potential students who might not otherwise consider studying 'at' college. The Idea Store, then, is neither a college nor just a local library, but an interesting intersection between both.

Taking learning seriously: the British Library, London

In a similar vein, but aimed at a different constituency, the British Library (BL) in London (designed by Colin St John Wilson and completed in 1997) has opened itself up to wider audiences compared with its previous relatively exclusive incarnation as the British Museum Reading Room. Again a series of study spaces are offered, from a canteen and café, to various 'corners' and corridors, as well as the main reading room itself, supported by a range of different furniture and settings, and giving access to a variety of exhibitions, collections and archives. What is most relevant to the arguments here is that, although very different in design to the Whitechapel building, the BL also offers an environment of relaxed but serious calm. These are both spaces that emphasise study as an interplay of distraction, relaxation and absorption as well as an activity that may be both collaborative and solitary. As such, they offer at least a dialogue with, if not a critique of, those learning spaces in universities that rely on beanbags, bright colours and the 'expression' of playfulness to indicate that informal learning is taking place.

The BL (especially now that it has opened up its entry requirements for readers) also raises questions about the extent to which an educational institution needs to provide its own resources. In a dense centre like London, the BL can offer specialised collections and facilities of a better quality than local university libraries – and potentially the associated study space as well. In such a context a 'university' could potentially become a much smaller, more fluid operation.

Education as inspiration: The Public, Walsall

I have written elsewhere about the value of 'thinking' learning through engaging with other providers, for example educators who work in galleries and museums (Boys 2010). The educational role of the museum and gallery has been explicitly challenged over the last decade – with considerable criticism of collections seen as based on the didactic transmission of expert knowledge to an (assumed) passive and homogeneous audience. As Eilean Hooper-Greenhill notes, this means that the biggest issue facing museums and galleries at the present time is the re-conceptualisation of their relationship to the people they serve (2000: 1). This is not simply about getting 'more bodies' in the door but also concerns changing understandings of the role of culture, identity and meaning in society; requires increased awareness of what diverse participants brings to their encounters in such spaces; and articulates learning around ideas of experience, interpretation and inspiration.

There are many differences in perspectives, histories and trajectories here, but also much potential for exploring and exploiting different disciplinary understandings creatively and constructively. This is both to open up the varying assumptions and approaches of post-compulsory education across its many locations to view, and to explore cross-site collaborations (Cook, Reynolds and Speight 2010). Similarly, while engagements with employers and other business organisations are often seen as an oppositional threat, these could instead be seen as offering the possibility of usefully articulating and negotiating those differences, rather than assuming that each community of practice offers a single coherent understanding of what post-compulsory education 'is'.

The Public in Walsall (Fig. 9.4), designed by Will Alsop (now Alsop Sparch Architects) and completed in 2008, is perhaps a problematic example of this genre as it has had a very troubled opening history. But it remains interesting for our purposes for two reasons: from its very inception the collection of interactive art works was intended to be user-centred, and also because its aim was for 'spaces for people

Fig. 9.4
Exterior and interior views of The Public, West Bromwich, England (Will Alsop, 2008). Photographs: Jos Boys.

to get together for virtually any purpose – cultural and educational exhibitions, live performances, social relaxation, community activities and clubs and major corporate or entertainment events' (http://www.thepublic.com/index.php/); that is, a complete intermixing of publicly and privately funded activities.

This includes office space for small businesses, a specially designed corporate entertainment space (the Longroom) and a doubling up of the main foyer for public use and for conference and business networking (branded as the PinkTank). Within a simple black rectangular shell dotted by jelly-bean-shaped windows trimmed in a deep pink, there are many deliberately different spaces across five floors, linked together by a long and winding ramp through the gallery itself. It was conceived, according to the architects, as a 'Box of Delights':

> The Public represents a radical gesture for community architecture, born from the conviction that art and architecture can be catalysts for regeneration and renewal. On five principal levels, the building is intended to give great scope to exhibition designers, artists, educators and users of all kinds, while encouraging and challenging all users to work in innovative ways. The Public is intended to inspire new ideas from its creative users rather than simply make way for them. [. . .]
>
> Inside, simplicity of form gives way to complexity: rugged, multi-faceted or curved forms appear to balloon into the space at random, sitting on, or suspended from a table structure – a wandering, large-scale ramp links the spaces. These forms are containers for the many different functions in the building. There are, for example, 'pods' for displaying art, as well as a huge 'sock' containing two large galleries; a 'ramp' contains a major proportion of the displays; an events space 'rock'; and a WC

'pebble'. At the top of the building, suspended from the roof, a series of 'lily-pads' – dish-shaped floors with brightly coloured interiors – house lettable workspaces.

(http://www.alsopsparch.com/)

As with many other galleries and museums, the building supports an educational programme, which aims to have IT and digital arts as a particular focus, and which they describe as follows:

> The learning team at The Public believe that learners should have the opportunity to work outside their normal learning environments and be creatively encouraged. The Public venue is an ambitious arts centre that provides visitors with new ways of viewing how site-specific learning and contemporary art can be harnessed to build skills for the future.
>
> (http://www.thepublic.com/index.php/learning/)

Thus, they position themselves as an extension to current learning spaces while, importantly, also giving value to being *differently* situated. Spaces such as these have the potential, then, both to blur boundaries between employment, leisure and learning 'internally' and to deliberately exploit their specialist, *separate* characteristics from other provisions.

Bringing the outside in: White Space, University of Abertay

Within the university sector in the UK, there has been a range of initiatives at the intersections between post-compulsory education, business and local communities. What makes White Space stand out is not its 'architectural' quality – it is a relatively basic conversion of an existing warehouse – but its multi-layered intersections across students, teachers, researchers and practitioners involved in computer arts, part of the University's School of Computing and Creative Technologies (Fig. 9.5). The space combines open tutorial and seminar areas with lecturers' workspaces and provision for local businesses. It houses a group working with contemporary and interdisciplinary artists from the UK and abroad as well as high-quality facilities for computer-generated art and studio production, intended to pull in top-level PhD and other research activities (Fig. 9.6):

> The White Space concept surrounds our students with the buzz of a real working environment, allowing them to share real-world knowledge and experience. Tutorials and lectures also take place here, which encourages lively discussions in the relaxation area with fellow students and staff afterwards. [. . .]
>
> White Space is about creating a set of essential, personalised assets and including their development in all of our programmes, so that they build your confidence and help get you a better job in the real world. These assets include creativity, the ability to work in teams, the ability to work within, across and between disciplines, an understanding of

the limits of knowledge and the significance of research, enterprise and entrepreneurship, and an ability to make correct and ethical decisions in the absence of all relevant facts.

(http://www.abertay.ac.uk/studying/schools/amg/)

Fig. 9.5
Entrance to White Space, University of Abertay. Photograph: Jos Boys.

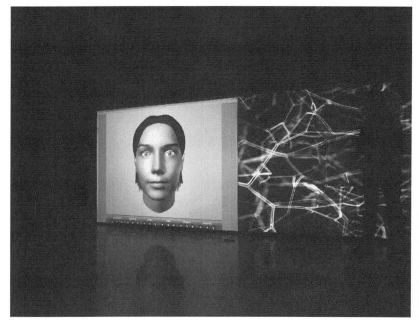

Fig. 9.6
'Human'-sized screens, computing facility, White Space, University of Abertay. Photograph: Jos Boys.

The space includes a masters course for business start-up, where each student has their own workspace, overlooking the shared seminar area (Fig. 9.7). Tutorials thus, literally, take place at the office. Interestingly White Space – which is perhaps one of the most innovative contemporary post-compulsory creative learning spaces in the UK – does not feature in many of the 'standard' taxonomies of new informal learning spaces (as illustrated, for example, in Chapter 1). Perhaps this is because it ignores the formal/informal divide, instead unpicking and then creatively and constructively remaking relationships between the different aspects of what education at post-compulsory level is *for*.

What makes a learning space? The Edible Campus, McGill University

The previous examples have focused on possibilities of shifting boundaries across and between public, community and business interactions with post-compulsory education. Other schemes have also explored community engagement and are, increasingly, acting as seedbed or 'enabler' locations for more widely socially purposeful and/or educational projects, which may not be merely about academic achievement or sit only within a specific subject discipline. These, perhaps, are most concerned with the Dearing Report's fourth purpose – 'shaping a democratic and civilised society'.

McGill University's Edible Campus, organised by Professor Vikram Bhatt, is an example of this. In the spring and summer of 2007, volunteers and researchers from a grouping of different organisations, including the School of Architecture at the university, began productive growing in a concrete-covered, prominent urban corner of one of the campuses:

The result was a 120 square meter container garden that involved citizens in the creation of green, edible community spaces. The Edible Campus has also demonstrated how productive planting can be woven into urban spaces without diminishing the utility or functionality, while exploring strategies for increasing food production in the city and improving spatial quality by exploiting under-utilised and neglected space.

(http://www.mcgill.ca/mchg/projects/ediblecampus/)

The intention has therefore been to re-use such corners and spaces across the public realm to grow produce and then to link this to a food collection and meal delivery system, creating a sustainable prototype that could potentially be expanded to other university campuses and across the city. Such a project, then, integrates design as a 'product' with design as a service, connecting the university with its locality not just through the garden scheme itself but also via a series of related community-based projects.

This idea has already been taken up and developed at other localities, for example by the Faculty of Arts at the University of Brighton, in this case linked to Katrin Bohn and Andre Viljoen's concept of the Continuous Productive Urban Landscape or CPUL (Viljoen 2005). The intention at Brighton is to activate an underutilised rooftop terrace (Fig. 9.8), making it productive by cultivating vegetables and herbs for use in the faculty restaurant and creating an attractive space for outdoor meetings and relaxation. Staff, students and local residents participate in the Edible Campus directly through a formal elective 'extension study', a student-led allotment society and the faculty's Environmental Action Network. Since establishing the project, restaurant staff have started to compost uncooked vegetable waste on-site with the aim of closing waste cycles. The goals of such a project then, go well beyond the existing boundaries of a university or college. They are articulated rather as an exemplar 'to make the benefits of cultivating in cities widely recognised in terms of its environmental, economic, social, recreational and health related roles, so that it can be used to its maximum potential by cities everywhere' (http://www. mcgill.ca/mchg/projects/ediblecampus/).

The 'place' of knowledge and the idea of the university

Although I have undertaken a brief exploration of built examples, the main proposition here is that proper research, creative methodologies and appropriate, constructive debate remain lacking, yet are all centrally important to the future design and development of new and better learning spaces for post-compulsory education. I have already outlined the kinds of conceptual frameworks and methods I suggest we need to better understand relationships between education and the spaces it occupies. In addition, I want to argue for the development of more 'meeting places' across and between different disciplines/communities of practice, both within post-compulsory educational institutions and beyond them. This is the space where our broadest conceptual assumptions about, and contestations over, what learning is take place. It is at the level of governmental and other stakeholder involvement and their often contradictory concerns about economic effectiveness, lifelong learning, workplace

Fig. 9.8
Edible Campus
project at the
University of
Brighton's
Faculty of Arts
and Design.
Photograph:
Andre Viljoen.

training and widening participation; about university, college and other educational providers' mission statements and their 'locations' within the wider context; and about different pedagogic models and their spatial implications. And it concerns basic philosophical issues about the status and authority of knowledge, and the role of knowledge creation and development in society. We need to have more debate about what constitute the 'normal' locations, boundary conditions, social and spatial practices and repertoires of post-compulsory education, so that we can also explore creative and effective alternatives. This is important, both for enhancing the quality of post-compulsory learning, teaching and research, and for better 'locating' the role of architecture in that process.

This brings us back to the value of the communities of practice framework, particularly if it is extended beyond examination of the *internal* dynamics of particular groupings *outwards*, to include both the tensions and productive intersections between groupings. As I have said before, understanding learning as taking place through communities of practice enables us to explore it as a situated process, firmly located in social interactions and engaging many participants – not just individual teachers and students. This is about 'the relational character of knowledge and learning, about the negotiated character of meaning, and about the concerned (engaged, dilemma- driven) nature of learning activity for the people involved' (Lave and Wenger 1991: 33). Yet these kinds of self-reflective, interactive and engaged interaction do not happen anything like enough between and across educationalists themselves, whether from different academic disciplines, different educational sectors, or from practice. We do not seem very good yet at learning from each other *about learning*. For Lave and Wenger, such intersections are constructive as well as problematic, and also have their own effects on the repertoires of learning communities:

> Because of the contradictory nature of collective social practice and because learning processes are part of the working out of these contradictions in practice, social reproduction implies the renewed construction of resolutions to underlying conflicts. In this regard, it is important to note that reproduction cycles are productive as well. They leave a historical trace of artefacts – physical, linguistic, and symbolic – and of social structures, which constitute and re-constitute the practice over time.
>
> (Lave and Wenger 1991: 58)

An important means of opening up these issues to debate and change is creative and constructive discussion between and across disciplines from within post-compulsory education. As the University of Lincoln's Learning Landscapes project puts it, headlining 'intellectualising the debate' as one of the key future activities for re-thinking learning space:

> The academic voice can be further enhanced by challenging academics to intellectualise the debate about teaching and learning space by reference to the custom and tradition, principles and preoccupations of their own subject areas. These debates can be generalised to include academics from other subject areas within an institution and from across the higher education sector. The subject of this generalised debate is teaching and learning space in the context of the role and nature of higher education. Situating the learning landscape debate within the context of academic

> values grounds the concept of innovation and design as part of an ongo-
> ing debate about 'the idea of the university'. This debate must be made
> accessible to all staff and students, and extend beyond the university
> campus.
>
> (Neary *et al.* 2010: 25)

In their online tool, the Learning Landscape team offer a history of the university building 'type' as one means of enabling discussion for 're-imagining university education'
(http://learninglandscapes.lincoln.ac.uk/the-idea-of-the-university-reimagining-higher-
education/beyond-vision-missions/).

In the current period, at least in some countries, post-compulsory education shares a similar and problematic 'location' in contemporary debates around
knowledge, authority, expertise and inclusion with other kinds of educational providers, particularly the public services such as libraries, community organisations, adult
education providers, museums and gallery educators. There have been many challenges to the status of the expert as a superior holder of 'special' knowledge when
this is used to exclude others – not just in knowing, but also in the kinds of meanings
they might want to make. Educators across these sectors have become increasingly
sensitive to such issues, and have examined how it might affect their activities.

But, as I began to suggest at the beginning of this chapter, the status
of knowledge in society, the 'place' of post-compulsory education in relation to
knowledge-production, and the position of the academic expert are currently neither obvious nor stable categories. With the added impact of the recent global
financial crisis, will the Dearing Committee's four purposes of education survive?
Will education continue to be about developing individual capacities to their highest
level, increasing knowledge and understanding (for its own sake) and helping to
shape a democratic society, as well as serving the needs of the economy? In the
UK, financial cuts to public provision, new forms of fee-paying by students and an
increasing move towards commercial educational services are again shifting how
and where (and for whom) post-compulsory education is available. But, crucially, the
response should not be a closing down, a defensive opposition by universities and
colleges, caught up in resisting the challenges to their assumed autonomy and current practices. Instead we need to take the opportunity to widen our angle of view,
to come together with other sectors – whether museums, galleries, businesses or
community organisations – to build new alliances that constructively and creatively
help us imagine viable alternatives.

At the same time, widening our angle of view can also challenge our own
assumptions about where education's most immediate problems are assumed to lie,
in particular by developing these conversations internationally. How does the dominant framing of change as from formal to informal learning spaces in mainly American,
British and Australian literature resonate (or not) with countries like Greece or Kenya?
Their particular histories of education are currently intersecting with social unrest: in
Greece because the police are banned from university campuses, which have thus
become potential 'free' zones for raves, some illegal activities and political organisation. In Kenya relationships between students in private and public universities

were recently being played out through the differential qualities and responses to both education and environment (Chepchieng *et al.* 2006). How does the emphasis on active learning relate to educational trends in Russia, China or India? And with the expansion of post-compulsory education in many of these places, what can be learnt from them?

Towards a conclusion

In previous chapters I have both critiqued the common-sense formal/informal framing of learning space design and offered an alternative conceptual framework, based on the work of Lefebvre. This accepts, but can also *illuminate*, the tensions and problematics in, across and between the three interweaving threads of: 'ordinary' social and spatial practices of learning; specific designed environments; and individual engagements with, and interpretations of, these practices and spaces. I have explored how contemporary theories from education and architecture, and methods from, for example, ethnography and ethnomethodology, can open up learning spaces in post-compulsory education to better view. Throughout, I have also argued that space is not central to learning (or any other form of occupation) but is one of the means through which we attempt to articulate new social and spatial practices, or to make concrete and 'obvious' existing ones. And just as learning is always more than the space in which it occurs, space is always more than just the activities it contains; it is a scarce resource and negotiable asset in its own right, with specific properties and 'affordances' that affect what it is capable of.

Finally, it is important to note the very real problems produced for architects in the common-sense links usually made between architecture and its occupation (of which the formal/informal learning space argument is one example); that is, where the designer's intentions somehow just 'become' the resulting scheme – without any problems in translation or other intervening variables. While giving them the appearance of a powerful role in social change, the setting of such high expectations for what new designed spaces are capable of (when buildings can hardly ever be 'ideal', when intention and reality don't match, when changing spaces does not, in reality 'automatically' change processes and practices) tends to lead to an endless, depressing cycle. Design is first hailed as the answer to some social and spatial issue. But when the building is complete it is criticised for its inability to achieve the expected social outcomes, and architects are then blamed for failing to understand the problem, or of not being interested in social issues.

As I noted in the introduction to this book, this has already been revealed by the UK Building Schools for the Future (BSF) programme, which could be seen as having set architecture up 'for a fall'. Here, architectural design was (and is) seen as having a huge potential to change and improve the quality of learning in the secondary schools sector. Then – as the complex processes of competitive tendering; consortia-building; efficiency planning through large, single purchasing deals; design participation and consultation; cost-cutting and various site and management deals take their course and result in a variety of relatively uncontrollable outcomes and unintended consequences – architects and designers are 'blamed' for the lack of obvious 'impact' on learning or design quality of the resulting schools. Despite

£35 billion spent on revamping secondary schools, 'a new generation of mediocre schools' is in danger of being produced, according to a Commission for Architecture and the Built Environment research report (2006).

While most architects both know and live with this aspect of their practice (and recognising that not all designers have the capacity to produce high-quality, appropriate buildings), I want to suggest that re-thinking relationships between architecture and its occupation can challenge such a common-sense framing by deliberately de-centring architecture from its supposed importance in making social change and by locating its 'place' in social and spatial processes more precisely.

So, finally, re-thinking learning spaces turns out not to be about making architecture central to, or the 'solution' for, perceived problems in contemporary post-compulsory education. Rather it is about three things. First, we need more research to help us better understand the relationships between architecture and occupation. Second, there are crucial debates about the location, nature and role of post-compulsory education which urgently need a 'space' for debate, particularly to help re-think relationships between and across the different boundary conditions, social and spatial practices and repertoires of the various educational communities of practice within and beyond the university. And finally, architects should resist being labelled as people who can solve the 'problem' of education through design. Instead we need to offer up architecture as just one mechanism – a part of the repertoire – through which attempts are undertaken to make concrete various (and often competing or ambiguous) understandings of learning, teaching and research. When space is articulated in this way – as integral to, but not central or singular in the challenges and arguments around the future of the university – the role of the architect and of design practices and processes subtly changes, requiring perhaps most crucially, that we begin to ask new and different kinds of questions about learning, space and design.

Bibliography

Abramson, P. and Burnap, E., 2006, *Space Planning for Institutions of Higher Education*. Scottsdale, Arizona: Council of Educational Facility Planners International.

Alfonso, A. I., Kurti, L. and Pink, S. (eds), 2004, *Working Images: Visual Research and Representation in Ethnography*. London: Routledge.

Archer, L. B., 1979, 'Whatever became of design methodology?' *Design Studies* 1(1), 17–20.

Archer, L., Hutchings, M. and Ross, A., 2003, *Higher Education and Social Class: Issues of Inclusion and Exclusion*. London: Routledge Falmer.

Arts Council England, 2004, *Space for Learning: A Handbook for Education Spaces in Museums, Heritage Sites and Discovery Centres*. Available online at: http://www.cloreduffield.org.uk/research/spaceforlearning/spaceforlearning0.html (accessed 26/03/10).

Atherton, J. S., (2009,) 'Learning and teaching: angles on learning, particularly after the schooling years'. Available online at: http://www.learningandteaching.info/ (accessed 06/10/10).

Augoyard, J.-F., 1979/2007, *Step by Step: Everyday Walks in a French Urban Housing Project*. Minneapolis/London: University of Minnesota Press.

Austerlitz, N. (ed.), 2008, *Unspoken Interactions: Exploring the Unspoken Dimension of Learning and Teaching in Creative Subject*. London: Clip Cetl/Edinburgh: Word Power Books.

Australian Teaching and Learning Council (ATLC), 2007, 'Teaching and learning spaces'. Available online at: http://www.altc.edu.au/carrick/go/home/pid/469 (accessed 07/02/09).

Barnett, R., 2000, *Realising the University in an Age of Supercomplexity*. Buckingham: Open University Press.

——, (ed.), 2005, *Re-Shaping the University: New Relationships between Research, Scholarship and Teaching*. Maidenhead: Open University Press.

——, 2007a, *The Idea of Higher Education*. Buckingham: Open University Press.

——, 2007b, *A Will to Learn: Being a Student in an Age of Uncertainty*. Buckingham: Open University Press.

Barnett, R. and Temple, P., 2006, 'Impact on space of future changes in higher education' (UK Higher Education Space Management Project, 2006/10). Higher Education Funding Council for England.

Barton, D. and Tusting, K. (eds), 2005, *Beyond Communities of Practice: Language, Power and Social Context*. Cambridge: Cambridge University Press.

Baudrillard, J., 1981, *For a Critique of the Political Economy of the Sign*. St Louis, MO: Telos Press.

Becher, T. and Trowler, P., 2001, *Academic Tribes and Territories*. Buckingham: Oxford University Press.

Beetham, H. K. and Sharpe, R., 2007, *Rethinking Pedagogy for a Digital Age: Designing and Delivering E-learning*. London: Routledge.

Bell, L., Stevenson, H. and Neary, M. (eds), 2009, *The Future of Higher Education: Policy, Pedagogy and the Student Experience*. London: Continuum.

Benjamin, W., 1999, 'The work of art in the age of reproduction', in *Illuminations*. London: Pimlico.

Bentley, T., 1998, *Learning Beyond the Classroom: Education for a Changing World*. London: Routledge/Demos.

Bhabha, H. K., 1994, *The Location of Culture*. London: Routledge.

Bibliography

Bickford, D. J., 2002, 'Navigating the white waters of collaborative work in shaping learning environments', *New Directions for Teaching and Learning*, 92: 43–52.

Biggs, J., 2003, *Teaching for Quality Learning at University: What the Student Does*. California: SAGE and Buckingham: Open University Press.

Boddington, A. and Boys, J., (eds), forthcoming, *Re-shaping Learning: A Critical Reader. The Future of Learning Spaces in Post-compulsory Education*. Rotterdam: Sense.

Boudon, P., 1979, *Lived in Architecture: Le Corbusier's Pessac Revisited*. Cambridge, MA: MIT Press.

Bourdieu, P., 1987, *Distinction: A Social Critique of the Judgement of Taste*. Cambridge: Harvard University Press.

Bourdieu, P. and Passeron, J.-C., 1990, *Reproduction in Education, Society, and Culture*. London/Newbury Park, CA: SAGE, in association with *Theory, Culture & Society*, Dept. of Administrative and Social Studies, Teesside Polytechnic.

Boyes, A., Cousens, C. and Stuart, H., 2008, 'Exploring the relationship between teaching and learning through practice', CETLD final report, March. Available online at: http://arts.brighton.ac.uk/__data/assets/pdf_file/0016/11482/CetLD-report-flash-final.pdf (accessed 02/05/10).

Boys, J., 2007, *Making Discursive Spaces: A Collaboration Between Deaf and Disabled Artists and Interior Architecture Students*. Available online at: http://www.discursivespaces.co.uk/domains/discursivespaces.co.uk/local/media/downloads/Discursive_Spaces.pdf (accessed 04/05/10).

——, 2008, 'Between unsafe spaces and the comfort zone? Exploring the impact of learning environments on "doing" learning', conference paper presented at *e-Learning and Learning Environments for the Future*, Solstice 2008, 5 June, Edge Hill University, UK.

——, 2009a, 'Beyond the beanbag? Towards new ways of thinking about learning spaces', *Networks* 8, (Autumn). Available online at: http://www.adm.heacademy.ac.uk/resources/features/beyond-the-beanbag-towards-new-ways-of-thinking-about-learning-spaces (accessed 28/03/10).

——, 2009b, *So What is Normal? Resources on Disability and Architecture for Higher Education*. Available online at: http://www.sowhatisnormal.co.uk (accessed 27/03/10).

——, 2010, 'Creative differences: deconstructing the conceptual learning spaces of higher education and museums', in Cook, B., Reynolds, R. and Speight, C. (eds), *Museums and Design Education: Looking to Learn, Learning to See*. London: Ashgate.

Boys, J. and Ford, P. (eds), 2006, *The e-Revolution and Post-Compulsory Education: Using e-Business Models to Deliver Quality Education*. London: Routledge.

Boys, J. and Shakespeare, P., 2009, 'Occupying (dis)ordinary space', conference paper presented at *Occupation: Negotiations with Constructed Space*, 2–4 July, University of Brighton.

Burbules, N. C., 1997, 'Aporia: webs, passages, getting lost, and learning to go on', *Philosophy of Education Year Book*. Available online at: http://www.ed.uiuc.edu/eps/pes-yearbook/97_docs/burbules.html (accessed 02/05/10).

Canter, D. and Lee, T. (eds), 1974, *Psychology and the Built Environment*. London: Architectural Press.

Caputo, J. (ed.), 1996, *Deconstruction in a Nutshell: A Conversation with Jaques Derrida*. New York: Fordham University Press.

Chepchieng, M. C., Kiboss, J. K., Sindabi, A., Kariuki, M. W. and Mbugua, S. N., 2006, 'Students' attitudes toward campus environment: a comparative study of public and private universities in Kenya', *Educational Research and Reviews* 1(6): 174–9. Available online at: http://www.academicjournals.org/ERR2/PDF/Pdf2006/Sep/Chepchieng%20et%20al.pdf (accessed 05/04/10).

Chism, N., 2006, 'Challenging traditional assumptions and rethinking learning spaces', in Oblinger, D. G. (ed.), *Learning Spaces*. Boulder, CO: Educause.

Clark, H., 2002, *Building Education: The Role of the Physical Environment in Enhancing Teaching and Research*. London: Institute of Education, University of London.

Clarke, A., 2009, 'The best use of infinity: open educational resources and the politics of knowledge', *Networks* 8, (Autumn): 20–3.

Clifford, J. and Marcus, G. (eds), 1986, *Writing Culture: The Poetics and Politics of Ethnography*. Berkeley: University of California Press.

Cockburn, C., 1991, *Brothers: Male Dominance and Technological Change*. London: Pluto Press.

——, 1998, *The Space Between Us: Negotiating Gender and National Identities in Conflict*. London: Zed Books.

Commission for Architecture and the Built Environment (CABE), n.d., '21st century schools: learning environments of the future'. Available online at: http://www.cabe.org.uk/files/21st-century-schools.pdf (accessed 07/02/09).

——, 2006, 'Assessing secondary school design quality: research report'. Available online at: http://www.cabe.org.uk/files/assessing-secondary-school-design-quality.pdf (accessed 03/05/10).

Conole, G. and Oliver, M. (eds), 2007, *Contemporary Perspectives in e-Learning Research: Themes, Methods and Impact on Practice*. London: Routledge Falmer.

Cook, B., Reynolds, R. and Speight, C. (eds), 2010, *Museums and Design Education: Looking to Learn, Learning to See*. London: Ashgate.

Cottam, H. (ed.), 2001, *Changing Behaviours*. London: Design Council.

Cousin, G., 2006a, 'An introduction to threshold concepts'. *Planet* 17, December. Available online at: http://www.gees.ac.uk/planet/p17/gc.pdf (accessed 27/03/10).

——, 2006b, 'Threshold concepts, troublesome knowledge and emotional capital: an exploration into learning about others', in Meyer, J. H. F. and Land, R. (eds), *Overcoming Barriers to Student Understanding: Threshold Concepts and Troublesome Knowledge*. London: Routledge Falmer.

——, 2009, *Strategies for Researching Learning in Higher Education: An Introduction to Contemporary Methods and Approaches*. London: Routledge.

Csíkszentmihályi, M., 1996, *Creativity: Flow and the Psychology of Discovery and Invention*. New York: Harper Perennial.

——, 1998, *Finding Flow: The Psychology of Engagement with Everyday Life*. New York: Basic Books.

Darley, G., 1991, 'Visions, prospects and compromises', *Higher Education Quarterly* 45(4): 354–66.

Darrouzet, C., Dirckinck-Holmfeld, L., Kahn, T., Stucky, S. and Wild, H., 1994, *Rethinking 'Distance' in Distance Learning*. Institute for Research on Learning.

Davidson, C. N. and Goldberg, D. T., 2009, *The Future of Learning Institutions in a Digital Age*. Cambridge, MA: MIT Press. Available online at: http://mitpress.mit.edu/books/chapters/Future_of_Learning.pdf (accessed 03/04/10).

De Certeau, M., 1979/1984, *The Practice of Everyday Life*. Berkeley: University of California Press.

Debord, G., 1995, *The Society of the Spectacle*. New York: Zone Books.

Delanty, G., 2001, *Challenging Knowledge: The University in the Knowledge Society*. Buckingham: Society for Research into Higher Education and Open University Press.

Deleuze, G., 1992, *The Fold: Leibniz and the Baroque*. Minneapolis: University of Minnesota Press.

Deleuze, G. and Guattari, F., 2000, *A Thousand Plateaus*. London: Athlone Press.

Dempsey, L., 2009, 'Systemwide organization of information resources: a multi-scalar environment', presentation at JISC Pre-Conference Forum, Edinburgh, March. Available online at: http://www.oclc.org/research/staff/dempsey/presentations.htm (accessed 07/07/09).

Derrida, J., 2001, *Writing and Difference*. London: Routledge Classics.

Dewey, J., 1934/2005, *Art as Experience*. New York: Perigee Trade.

Dober, R., 1992, *Campus Design*. New York: John Wiley.

Dodgson, M., Gann, D. and Salter, A., 2005, *Think Play Do: Technology, Innovation and Organisation*. Oxford: Oxford University Press.

Doel, M., 1999, *Poststructuralist Geographies: The Diabolical Art of Spatial Science*. Lanham, MD: Rowan & Littlefield.

Dudek, M., 2000, *The Architecture of Schools: The New Learning Environments*. Boston: Architectural Press.

Bibliography

Duffy, F. and Powell, K., 1997, *The New Office*. London: Conran Octopus.

Dugdale, S., 2009, 'Space strategies for the new learning landscape', *Educause Review* 44(2): 50–2.

Edgerton, E., Romice, O. and Spencer, C., 2007, *Environmental Psychology: Putting Research into Practice*. Cambridge: Cambridge Scholars Publishing.

Edwards, B., 2000, *University Architecture*. London: Spon.

Edwards, R., 1997, *Changing Places? Flexibility, Lifelong Learning and a Learning Society*. London: Routledge.

Edwards, R. and Usher, R. (eds), 2003, *Space, Curriculum and Learning*. Greenwich, CT: Information Age Publishing.

——, 2008, *Globalisation and Pedagogy: Space, Place and Identity*. London: Routledge.

Empson, W., 1930, *Seven Types of Ambiguity*. London: Chatto & Windus.

Enquire, 2006, 'Inspiring learning in galleries 02'. Available online at: http://www.en-quire.org/research. aspx (accessed 26/03/10).

Entwistle, N., 1984, 'Contrasting perspectives on learning', in Marton, F., Hounsell, D. and Entwistle, N. (eds), *The Experience of Learning*. Edinburgh: Scottish Academic Press.

Evans, M., 2005, *Killing Thinking: The Death of the Universities*. London: Continuum.

Evans, R., 1997, 'Figures, doors and passages', in *Translations from Drawing to Building and Other Essays*. London: AA Publications.

Foucault, M., 1970, *The Order of Things: An Archaeology of the Human Sciences*. New York: Pantheon Books.

——, 1997/1995, *Discipline and Punish: The Birth of the Prison*. New York: Vintage.

Frichot, H., 2005, 'Stealing into Deleuze's Baroque House', in Buchanan, I. and Lambert, G. (eds), *Deleuze and Space*. Edinburgh: University of Edinburgh Press.

Futurelab, 2006, 'What if . . . ? Re-imagining learning spaces'. Available online at: http://www.futurelab. org.uk/resources/publications_reports_articles/opening_education_reports/Opening_Education_ Report128 (accessed 07/02/09).

Garfinkel, H., 1967, *Studies in Ethnomethodology*. Cambridge: Polity Press.

Gaver, W., Boucher, A., Pennington, S. and Walker, B., 2004, 'Cultural probes and the value of uncertainty', *Interactions* 11(5): 53–6. Available online at: http://mars.gold.ac.uk/media/30gaver-etal.probes+uncertainty.interactions04.pdf (accessed 02/05/10).

Geertz, C., 1973, 'Thick description: toward an interpretive theory of culture', in *The Interpretation of Cultures: Selected Essays*. New York: Basic Books.

Ghirado, D. (ed.), 1991, *Out of Site: A Social Criticism of Architecture*. Seattle, WA: Bay Press.

Gibson, J. J., 1977, 'The theory of affordances', in Shaw R. E. and Bransford, J. (eds), *Perceiving, Acting, and Knowing*. Hillsdale, NJ: Lawrence Erlbaum Associates.

——, 1979, *The Ecological Approach to Visual Perception*. Boston: Houghton Mifflin.

Goffman, E., 1959, *The Presentation of Self in Everyday Life*. London: Penguin.

Gosling, D., 2008, 'JISC study on how innovative technologies are influencing the design of physical learning spaces in the post-16 sector', unpublished report.

Haggis, T., 2003 'Constructing images of ourselves? A critical investigation into "approaches to learning" research in higher education', *British Educational Research Journal* 29(1): 89–104.

——, 2004, 'Meaning, identity and "motivation": expanding what matters in understanding learning in higher education?', *Studies in Higher Education* 29(3): 335–52.

Harding, J. and Hale, L., 2007, 'Anti-creativity, ambiguity and the imposition of order creativity or conformity?' Conference paper at *Building Cultures of Creativity in Higher Education*, 8–10 January, University of Wales Institute, Cardiff.

Harris, S. R. and Sheswell, N., 2005, 'Moving beyond communities of practice in adult basic education', in Barton and Tusting (eds), *Beyond Communities of Practice: Language, Power and Social Context*. Cambridge: Cambridge University Press.

Harrison, A., 2006, 'Working to learn, learning to work: design in educational transformation', 4th

Annual Foundation Lecture. Available online at: http://www.degw.com/knowledge_lectures.aspx (accessed 10/10/09).

Harrison, A. and Cairns A., 2009, 'The changing academic workplace', DEGW UK Ltd. Available online at: http://www.exploreacademicworkplace.com/downloads/the_changing_academic_workplace_2008.pdf (accessed 07/02/09).

Harrison, A., Wheeler, P. and Whitehead, C., 2004, *The Distributed Workplace: Sustainable Work Environments*. London: Spon Press.

Harvey, D., 1989, *The Condition of Postmodernity: An Enquiry into the Origins of Cultural Change*. Oxford: Wiley-Blackwell.

——, 2000, *Spaces of Hope*. Berkeley: University of California Press.

Hein, G. E., 1998, *Learning in the Museum*. London: Routledge.

Heppell, S., 2009, 'Space the final frontier', introductory video for *SPACE: ADM-HEA Annual Forum*. 29 April–13 May, Wales Millennium Centre, Cardiff. Available online at: http://www.adm.heacademy.ac.uk/events/our-events/space-video-presentations/space-the-final-frontier (accessed 02/05/10).

Hickman, W., 1965, 'Campus construction for academic survival', *Journal of Higher Education* 36, 322–30.

Higher Education Funding Council for England (HEFCE)/Joint Information Systems Committee (JISC), 2007, 'In their own words: exploring the learner's perspective on e-learning'. Available online at: http://www.jisc.ac.uk/whatwedo/programmes/elearningpedagogy/intheirownwords.aspx (accessed 05/04/10).

Holston, J., 1989, *The Modernist City: An Anthropological Critique of Brasilia*. Chicago: University of Chicago Press.

Hooper-Greenhill, E., 2000, *Museums and Visual Culture*. London: Routledge.

Howell, C., 2008, 'Thematic analysis: space learning landscape project'. University of Cambridge. Available online at: http://www.caret.cam.ac.uk/blogs/llp/?page_id=41 (accessed 05/04/10).

Hughes, J., Jewson, N. and Unwin, L., 2007, *Communities of Practice: Critical Perspectives*. London: Routledge.

Hunter, B., 2006, 'The espaces study: designing, developing and managing learning spaces for effective learning', *New Review of Academic Librarianship* 12(2): 61–81.

Innovation Unit, 2008a, 'Learning futures'. Available online at: http://www.innovation-unit.co.uk/content/view/446/973/ (accessed 07/02/09).

——, 2008b, 'What's next? 21 ideas for 21st century learning'. Available online at: http://www.innovation-unit.co.uk/about-us/publications/whats-next.html (accessed 07/02/09).

Jameson, F., 1992, *Postmodernism or the Cultural Logic of Late Capitalism*. Durham, NC: Duke University Press.

Jamieson, P., 2008, 'Creating new generation learning environments on the university campus', *Woods Bagot Research Press*. Available online at: http://www.woodsbagot.com/en/Documents/Public_Research/WB5307_U21_FA-7_final.pdf (accessed 07/02/09).

Johnson, C. and Lomas, C., 2005, 'Design of the learning space: learning and design principles', *Educause Review* 40(4): 16–28. Available online at: http://connect.educause.edu/Library/EDUCAUSE+Review/DesignoftheLearningSpaceL/40557 (accessed 26/03/10).

Joint Information Systems Committee (JISC), 2006, 'Designing spaces for effective learning'. Available online at: http://www.jisc.ac.uk/eli_learningspaces.html (accessed 07/02/09).

——, 2009, 'A study of effective evaluation models and practices for technology supported physical learning spaces'. Available online at: http://www.jisc.ac.uk/media/documents/projects/jels_final_report_30.06.09.doc (accessed 26/03/10).

Keating, M. C., 2005, 'Negotiating the experience of self', in Barton, D. and Tusting, K. (eds), *Beyond Communities of Practice: Language, Power and Social Context*. Cambridge: Cambridge University Press.

Kolb, A. Y. and Kolb, D. A., 2005, 'Learning styles and learning spaces: enhancing experiential learning in higher education', *Academy of Management Learning & Education* 4(2): 193–212.

Bibliography

Koolhaas, R., 1997, *Delirious New York: A Retroactive Manifesto for Manhattan*. New York: Monacelli Press.

Koolhaas, R. and Mau, B., 1997, *S. M. L. XL*. New York: Monacelli Press.

Krauss, A., 2008, *Hidden Curriculum*. Rotterdam: Episode Publishers.

Kress, G. R., 2003, *Literacy in the New Media Age*, London: Routledge Falmer.

Kuh, G. D. and Pike, G., 2006, 'Relationships among structural diversity, informal peer interactions and perceptions of the campus environment', *Review of Higher Education*, 29(4): 425–50.

Kuh, G., Kinzie, J., Schuh, J. and Whitt, E., 2005, *Student Success in College: Creating Conditions that Matter*. San Francisco: Jossey-Bass.

Kwon, M., 2004, *One Place After Another: Site-Specific Art and Locational Identity*. Cambridge, MA: MIT Press.

Land, R., Cousin, G., Meyer, J. H. F. and Davies, P., 2005, 'Threshold concepts and troublesome knowledge (3): implications for course design and evaluation' in Rust, C. (ed.), *Improving Student Learning: Equality and Diversity*. Oxford: OCSLD.

Land, R., Meyer, J. H. F. and Smith, J. (eds), 2008, *Threshold Concepts in the Disciplines*. Rotterdam: Sense Publishers.

Laurillard, D., 2001, *Re-thinking University Teaching: A Framework for the Effective Use of Learning Technologies*. London: Routledge Falmer.

——, 2002, 'Re-thinking teaching for the knowledge society', *Educause Review* 37(1): 16–25.

Lave, J. and Wenger, E., 1991, *Situated Learning: Legitimate Peripheral Participation*. Cambridge: Cambridge University Press.

Lawson, B. R., 2001, *The Language of Space*. Oxford: Architectural Press.

Learning Theories Knowledgebase, 2010, [website]. Available online at: http://www.learning-theories.com/ (accessed 27/03/10).

Lee, G., 2009, 'Learning spaces: student writing competition', *Networks* 8, (Autumn). Available online at: http://www.adm.heacademy.ac.uk/awards/student-essay-competition/georgina-lee-learning-spaces/ (accessed 05/04/10).

Leesig, L., 2005, *Free Culture: The Nature and Future of Creativity*. New York: Penguin.

Leitch Review of Skills, 2006, 'Prosperity for all in the global economy: world class skills', Final Report, December, HMSO.

Lefebvre, H., 1991, *The Production of Space*. Oxford: Blackwell.

Loughborough University, 2005, 'The VALiD practice manual'. Available online at: http://www.valueindesign.com/downloads/VALiD_Practice_Manual.pdf (accessed 19/05/10).

Lyon, P., forthcoming, *Learning and Teaching Through Design: An Anthology Of Models, Approaches and Explorations*. London: Gower.

McGill University, Montreal, n.d, 'Making the edible campus'. Available online at: http://www.mcgill.ca/files/mchg/MakingtheEdibleCampus.pdf (accessed 02/05/10).

McKean, J. M., 1972, 'University of Essex: case study', *Architects' Journal* 20, September, 645–67.

McLean, M., 2006, *Pedagogy and the University*. London: Continuum.

Melhuish, C., 1996, *Architecture and Anthropology*, Architectural Design Profile 124, London: Academy Editions.

——, 2007, 'Inhabiting the image: architecture and cultural identity in the post-industrial city. A study of the Brunswick, London', unpublished PhD thesis, Brunel University.

——, 2010a, 'Ethnographic case study: perceptions of three new learning spaces and their impact on the learning and teaching process at the universities of Sussex and Brighton', unpublished report, CETLD/InQbate.

——, 2010b, 'Ethnographic case study: literature review and bibliography', unpublished report, CETLD/InQbate.

Meyer, J. H. F. and Land, R., 2003, 'Threshold concepts and troublesome knowledge (1): linkages to ways of thinking and practicing', in Rust, C. (ed.), *Improving Student Learning: Equality and Diversity*. Oxford: OCSLD.

—— (eds), 2006, *Overcoming Barriers to Student Understanding: Threshold Concepts and Troublesome Knowledge*. London: Routledge.

Mitchell, C., 2007a, 'CETLD evaluation report: Spotlight project'. Available online at: http://arts.brighton. ac.uk/__data/assets/pdf_file/0007/8773/Spotlight-Final-Report.pdf (accessed 04/05/10).

——, 2007b, 'The art of learning online: engaging students', conference paper at *Designs on e-Learning*, 12–14 September, University of the Arts, London. Available online at: http://www. designsonelearning.net/conferences/face_to_face/sept2007/2007_papers/ps5_papers/chris_ mitchell.pdf (accessed 04/05/10).

Mitchell, W. J., 1996, *City of Bits: Place, Space and the Infobahn*. Cambridge: MIT Press.

——, 2007, *Imagining MIT: Designing a Campus for the Twenty-First Century*. Cambridge: MIT Press.

Moore, K., 2009, *Overlooking the Visual: Demystifying the Art of Design*. New York: Routledge.

Muthesius, S., 2000, *The Postwar University: Utopianist Campus and College*. New Haven: Yale University Press.

Myerson, J. and Ross, P., 2006, *Space to Work: New Office Design*. London: Laurence King Publishing.

Naisbitt, J., 1999, *High Tech, High Touch: Technology and Our Search for Meaning*. New York: Broadway Books.

Nancy, J.-L., 1996, *The Muses*. Stanford, CA: Stanford University Press.

——, 2000, *Being Singular Plural*. Stanford, CA: Stanford University Press.

National Committee of Inquiry into Higher Education (NCIHE), 1997, 'Higher education in the learning society: report of the National Committee of Inquiry into Higher Education'. NCIHE.

Neary, M., 2010, 'Learning landscapes in higher education: the struggle for the idea of the university: between research and reflexivity', conference paper at *Learning Landscapes and the Idea of the University: Efficiency, Effectiveness and Expression*, 13 April, Queen Mary, University of London.

Neary, M., Harrison, A., Crelin, G., Parekh, N., Saunders, G., Duggan, F., Williams, S. and Austin, S., 2010, 'Learning landscapes in higher education', Centre for Educational Research and Development, University of Lincoln. Available online at: http://learninglandscapes.blogs.lincoln.ac.uk/files/2010/04/ FinalReport.pdf (accessed 02/05/10).

Nonaka, I. and Konno, N., 1998, 'The concept of "Ba": building a foundation for knowledge creation', *California Management Review*, 40(3): 40–54.

Norman, D. A., 1988, *The Psychology of Everyday Things*. New York: Basic Books.

——, 1990, *The Design of Everyday Things*. New York: Doubleday.

Oblinger, D. G. (ed.), 2006, *Learning Spaces*. Educause. Available online at: http://www.educause.edu/ LearningSpaces/10569 (accessed 07/02/09).

Office for Economic Co-operation and Development (OECD), 2007, *Moving UP the Value Chain: Staying Competitive in the Global Economy*. Available online at: http://www.oecd.org/dataoecd/24/35/ 38558080.pdf (accessed 12/10/09).

Oseland, N., 2008, 'The evolving workplace', *PFM*, October, 14–16. Available online at: http:// aleximarmot.com/layout_images/1235725048.pdf (accessed 29/03/10).

Paechter, C., Edwards, R., Harrison, R. and Twining, P., 2001, *Learning, Space and Identity*. London: Sage.

Parlett, M. and Hamilton, D., 1972, *Evaluation as Illumination: A New Approach to the Study of Innovative Programs*, occasional paper, Edinburgh University Centre for Research in the Educational Sciences/ Nuffield Foundation. Available online at: http://www.eric.ed.gov:80/ERICWebPortal/custom/ portlets/recordDetails/detailmini.jsp?_nfpb=true&_&ERICExtSearch_SearchValue_0=ED167634 &ERICExtSearch_SearchType_0=no&accno=ED167634 (accessed 02/04/10).

Patel, D., Powell, J. and Boys, J., 2006, 'Getting from here to there; improving processes and adding value', in Boys, J. and Ford, P. (eds), *The e-Revolution and Post-Compulsory Education: Using e-Business Models to Deliver Quality Education*. London: Routledge.

Bibliography

Payne, G. C., 1976, 'Making a lesson happen: an ethnomethodological analysis', in Hammersley, M. and Woods, P. (eds), *The Process of Schooling*. London: Routledge.

Perry Chapman, M., 2006, *American Places: In Search of the Twenty-First Century Campus*. Washington, DC: American Council on Education/Phoenix, AZ: Oryx Press.

Pink, S., 2006, *Doing Visual Ethnography: Images, Media and Representation in Research*, 2nd edn. London: Sage.

Prosser, M. and Trigwell, K., 1999, *Understanding Learning and Teaching: The Experience in Higher Education*. Philadelphia, PA: Society for Research into Higher Education and Open University Press.

Ramsden, P., 1992, *Learning to Teach in Higher Education*. London: Routledge.

Ratcliffe, D., Wilson, H., Powell, D. and Tibbetts, B. (eds), *Learning Spaces in Higher Education: Positive Outcomes by Design*. Brisbane: University of Queensland.

RIBA Higher Education Forum, 2007, 'Distinction by design'. Available online at: http://www.architecture.com/Files/RIBAHoldings/PolicyAndInternationalRelations/ClientForums/Higher/Resources/HEDQF2007ExhibitionCatalogue.pdf (accessed 07/02/09).

Robertson, J. and Bond, C., 2005, 'Being in university', in Barnett R. (ed.) *Reshaping the University: New Relationships between Research, Scholarship and Teaching*. London: Open University Press.

Rorty, R., 2000, *Philosophy and Social Hope*. New York: Penguin.

——, 2008, *Philosophy and the Mirror of Nature*, 30th Anniversary edn. Princeton, NJ: Princeton University Press.

Rose, G., 2006, *Visual Methodologies: An Introduction to the Interpretation of Visual Materials*. London: Sage.

Rust, C. (ed.), *Improving Student Learning: Equality and Diversity*. Oxford: OCSLD.

Rust, I., 2009, *Halycon Daze*, Digital Video, CETLD. DVD available from ike.rust@rca.ac.uk.

——, 2010, Presentation paper on *Halycon Daze*, 19 February, British Higher School of Art and Design, Moscow. Available online at: http://arts.brighton.ac.uk/research/cetld/speaking-and-writing-the-visual/visual-pedagogy (accessed 02/0510).

Ryave, A. L. and Schenkein, J, N., 1974, 'Notes on the art of walking', in Turner, R. (ed.), *Ethnomethodology*. Harmondsworth: Penguin.

Sacks, H., 1984, 'On doing being ordinary', in Atkinson, J. M. and Heritage, J. C. (eds), *Structures of Social Action*. Cambridge: Cambridge University Press.

——, 1992, *Lectures on Conversation*, Vol. 1. Oxford: Blackwell.

Sagan, O., 2008, 'Playgrounds, studios and hiding places: emotional exchange in creative learning spaces', in Austerlitz, N. (ed.), *Unspoken Interactions: Exploring the Unspoken Dimension of Learning and Teaching in Creative Subjects*. London: Clip Cetl/Edinburgh: Word Power Books.

——, 2009, 'Open disclosures: learning, creativity and the passage of mental (ill) health', *International Journal of Art and Design Education* 28(1).

Saint, A., 1987, *Towards a Social Architecture: The Role of School-Building in Post-War England*. London: Yale University Press.

Salmon, G., 2000, *e-Moderating: The Key to Teaching and Learning Online*. London: Routledge.

Savin-Baden, M., 2008, *Learning Spaces: Creating Opportunities for Knowledge Creation in Academic Life*. Buckingham: Open University Press.

Schechner, R., 1993, *The Future of Ritual: Writings on Culture and Performance*. New York: Routledge.

Schön, D. A., 1987, *Educating the Reflective Practitioner: Toward a New Design for Teaching and Learning in the Professions*. San Francisco: Jossey-Bass.

Schunk, D. H., 2007, *Learning Theories: An Educational Perspective* (5th edn). New York: Prentice Hall.

Scott, P., 1995, *The Meanings of Mass Higher Education*. Buckingham: Society for Research into Higher Education and Open University Press.

Scottish Funding Council, 2006, 'Spaces for learning: a review of learning spaces in further and higher education'. Available online at: http://aleximarmot.com/research/ (accessed 07/02/09).

Scott-Webber, L., 2004, *In Sync: Environmental Behaviour Research and the Design of Learning Spaces.* Ann Arbour, MI: Society for College and University Planning (SCUP).

Seamon, D., n.d., 'Phenomenology, place, environment and architecture: a review', in *Environmental and Architectural Phenomenology Newsletter.* Available online at: http://www.phenomenologyonline.com/articles/seamon1.html (accessed 06/10/10).

Seely Brown, J., 2005, 'New learning environments in the 21st century'. Available online at: http://www.educause.edu/ir/library/pdf/ff0604S.pdf (accessed 07/02/09).

Seely Brown, J. and Duguid, P., 1997, *Universities in the Digital Age.* Palo Alto, CA: Xerox Palo Alto Research Center.

Shanahan M. and Meyer, J. H. F., 2006, 'The troublesome nature of a threshold concept in economics', in Meyer, J. H. F. and Land, R. (eds), *Overcoming Barriers to Student Understanding: Threshold Concepts and Troublesome Knowledge.* London: Routledge.

Shattock, M. (ed.), 2009, *Entrepreneurialism in Universities and the Knowledge Economy.* Maidenhead and New York: Open University Press.

Shreeve, A. and Sims, E., 2006, 'Evaluating practice-based learning and teaching in art and design'. Available online at: http://www.arts.ac.uk/docs/cltad_pedrespapshreevesims.pdf (accessed 15/04/10).

Smith, A. and Webster, F. (eds), *The Postmodern University? Contested Visions of Higher Education in Society.* Buckingham: Society for Research into Higher Education and Open University Press.

Smith, H. C. and Boys, J., forthcoming, 'What do we know about what is being built? Constructing a taxonomy of new learning spaces', in Boddington, A. and Boys, J., (eds), *Re-shaping Learning: A Critical Reader. The Future of Learning Spaces in Post-compulsory Education.* Rotterdam: Sense.

Soja, E. W., 1989, *Postmodern Geographies: The Reassertion of Space in Critical Social Theory.* London: Verso.

Space Management Group (SMG), 2006a, 'UK higher education space management project: summary'. Available online at: http://www.smg.ac.uk/resources.html (accessed 26/03/10).

——, 2006b, 'UK higher education space management project: phase 2 reports'. Available online at: http://www.smg.ac.uk/resources.html (accessed 26/03/10).

Steedman, C. K., 1987, *Landscape for a Good Woman: A Story of Two Lives.* New Brunswick, NJ: Rutgers University Press.

Sternberg, R. J. and Lubart, T., 1995, *Defying the Crowd: Cultivating Creativity in a Culture of Conformity.* New York: Free Press.

Strange, C. and Banning, J. H., 2001, *Educating by Design: Creating Campus Learning Environments That Work.* San Francisco: Jossey-Bass.

Stratford, H. and Wesser, D., 2009, 'Choreographing knowledge' in *Urban (Col)laboratory: Public Interventions.* Available online at: http://www.urbancollaboratory.net/ (accessed 19/05/10).

Swales, J. M., 1998, *Other Floors, Other Voices: A Textography of a Small University Building.* London: Routledge.

Taylor, P. and Wilding, D., 2009, *Rethinking the Values of Higher Education: The Student as Collaborator and Producer? Undergraduate Research as a Case Study,* The Reinvention Centre for Undergraduate Research, University of Warwick. Available online at: http://www.qaa.ac.uk/students/studentEngagement/Rethinking.pdf (accessed 19/05/10).

Temple, P., 2008, 'Learning spaces in higher education: an under-researched topic', *London Review of Education* 6(3): 229–41.

——, 2010, 'Learning landscapes in higher education in the 21st century', conference presentation at *Learning Landscapes and the Idea of the University: Efficiency, Effectiveness and Expression,* 13 April, Queen Mary, University of London.

Bibliography

Temple, P. and Barnett, R., 2007, 'Higher education space: future directions', *Planning for Higher Education* 36: 5–15.

Tertiary Education Facilities Management Association (TEFMA), 2006, 'Learning environments in tertiary education'. Available online at: http://www.tefma.com/infoservices/publications/learning.jsp (accessed 07/02/09).

Thackara, J., 2001, *The New Geographies of Learning*. Amsterdam: Hogeschool van Amsterdam.

——, 2006, 'Chapter 7: Learning', in *In the Bubble: Designing in a Complex World*. Cambridge, MA: MIT Press.

Thody, A., 2008, 'Learning landscapes for universities: mapping the field working paper 1', Centre for Educational Research and Development, University of Lincoln. Available online at: http://eprints.lincoln.ac.uk/1597/ (accessed 05/04/10).

Thrift, N., 2008, *Non-Representational Theory: Space, Politics, Affect*. London: Routledge.

Till, J., 2009, *Architecture Depends*. Cambridge, MA: MIT Press.

Tschumi, B., 1994, *The Manhattan Transcripts* (2nd edn). New York: John Wiley & Sons.

——, 1996, *Architecture and Disjunction*. Cambridge, MA: MIT Press.

Turner, R. (ed.), 1970, *Ethnomethodology*. Harmondsworth: Penguin.

University of Strathclyde and DEGW, 2008, 'Explore it: effective spaces for working in higher and further education'. Available online at: http://www.exploreacademicworkplace.com/index.php/site/introduction (accessed 02/05/10).

Van Schaik, L., 2008, *Spatial Intelligence*, AD Primer. Hoboken, NJ: John Wiley & Sons.

Viljoen, A., (ed.), 2005, *Continuous Productive Urban Landscapes: Designing Urban Agriculture for Sustainable Cities*. Oxford: Architectural Press.

Watson, L., 2006, 'Where are we now?' in Boys, J. and Ford, P. (eds), *The e-Revolution and Post-Compulsory Education: Using e-Business Models to Deliver Quality Education*. London Routledge.

Wenger, E., 1998, *Communities of Practice: Learning, Meaning and Identity*. Cambridge: Cambridge University Press.

——, 2009, *Social Learning Capacity: Four Essays on Innovation and Learning in Social Systems*, Copies available by email to etienne@ewenger.com.

Whisnant, D., 1971, 'The university as a space and the future of the university', *Journal of Higher Education* 42: 85–102.

Woolf, V., 1929/1989, *A Room of One's Own*, Mariner Books.

Worthington, J., 2006, *Reinventing the Workplace*. New York: Architectural Press.

Index

Index

Index